Brian Bigg is an Australian journalist, television and movie producer, publisher, editor, writer and author. He has travelled extensively and wrote about his Camino pilgrimage in *Walking the Camino: My Way* (released September 2020). This second book, about his adventures making television shows throughout Europe, *Making Television: My Way* was due for release in December 2022.

Brian is also considered to be the world's foremost expert in producing the record-breaking television quiz format *Who Wants to be a Millionaire?* He will chronicle what makes that show so successful in his third book *Making a Millionaire: My Way* (due in 2023).

Brian normally lives in Sydney with two of his three children and their rabbit. But during the COVID crisis he is in Europe, chasing other dreams.

CACHEKAT

Reviews of
Walking the Camino: My Way

The book is a real page-turner and once you start reading,
I guarantee you will have trouble putting it down.
P. Teese

Brian has created an absolute gem unlike any other Camino
book out there, and I've read a few! Highly recommended!!
Justin Gendle

Enjoyable and entertaining easy read.
Commondenominator

Having walked the Camino myself I found this to be one
of the funniest, honest and realistic views of the journey to
Santiago.
Kindle customer

Fantastic book that I didn't want to put down.
A good description of the route he took, his personal
experience of the walk and the people he met.
It was very uplifting and very, very funny.
Brenda Surtees

MAKING TELEVISION: MY WAY

By BRIAN BIGG

Table of Contents

	Before we get started	15
1	Feeling shaky	22
2	So how did you become king then?	27
3	Brian's law	33
4	First time in Hungary	40
5	A walking bible	51
6	The rise of formats	54
7	What is a format?	63
8	The American way	68
9	A new world record	74
10	Travelling isn't always fun	86
11	It's how you sell it	100
12	Courting La Diva	117
13	Getting belted	125
14	Killer robots	134
15	Addressing the conference	145
16	The most handsome man I know	154
17	Body language	176
18	Hiring staff	186
19	Finland fish	191
20	The national anthem	198
21	The murder next door	210
22	Learning a new language	215
23	Eating out	220
24	And the winner is …	226
25	Delivering the good news	236
26	Finnish sauna	243
27	Lithuania all over again	247

28	Doing backflips	254
29	Bless you my son	263
30	Forgetting	271
31	An old saying	281
32	The trouble with being a 'yes' person	287
33	And finally	294
	Acknowledgements	297

Author's note:

This book is a collection of my experiences in the mid to late 1990s in a variety of countries making television for a company which no longer exists in its original entity, save for its name.

My experiences, reflections and judgments are my own, and are not meant to be construed as absolute fact: just how I saw, heard or was told and how I remembered a fascinating time in history and in television production.

11

For Alison, Charlie and Laren

Before we get started

My friend and long-time colleague, Peter, turned to me from a conversation he was having with someone at his poolside barbeque in Sydney.

"Brian, tell him about the time you gave the game show contestant a blood transfusion so he could appear on your show."

Admittedly, I'd swallowed a few beers by that stage, but I couldn't for the life of me remember what the hell he was talking about.

Peter had worked with me in Europe on some TV shows in the late 1990s. According to him, he had a clear recollection of the incident, so he regaled the barbeque guests with the story. I chipped in with background details where I could, which wasn't a lot. As it turned out, there was good reason for my scepticism.

I had been supervising the production of a television show for one of the first commercial free-to-air television networks in a particular former Soviet republic, which shall remain nameless. The program was called *Forgive Me*. Developed by Endemol in the Netherlands, I had supervised the roll out of the program across much of Europe, by and large, quite successfully.

Forgive Me is a female friendly talk show, disguised as a sort of game show. The central theme is quite clever, if a little complicated: two people, who have been friends for some time, have a fight and no longer talk to each other.

Neither person wants to be the one to apologise, believing the other to be the cause of the argument. Eventually, one of the two approaches the show.

That person (let's call them person A) is invited to the studio and asked to tell the audience about the friendship and the fight which ended it. Generally, that's where the tears begin.

The presenter then shows person A, and the audience obviously, a video of what happened when the presenter took a special bouquet of flowers to person B in order to say "sorry" on behalf of person A.

Still following?

On the video, the presenter tells person B that "someone wants to say sorry to you by giving you flowers". The presenter asks person B to speculate on who might be the apologist.

Most times person B correctly guesses it's their friend, person A. The host then asks person B if they are willing to accept the flowers and forgive their former friend.

When the answer is "yes" – which it is most of the time – the camera shows the happy and surprised emotional reaction of person A in the studio. Then, to the further surprise of person A and the audience, the presenter then announces that person B has also come to the studio!

Person B comes in and the two former friends hug, kiss and make up. They each tell the audience how happy they are now because the show has repaired their friendship and usually everyone goes home with a warm and fuzzy feeling.

Forgive Me is a relatively cheap show to produce and is always good fodder for the mid-morning women's interest programs, which most television networks in the world put to air.

The program is usually also quite successful in the ratings.

The success or failure of a program such as *Forgive Me* relies on good research. The quality of guests for such a show depends on the skill of the researcher whose job it is to find the guests and investigate their stories. That process is often quite difficult and stressful. Being a television program researcher can be a quick path to an early grave.

Many, many potential television contestants tell lies just to get themselves chosen. They call a program hotline and are usually willing to say anything to see their own faces on screen.

They might lie merely to cover up embarrassing facts about themselves, or so they don't disappoint the researcher who has shown an interest in them.

It's the researcher's task to go through the calls made to the show, identify the best potential stories and flesh them out; to use detective skills to establish if the caller has a real story or not. Or is the caller just one of the many, many people with mental health problems who believes he or she deserves their 15 minutes of fame?

But, despite the importance of their work, researchers are on the bottom rung in a production office. The majority of them are willing and very professional. But not all. They are the lowest paid people in the room and, even these days, some are chosen purely because of their looks, rather than their resumes. Men *and* women, in case you were wondering.

As everyone knows, the hardest part of getting a job in the entertainment business is getting a foot in the door. Good researchers use the springboard they are given and go on to more important and better paying jobs in the industry.

Many go all the way to the top. If you can survive being a researcher, every other job is relatively easy.

So a program is often only as good as the quality of its weakest link (hmm, that's a good name for a show).

In a normal day's production schedule, we might need to record up to four separate episodes, which might mean moving up to 20 guests through the studio. To save money, some quiz and game shows record their entire 13-episode season in a week. That means a lot of guests and contestants to move through. You need a well-oiled machine to ensure it all stays on track.

Depending on the researcher involved, there will be a percentage of the guests in each episode who aren't what we have been told to expect. A producer often needs to move heaven and earth to ensure the taping of each show stays on schedule and to ensure the quality of each episode isn't compromised, even when a guest or two doesn't measure up.

The well-researched and easy guests or contestants are moved into the studio first. The more difficult ones are moved back in the schedule or replanned into other episodes, so last-minute research can be done on them, or a replacement found.

On recording day, no one is allowed to drop out, no matter how bad things get, because there is almost no room for manoeuvring. The schedule is that tight.

Sometimes, guests succumb to stage fright and withdraw without telling anyone. They just don't turn up on the day and refuse to answer their phones. It should be legal to hunt these people down and kill them slowly.

One time during a live show, I had a guest sitting outside the studio door, already with make-up on and wearing a lapel microphone. In the commercial break before he was due to go onto the set, he jumped up and ran out. Not only did we have to suddenly fill a three-minute hole in a live program, we had to track the guest down to get our microphone back.

So, to ensure we get 20 guests through in a day, we might schedule 23, just to be on the safe side.

If all 23 turn up and their stories make sense, it's a rare day. But regardless of how well you plan, by the end of three or four days of recording, you are generally down to the dregs, guests whose stories need to be 'massaged' to make them palatable ("Just don't mention the prison sentence" or "Can we cover up those tattoos, please?") or those who need to be - speaking plainly - bribed to make up the numbers.

Peter took up the story.

"By the morning of the last day of recording, Brian had most of the episodes completed and was down to just a few guests remaining to be scheduled on the final afternoon.

"One of these was a man whose wife had left him because of his hard-drinking ways. He wanted to surprise her in the studio, where she had been invited to be an unsuspecting audience member. He would appear unexpectedly and promise her that, if she would take him back, he would remain sober for the rest of his life. A great heart-warming story except for one small thing.

"The man turned up to the studio paralytically drunk and had to be almost carried into the production rooms!

"Brian turned to the researcher responsible for the guest and told her (they are usually 'her') that, because we were at the end of a long recording period, there were no back-ups or stand-by guests left to cover any hole.

"He told her he would move the drunk to the end of the schedule in the afternoon, but if the drunk wasn't in good shape to go into the studio by then, the researcher would be in trouble. The recording went on and, eventually, the lunch break was called. Everyone went out.

"When Brian returned to the production office afterwards, he received a big surprise. The drunk was standing in the preparation room, apparently sober and smiling sheepishly.

"He was also soaking wet, including all his clothes and hair.

"The hairdressing and make-up people went to work on him and, looking very dapper, the man strode into the studio to give his wife her big surprise. It was a lovely moment and she tearfully agreed to have him back, much to the delight of the presenter, the audience, and the man himself.

"Brian had the episode in the can.

"The researcher later claimed that she had a relative who worked at a local hospital. She had taken the drunk there and the relative had given him a full blood transfusion during the lunch break."

"They had laid him in a bath of icy water (which apparently you have to do when you get a blood transfusion) fully clothed, without asking for, or receiving, the drunk's permission.

"And one hour later, voila!

"No more drunk.

"The segment was a success and the researcher impressed Brian enough with her initiative that he later promoted her. "And he has always refused to say whether or not he reimbursed her for paying the hospital worker $500 for all the trouble."

The barbeque guests were suitably horrified and laughed in all the appropriate places.

So that was the story, as told by Peter.

As I said at the beginning, I had no memory of the event because the day it happened was only another day in a long stream of noteworthy or terrifying days which was my life at the time.

And, as it turned out, I had good reason for my memory lapse. The story was absolute nonsense, of course.

A blood transfusion, if anyone was even willing to do it, would not sober you up. Alcohol is present in many parts of your body and, if you did completely change your blood, it would leach back and get you drunk again.

A blood transfusion is generally adding blood after blood loss. So you would have to remove all the drunk's blood and replace it with new blood, which would take many hours.

Longer than it would take to sober up naturally.

The researcher had actually taken the drunk into the hospital for a saline infusion, a quick and dirty but tried and true method for getting people sober fast. Still without his permission, mind you. But that story about me had transfused from myth to reality over many retellings.

After that barbeque, I realised that if I was to tell all my stories properly, I'd better do it myself. That was the inspiration for this book. To tell the events I experienced, of a time period in Europe after the Berlin wall came down, when I was at the centre of television production in many countries.

So *Forgive Me* my arrogance. Here are a few of my stories. They are all true, although I have changed a name here and there (and the name of a country here and there, too) to protect the innocent, or to ensure some people I like will remain my friends for a while longer.

By the way, I do remember that the day after the recording, the drunk called the production office. He and his wife had celebrated their glorious reunion by going out for dinner, whereupon he had proceeded to get very drunk. She'd kicked him out, again. He sheepishly asked if he could come onto the show to try again, please?

Ah, no. As you are about to read, reality television is rarely the same as reality.

1. Feeling shaky

I knew there was a serious problem even before I opened my eyes. For a start, I was face down on the floor, and not in the bed of my very expensive international hotel room in Istanbul. Secondly, I had dirt in my mouth, which is never a good thing. And finally, I had a huge headache, warning me not to open my eyes under any circumstances. The last of these was the most easily explained.

My job involved travelling from country to country helping local television producers make shows bought from my employer company. We invented the program, a television company bought the idea of the program from us and the locals got me as a sort of walking bible on how to make it.

I had been in Turkey several times before, helping to prepare one of our big game shows for a local production company. The first episode of the program had been broadcast the previous night and had been a major hit. The network was happy, the local producer was happy and so was the presenter, a bull-like Turkish man who was professionally unshaven and unprofessionally smelled like a garlic factory.

The presenter was over the moon at his newfound fame. So, after the program had been to air and we had wrapped for the night, he insisted on taking the local producer and I to dinner to celebrate.

He brought along a large bottle of Johnnie Walker Black Label whiskey to keep us company. As a result, the end of the evening was deep in the mist. I remember him kissing me at one point. Turkish men like to kiss you for some reason. It takes a bit to get used to. It takes a lot of Johnnie Walker whiskey to get used to.

The long celebrations explained my throbbing headache, but why did I have dirt in my mouth? Despite the warnings from my fluid-deprived brain about the pain which would hit me, I cracked one eye open. I had to risk it. I had a plane to catch.

The picture was not pretty. I was face down on the carpet in my hotel room. Hmmm. Next to me lay pieces of a beautiful crystal vase which, the previous day, had sat on the expensive windowsill of my expensive room. Now it was in pieces. Worse still was that I could see that the expensive flatscreen television, which had perched next to the expensive vase, was also on the carpet in pieces. Lots and lots of pieces. What the hell?

I sat up abruptly, which turned out to be a mistake. It was several moments before I could get my eyes to focus on the scene around me. I couldn't get the message into my whiskey-soaked brain. Every object in my room was on the floor and broken. My clothes were scattered about and the mini bar fridge door was open, its contents spilled haphazardly onto the carpet. How could that be? What had I been up to?

For the record, I am a very placid drunk. Whenever I have too much, I just fall asleep. I don't get into fights. I don't get rowdy. I tend not to do too many embarrassing things because I go to sleep before they can happen (although there have been several noteworthy exceptions, if I'm honest). I don't get violent. I don't trash hotel rooms.

Specifically, I don't trash expensive hotel rooms when I'm on a work trip. I gingerly climbed to my feet, cautiously stepped around the broken glass and made my way to the bathroom. The scene in there was just as bad. The widescreen mirror was cracked in several places and the expensive-looking complimentary toiletries scattered around and smashed.

The only explanation I could come up with was that I must have gone berserk for some drunken reason. But what could have set me off? Did it mean I was going mad? I kept shaking my head as if to make it all go away.

Then a second, more important, realisation hit me. I was on a work trip. Imagine the surprise of my assistant when she tried to book me into this hotel again in a few months' time and they refused to take me. And told her why.

Trashing a hotel room might be okay if you're an international rock star, but it is not considered wise practice for television producers – certainly not for the people who employed me. And even more worrying, the damage was going to cost thousands of dollars to repair. The only money I had was in the form of company credit cards.

I would definitely have to pay for the damage (once the maid had knocked, entered and taken one look – her hand going to her open mouth in shock). As soon as the company accountant saw my credit card statement in a few weeks' time, I would be fired immediately. No question.

I spent half an hour trying to think a way out of my predicament, all the while battling a savage headache and waves of self-pity. I considered inventing a story involving the Turkish men coming back to my room to celebrate boisterously. Ultimately, I came to the conclusion that I would just have to take my medicine like a man. Own up to what I had done and face the accountant's wrath.

My job had been a good run, but now it was over. Because of my own stupidity.

I showered and cleaned myself up as best I could. Then I went around the room picking things up from the floor and creating neat little piles of rubble, trying to make the room look as nice as possible for the poor maid who was about to get a nasty surprise.

Then I headed to the elevator and pressed the button for the lobby, my head throbbing and my heart heavy.

On ground level, there were a lot of people milling around, the usual sort of busy checkout time at an international hotel. As I walked towards the desk, the same young receptionist who was on duty when I had checked in the day before, looked up at me and smiled.

"Good morning Mr Bigg," she said cheerily.

"How did you go in the earthquake last night?

"I hope it wasn't too frightening for you?"

Earthquake? Earthquake!

My mouth fell open and my legs came to a stop all on their own. There'd been an earthquake? For a few moments my mind held a blissful peace. Then a broad grin spread across my face. An earthquake! A wonderful, destructive earthquake! Yes! You bloody beauty!

To the amazement of the crowd standing around the reception desk, I started dancing in circles, pumping the air and singing the word "Earthquake" loudly. An earthquake! A miracle! Praise be! The crowd edged away from me as if I was a madman. I didn't care. I was saved. I went home a happy but hungover.

As unbelievable as it may seem, a similar thing happened to me several months later, again in Istanbul after another show.

The second earthquake wasn't as bad, just shook things a

25

little and didn't bother me in the least.

But it has allowed me forevermore, to be able to say that I've slept through two earthquakes in Istanbul, thanks to the wonderful anti-earthquake medicine made by Johnnie Walker.

2. So, how did you become king then?

For six years, starting in the mid-1990s, I travelled backwards and forwards across Europe, five and six days a week, helping people make television programs. For years I was in and out of airports, in and out of hotels, in and out of television recording studios.

I spent the years going to places most people pay a lot money to visit, or often pay a lot of money to avoid. The worst part was that I rarely got to see any of the local sights. At one stage, I realised I had driven past the Acropolis in Athens at least 50 times, but had never once been to visit.

All my hectic hither and froing was part of my job to help a relatively small Dutch television production company called Endemol, grow from being merely the biggest television production company in the Netherlands to become the biggest television production company in the world.

We were responsible for giving the world *Big Brother* and literally hundreds of other television shows, in just about every country of the world.

I was employee number 12 at Endemol International and its first foreigner. I was something of an oddity in what had been, up until then, a fiercely Dutch-only company. Years later, when I left to return to Australia, there were thousands of us foreigners scattered in dozens of offices around the world.

The company had grown that fast. At one stage, we joked we were hiring people so quickly, you only needed to be able to spell the word "television" to be given a producer's job.

It was an exciting time and I was near the centre of the vortex. It was also an exciting time to be in Europe. The Soviet Union had collapsed spectacularly a few years earlier and the countries that had been part of its united republics were still working out what democracy actually meant.

Very few middle and eastern European countries had experienced any lengthy period of self-rule. One dictator after another had been in charge since the days Jesus was in short pants.

With no longer any guiding hand telling the people what to do, life proved to be rather scary in many of these countries.

Oddly enough, people from many of these countries told me the same story; that one of the hardest things about democracy was actually making a decision. Formerly, making decisions was someone else's job. There was always someone above you to second guess any decision you made or to criticise you for the decision you had made.

From their stories, it was clear that democracy, being left to their own devices for the first time, was actually like being a prisoner released from jail after a lengthy sentence. Having three meals a day and getting lights out at the same time every night actually becomes comforting to the institutionalised. It's hard to readjust to the outside world.

By the 1990s, we in the West had been telling them in the East that if they gave up the evil communism, they would get cars and boats and Nike shoes and televisions. These things were just falling out of the trees, we assured them. When they finally listened to us and did step out on their own, they discovered we had hadn't been telling them the complete truth.

We forgot to mention that freedom to choose your own leaders and lifestyle, also meant freedom to go hungry if you had no money, go homeless if you couldn't afford the rent or sit in the dark and freeze if you couldn't afford to pay the energy bill. That was a huge shock to them.

The cars and sports shoes we promised them were certainly there in abundance, but they weren't free, or even affordable. And most of the people in former Soviet Union countries quickly and painfully realised they probably wouldn't be getting those things any time soon.

The factories, where most of them had worked their entire adult lives, were often unable to compete with the factories of the West and many shut down overnight after communism stopped. Any decent profitable business was stolen by former agents of the secret police. Many times I met former KGB officers who somehow had become respected rich owners of former state oil companies or banks. I always felt like wiping my hand on my pants or washing my hands in the bathroom washbasin after shaking hands with them. Few of these men would look you in the eye. They were creepy and always trying to rob you in business deals.

For normal people, things were worse.

It was desperately sad for me to get driven to work in Warsaw each morning and see hundreds of men, in bright-coloured plastic pants and plastic waterproof jackets, standing by the tram stations alongside the road.

My driver told me some of the men were too embarrassed to tell their families that their factory had shut down, so they stayed at the tram station all day drinking vodka.

Fortunately, or not, depending on your social status, vodka in Poland in those days was cheaper than water, but more dangerous for your insides than battery acid.

Democracy and capitalism were a nasty shock to the people in the East. Some of them turned to crime as a quick way to get money. By the time I naively wandered onto the scene, the authorities in most of these places had realised television was an excellent way of keeping the increasingly angry masses quiet and in place. After all, television shows demonstrate how 'normal' people live and how 'normal' people should behave. And the former Soviet citizens had longed to be 'normal' like us.

Forgive me a brief cynical opinion. At its most basic, television demonstrates to the poor and working classes how other people conduct themselves. None of the good guys on television take part in riots or go on strike for higher pay. Governments like television because it babysits the population so it can get on with governing.

Consider the shows you like to watch.

Doesn't every character in them lead relatively normal middle class lives (unless you are a *The Walking Dead* fan, of course) and don't they already own all the important consumer goods, such as cars and kitchen appliances? Part of television's job is to hold out the big carrots to ordinary people and tell them that, if they play by the rules, they will get those same goodies, the same easy life, as they see in their favourite shows.

Most people buy into it. I remembered the graffiti I'd seen on walls around inner Sydney in the 1980s which said 'consume, be silent, die'. So appropriate.

Driving past all these sad men in Warsaw each morning used to depress me until, being the thoughtful and sensitive man that I am, I asked the driver to take me a different way to work.

And that will be the only serious bit in the book, I promise. I wanted to get it off my chest.

The rest of the book should be funnier.

So, there were still many, many angry people in the countries I was tasked to visit. In several, I needed a bodyguard and, a couple of times, I came close to becoming a statistic.

The first year I went to Poland, for instance, a US magazine featured a story revealing that 385 foreign businessmen had been kidnapped in Warsaw that year.

That was more than one a day!

The kidnappers revealed their true capitalistic nature through the outcomes of these kidnappings. Only two of the businessmen were killed. All the others had kidnap and ransom insurance, which was what the kidnappers were after.

Many of the victims were stripped to their underwear and released near a freeway off-ramp after the ransom was paid. There were so many victims, one of the local newspapers joked it had a photographer posted permanently at the off-ramp, just in case.

My company wouldn't pay for kidnap and ransom insurance for me. When I was in Poland, I got a driver/bodyguard called Marc. Marc was smaller than my mother and most likely would not have beaten her in a fist fight.

Marc spoke almost no English, drove worse than my teenage daughter. His hand was too small to fit around the large pistol he carried in his pants.

What was worse, sometimes he left the gun on the floor of the car. Because the gun rattled and bumped around as we drove, I was terrified we would hit a pothole and I would get my testicles shot off. And because it was rattling around the floor, how was Marc going to reach it in any emergency?

The people doing the kidnapping were apparently mostly gangsters and former special forces soldiers with proper military training. How would little Marc defend me? And why would he?

We paid him a pittance, so he was totally open to betraying me to the kidnap gangs if they offered him more than about $1.50.

I resolved to always wear new and clean underwear in Poland, in case I had to jog in them down the off-ramp.

I was assured the house in which I was living in Warsaw had both interior and perimeter alarm systems for my safety. But no one knew the code for the interior alarm, so I never found out if it worked or not.

I know the perimeter alarm didn't.

One morning in the middle of winter, as I left for work, I noticed fresh footprints in the snow all the way around the house, with big disturbances near the windows. The perimeter alarm turned out to be a wire on a peg, which was half a metre under the snow.

Marc was actually more protection for me than that. My mother would have been even more effective. I bought more underwear just incase.

So that was the scene in Eastern Europe at the time I danced into view, carrying all the West's best game shows and entertainment programs for their amusement and distraction.

No longer communist, but not quite western either.

As I discovered, few people in either eastern or western Europe knew how to deal with a devilishly handsome red-headed producer from Australia.

3. Brian's law

International travel can be a nightmare. The first time I was scheduled to journey from the Netherlands to Portugal I was all excited. I cleverly gave myself 1 hour 40 minutes to get to the airport, for what is usually a 40-minute taxi ride.

But then things turned sour.

The taxi I was travelling in moved 100 metres onto the freeway, then we found ourselves stopped behind 1,000 other cars. The radio reported that somewhere up ahead, a driver had suffered a heart attack at the wheel and caused a major crash.

So we sat in the traffic jam, moving one car at a time.

An hour later, and just as I was about to tell the driver that I couldn't make it so we might as well go back, we moved forward and the jam cleared. The driver (who apparently drove Formula 1 cars on his days off) then took it as a personal challenge to get me to the airport on time. It was a gut-wrenching trip to Schiphol.

I arrived in front of the airport travel desk my company used at exactly the time my plane had been scheduled to depart. As the woman behind the travel counter handed me my tickets, she knowingly commented, "You'll never make it".

I replied "Wanna bet?" and ran off.

Of course, I didn't count on Brian's Law, the first part of which states: When you arrive at the airport two hours early for a flight, there are never any queues at customs and your aircraft is scheduled to leave from gate A-1, which is usually only 2 meters from the customs barrier.

However, the second part of Brian's Law states: If you arrive at the airport late, there will always be a little old lady at the front of the customs line prepared to spend all day, if necessary, to arguing with the customs officer why she should be allowed out of the country, even though she has a bag full of illegal food products and doesn't have the correct visa.

Every other line moved through customs quickly, but mine just stayed as still as if we were all welded to the floor. I got increasingly agitated and hopped from foot to foot quietly cursing the little old lady.

"Come on lady. Come on! Look, just get the fuck out of the line, will you? Someone hit her. COME ON!"

Finally, I burst through customs to discover the third part of Brian's Law: When you are very, very late to arrive at the airport, your plane will always leave from gate Z-235 which is slightly further than the Olympic marathon distance from where you are standing.

I had a heavy overnight bag over my shoulder and I was wearing a good suit. I quickly discovered why athletes don't wear these when competing.

I ran and ran and ran until I thought my lungs would burst. It felt like kilometres.

Finally … pant, pant … I got to the … pant, pant … gate where the … gasp, gasp … chief steward was standing at the half closed aircraft door, looking at her watch … pant, pant … clutch the chest, bend forward, open the mouth … gasp for breath.

"Please take your seat," she said with a barely concealed snarl.

"You've only just made it."

I had a whistling sound in my ears and my face was so red, the aircraft smoke detectors started to twitch … gasp, gasp, sweat. I hobbled down the aisle and collapsed into my seat.

I must have looked pretty bad because the steward for my section came by every 30 seconds to offer me orange juice. And, I'm sure, to check I didn't die in her section.

I cursed to hell the bastard who'd suffered the heart attack on the freeway and quietly promised between gasps that, if I died on the plane, I would find him in hell and kick him. Of course, he would be safe if he had lived a good life and was in heaven. I won't be allowed in there.

After a while I recovered and, ignoring dirty looks from other passengers around me – after all, I had caused a 15-minute delay to our departure – I sank into a book.

When the plane descended a few hours later, it was extremely early according to the schedule given to me by the travel office. And, quite frankly, when I looked out the window, Lisbon, the capital of Portugal, did not look as big a city as I thought it might be.

However, when we landed, I ignored all the arrival announcements, grabbed my bag from the overhead locker and left the plane.

The friendly man at the customs desk tried to tell me something, but I've found with these people that if you act confident and just go past, they'll generally let you go.

Which I did.

And he did.

I went to a cash machine in the terminal, waited my turn to use the machine then came to a complete standstill. To the people behind me in the queue (no doubt some of them swearing quietly at their own version of Brian's Law), it must have appeared as if I had suffered a stroke, because I just stood there with my finger poised above the keypad. Inside, I was experiencing a cascade of depressing realisations about how ill-prepared I was to be an international television producer.

The machine offered to give me 10,000 escudos, the Portuguese money at that time. It sounded like a lot, but I realised that I had no idea how much that was in guilders, the Dutch money at that time. But I thought to myself I could always give it back to my office administrator if it was too much.

Then I was struck by another thought.

What if 10,000 escudos wasn't very much at all?

Maybe 10,000 escudos wouldn't even buy me a sandwich.

Who the hell knew?

And more importantly, I wondered if it would be enough to pay for a taxi to get me to our Lisbon office.

Then I was struck by yet another thought.

"Where was our office in Lisbon?" I'd come away without writing down the address. So, I went out onto the footpath near the taxi rank and called the Lisbon office.

At least I'd had the sense to bring the phone number.

"Just checking I've written the correct address of your office," I said to the woman who answered the phone.

"Can you read it to me, so I can double check what I have obviously written down on my piece of paper here?"

"Just being efficient, you know."

The woman on the other end of the call read out the address, which was a disaster.

She said something like, "Chinqua chinqua chinqua hose del la compandandananandndnda".

I said, "Hold on, I'm trying to write that down", at which the woman said, "I thought you already had it written down?"

"Ah yes," I blustered.

"Just checking I have the spelling right."

"Why do you need to spell it?" She obviously thought I was an idiot. If she only knew the rest of the story.

Armed now with the address, I jumped into the taxi at the front of the line and confidently showed the driver the piece of paper, upon which I'd just written the address.

"Could you take me there, please, and how much in escudos would it be?" He had almost no English. He fired off some rapid Portuguese and looked at me in a funny way.

"You want to go to that address," he asked? "Is in Lisboa."

"Yes," I said, a little irritated.

"I know it's in Lisboa. That's why I want to go there."

He fired off more Portuguese. I shook my head and pointed to the address again. We were still in the taxi line and people behind us were beginning to get antsy. Brian's Law again. There's always an idiot at the front of the line. It's me again.

Unable to communicate what he wanted to say to me, the driver climbed out of the taxi and beckoned another driver over. He showed him my piece of paper and they discussed it at length. The second driver approached me.

"Is in Lisboa," said the second driver.

"Both of them are masters of the bleeding obvious," I thought, but smiled politely. Then my driver sighed deeply and beckoned me to follow him inside to the airport tourist desk.

The girl with perfect English behind the counter, after being appraised of the situation in a 10-minute stream of Portuguese, turned to me and told me with a cheery smile,

"Yes, that address is definitely in Lisbon."

"Well, why won't the driver take me there?" I asked.

"Because," she replied, "Lisbon is 300 km away."

"He says he has to be back to his family tonight and he won't be back in time if he goes there."

"Wait. What? Where am I then?"

"You are in Porto, senor. A city in northern Portugal."

Jesus Christ!

Without a word of thanks or backward glance, I grabbed my bag and ran to the KLM counter, where I learned my plane was just leaving on the second stage of the trip to Lisbon.

"It always stops in Porto first on Tuesdays and Thursdays," the kind woman behind the counter informed me.

"I'll try to get you back on board, but I can't promise."

I didn't wait to hear anything more. I turned and ran into the departure area. I was still running when I went past the original customs officer, who smirked at me.

"Told you so," his smile clearly told me.

I sprinted out onto the tarmac. They were about to pull away the stairs.

"Wait!" Up the stairs I clambered, past the astonished chief steward standing at the half-closed aircraft door once again and down the aisle where I flopped into my original seat.

Holy . . . gasp, gasp . . . hell . . . pant, pant . . . that was . . . gasp, gasp . . . a close one . . . gulp for air . . . lean forward. Gasp, sweat.

Out of the corner or my eye, I could see the other passengers staring at me as if I was some sort of circus freak. Several of them had covered their open mouths in shock at the sight of me.

The steward for my section was there, holding out another tray of orange juice. She was also staring at me as if I was some sort of bad dream.

I'm sure she thought the airline was conducting a secret test on her. Or was the apparently insane passenger actually one of those rare fitness freaks who whipped out for a quick run every time the plane landed?

There are those people aren't there?

He couldn't just be a dickhead. Could he?

On arrival soon afterwards in Lisbon (a very big city as it turns out) I sat up and listened carefully to all the announcements. When we disembarked, other passengers kept well back from me and let me disembark first.

In case I felt the need to go for another quick jog in full suit and overnight bag, I guess. Or, more likely, if I went truly mad and started throwing my faeces at them.

I didn't completely recover my wits until I saw at least five signs that said: "Welcome to Lisbon."

Yeah, right.

4. First time in Hungary

Bloody hell. It took nearly 10 hours for me to get from the Netherlands to Budapest. I could have walked there faster. I had discovered during the week that, as an Australian, I would need a visa to get into Hungary.

When I telephoned the Hungarian embassy in the Netherlands, they told me that if I didn't have time to go to the embassy in The Hague, I could easily pick up a visa at the airport in Budapest on arrival.

Naturally, I believed them. Ha!

When I got to Schiphol Airport, the two colleagues with whom I was to travel, Matthew and John (very biblical) had already checked in for the flight.

They don't travel as much as I do and had arrived in time to do some shopping.

As you will have read elsewhere, I usually arrive with only seconds to spare.

It's a fine art I've perfected.

I've only missed two flights so far and saved myself thousands of hours waiting pointlessly at airports. However, the woman at the KLM check-in counter cheerfully told me that, before they would let me on the plane, I would need a letter to prove I was eligible to get a visa when I arrived in Hungary. KLM couldn't put me on the flight without it.

I begged, pleaded and threatened, but the damned woman was unmoved. So I missed the flight and was forced to wait five hours for the next one, while my travel office arranged for the visa permission letter. It was also bad news for Matthew and John, who had boarded the plane, well in time and with an armload of goodies from the duty-free stores.

I was carrying all the tapes we planned to use in our meetings in Budapest and, even worse, I was carrying the great big wad of Hungarian cash they would need to pay for a taxi from the airport.

So I waited in the Schiphol Airport lounge for five hours drinking cup after cup of free coffee.

Finally, the visa permission letter came through, and I boarded the next flight. KLM tried to suck up by upgrading me to business class. Nice try KLM but I can't be bought so cheaply. I silently told them that while shoveling down the free sandwiches and champagne.

After a short, uneventful flight, I finally arrived in Budapest.

Budapest Airport in those days was quite cute.

It looked just like the pictures you see of Soviet Airports in the 1950s. Buildings put up quickly and cheaply – and badly – after World War 2 and not touched by man or beast since.

It was staffed by people who looked to me like criminals, each of them badly-dressed and surly. The customs staff all looked dumpy and square (I now know what members of the Russian Olympic shot-put team do when they retire – advise Hungarian airport officials on diet and clothing).

The men all looked swarthy and suspicious.

I kept a firm hand on my huge wad of Hungarian money. Matthew and John, I discovered, had called the local office and a car had been sent for them, so they hadn't needed the cash.

The Soviets may have left Hungary, but their super-efficient way of running things was still in evidence at the airport.

I fronted up before the visa counter and was brusquely told by the surly shot-putter behind the screen to fill in two great long forms. The forms were intrusive. I was asked who I was, why I was there, where was I planning to stay and how many times a day did I plan to go to the toilet while there? Maybe not that last one, but it felt like it.

I got stuck on one particular question.

The travel person at my office in the Netherlands had told me I was not allowed to bring Hungarian money out of the country, so I should not tell them how much I was bringing in.

So on the form where it asked how much Hungarian money I was carrying, I wrote "0" even though any alert official could have easily noticed I had developed a limp from carrying several kilograms of Hungarian cash in my right pocket. After spending half an hour filling out the forms, I handed them to the shot-putter. She asked me to pay for the visa. I put on my most charming voice and asked if I could pay by credit card.

"No," she replied, "just in US dollars."

"I have no dollars," I replied, with my best smile.

She just shrugged.

We stared at each other for several seconds, neither or us willing to be the first to cave in.

Then I caved in. Obviously.

"In that case," I said resignedly, "I will pay in forints."

She looked down for a long moment at the form where I had written under "Hungarian money being carried – 0" and told me I would have to pay extra if I insisted on paying in forints.

Even the Hungarians knew their local money had no value.

I was sure she was ripping me off, but I had begun to have

visions of being slapped in a Soviet-era jail, until I could adequately explain how it came to be that I had approximately 82 kilograms of Hungarian money in my pocket.

So I didn't say anything more.

She hashed at an ancient calculator for several seconds and then told me it came to 15,500 forints. That was about US$60 and, what was more of a relief, it relived me of about half of my stash of notes.

She gathered up the pile of money, my passport, and the forms I had obviously told lies on and disappeared to an office at the back.

She didn't come back.

Eventually, every other passenger from my plane and all the customs people left the area. I was alone in the airport and convinced I would be sleeping there.

While waiting, I heard and then saw a group of 200 soldiers, fully armed and dressed in their best Bolivian Army-style uniforms, march onto the tarmac in front of the terminal and line up. With nothing to do while I waited and with no one there to tell me I couldn't, I wandered back out onto the tarmac to watch the show.

The commanding officer looked like a peacock in his fancy uniform, red stripes and big hat.

He made the soldiers stand to attention, then at ease, then to attention again – and so on, for ages and long past the point where I would have yelled out "make up your bloody mind!" had I been a private in the Hungarian army.

While most of the soldiers practiced their drill, others laid a red carpet half-way across the tarmac. Still others strained under the weight of big plastic trees in large pots, which they carried out and placed alongside the red carpet at regular intervals, to

43

give the whole scene a nice, homey feel.

It was amusing to watch and it was with some disappointment that I noticed at the visa counter inside the terminal, that the shot-putter had finally returned. She thrust my passport at me and told me I could go. I found out later the soldiers were there to be an honour guard for the Austrian President who was due soon for a state visit.

Anyway, I made it through to the main passenger terminal to discover that, not surprisingly, none of the taxies had waited for me. Another surly shot putter (this one also swarthy) sat behind the airport bus shuttle counter and was most irritated when she was forced to order a bus just for me.

It seems I had ruined everyone's day by taking forever to come through customs.

Just who did I think I was?

The President of Austria?

I sat patiently for another 45 minutes until my special 'Just For Inconsiderate Bastards' shuttle bus arrived (I'm sure they made him park down the road for half an hour just to make me wait).

The driver was a surprisingly pleasant man, neither surly nor swarthy, and he spoke reasonable English. He whizzed me into town where I arrived at 5 pm, a mere 10 hours after leaving home, a lot less sweaty.

Budapest on the day I arrived, looked rundown and grimy. The last paint company in the region apparently had gone broke shortly after World War 2.

As far as I could see, nothing had been painted in the whole city since, even though it was obvious the local graffiti artists managed to find a regular supply of paint somewhere.

The cars were mostly East German Ladas (I suppose the

poor Hungarians were made to buy them to show solidarity with their Soviet comrades) and East German Trabants (both cars looked like they were designed by disabled children using crayons).

The cars emit a lot of pollution, so the air was warm and brown. On the plus side, there were also a lot of modern German sedans and even some Japanese and Korean hatchbacks.

The streets looked as neglected as the buildings.

It was obvious they hadn't been touched by a road repair crew since the boys of the Sixth Panzer Regiment rolled out of town in 1945.

Despite this, there were signs of modem capitalistic life starting to emerge. What always surprises me when I travel is that, even in the most remote and backward of countries, places where there might be no reliable electricity or education system, the people from McDonalds, Pepsi, Nike and Mercedes have already been there.

Budapest was no exception. Big, modern stores were growing among the old stone houses. Whopping modern advertising billboards sprouted every 10 meters along the main roads.

I'm sure that when Captain Cook first sailed up the east coast of Australia, the Aborigines waving spears at him were all wearing tee-shirts advertising Hyundai.

The buildings in Budapest were all made from stone and, outside the CBD which looked very modern, many buildings looked like no one had repaired them since the war.

Amazingly, though, on even the most dilapidated, run down and abused old building, where the poorest of the poor undoubtedly lived, there were one, two or even sometimes three, satellite dishes.

Once the Soviets left, everyone developed a taste for television and until the local industry developed (which is something I was going to help with), they got most of their TV from the satellites which showed them German channels.

I got another surprise, arriving at the company office where we were due to meet, to discover hardly anyone spoke English but, because of the satellite dishes, everyone spoke German (as well as Hungarian, obviously).

So, for the next two days, I would have to do business in German. I learned the language when I was younger, but I couldn't remember much of it. If you had asked me if I would remember enough to work in the language, I would have scoffed and called you an unwashed scoundrel.

But I found I understood most of what they were saying and could get by well enough. And the more I was forced to speak the language, the better I became with it..

I had several quick meetings to make up for the fact that I had arrived very late and went on a tour of their studio facilities, which were built in 1917 and looked it.

The company we were dealing with, according to Matthew and John, was the local favourite to secure a license to establish a new commercial television station.

Our plan was to set up a joint venture with them to make the programs they would need to fill the airtime on that channel.

Big business for us, but first we had to work out if they were legitimate. My colleagues had to look over the books and finances. My job was to look at their production facilities and try and work out if they had the people to make our shows properly.

I have to say, although I arrived very late (yes, yes, you can stop telling us that) I didn't see anything early in my visit which indicated they were remotely qualified to run a TV station.

But I was told the company's owner and the chairman were

very well connected (wink, wink) with the new government.

If they were powerful enough to convince the government to give them a license to set up a television station, I was sure they would be powerful enough to get it up and running on time.

It wasn't like Hungarian television was the height of sophistication. Until recently, if a company, for example a refrigerator manufacturer, took an advertisement on Hungarian television, they paid not in cash, but in fridges. The television companies set up their own stores to sell all the stuff they'd been paid with.

That system grew up mainly because the good old forint wasn't worth a damn. Anyway, my company planned to change this system and get everyone to pay in cash, specifically the Euro.

We expected a few arguments about it.

Matthew, John and I, were installed in the comfort of a big, old conference room in the company's ground floor and supplied with unending coffee and biscuits. We stayed there the whole first evening and the people we were scheduled to meet trooped in one after the other on a tight schedule. In between these meetings, we were left alone in the room.

About 7 pm, the boss of the company drove us to our hotel, which was nice and modem in the centre of the city and which we were lucky to get, because apparently there were 4,000 doctors in town for a conference. The next day we were again parked in the big conference room with staff marched in to speak to us.

John became more upset as the day wore on.

He was in charge of checking the finances and much of the money we planned to make in Hungary depended on the locals being ready to broadcast programs the moment they got their license approval.

This was supposed to be only a few months away, but none of us could see any sign of anyone working on shows to be ready on time. John got vague and different answers each time.

Once, when we were in the conference room on our own, he grouched to Matthew and I that he was going to keep asking until he got an answer he was happy with.

For some time before this, I had been getting the strangest feeling. The room had a big thick door and, from outside, you couldn't hear anything which went on inside. Similarly, from inside, you couldn't hear anything going on outside. I kept getting the distinct feeling someone was watching me.

I remembered I had also felt this way the evening before.

I also realised that, without consciously meaning to, I had begun to be careful about what I was saying. I kept looking around the room for a security camera or a microphone.

At lunchtime, they left us alone in the room, again with the big door closed. John started grizzling again about how people were avoiding answering his questions about the broadcasting preparations. I felt quite weird, so I shushed him and told him quietly to be a bit careful how he spoke. Matthew admitted he'd also felt something was not quite right.

I picked up the newspaper I was reading and coincidently saw a story that claimed 35 per cent of American companies spied on their employees. We laughed and decided we must be getting paranoid.

But we didn't talk about work anymore when we were on our own. And now we were suspicious, we noticed during the afternoon meetings how many of the Hungarians who came into the room spoke very softly or not at all, unless specifically spoken to.

And that the boss, when he was in there, spoke as if everything he said could be used against him in court.

At the end of the day, as we prepared to leave, the chairman of the company (who had apparently been away all day, wining and dining the communications minister, which you need to do if you are to win a television broadcasting license), strode into the room and made a speech thanking us for being there and helping them on their way to greatness.

"By the way," he said, "I'm sorry we haven't had a chance to take you to the other building across town where there is a big team of people working to get the television station ready to go on air in time. Maybe you will get to see them on your next visit."

Matthew, John and I exchanged a look. It was way too convenient. We had already asked about all their buildings and studios and staff. Now suddenly there was another building?

As we were walking out to get into a taxi, Matthew made a comment about how beautiful the conference room was and how thick a door it had. The chairman agreed it was beautiful and told us it was the one office left untouched from the Soviet era (the place was formerly a film studio). He said they had renovated everything except this particular room.

The door was thick, he explained, because the film people had wanted to make sure no one could hear their conversations. But then he laughed and said, "but of course, with all the things there" (here he waved his hand towards the ceiling), "everyone heard every word of what was going on anyway".

Matthew and I looked at each other. Was this man admitting that the room really was bugged, and that he'd been one of those who'd done the bugging? (I guess that would put him in the enthusiastically communist-turned-capitalist category).

It might also explain the disproportionate influence this small, inexperienced company seemed to have in Hungary. Were we bugged? Who knows?

By the way, the boss offered to get me free tickets to a concert by the American rock group Kiss, which was planned for Budapest the following week. I had told him I was a fan of Kiss but had never seen them in concert. He said he knew someone who could get me tickets and backstage passes, so I could meet the band. I told him I had to be in London that particular day.

Maybe because Matthew and John were asking all the tough questions and I played Mr Nice Guy (which were the roles we'd agreed on beforehand), the locals thought I might be the easiest mark for them to win over.

Kiss tickets and a backstage pass? Damn you Hungary.

I can't be bought so cheaply. Although. Although.

Backstage passes and meeting the band?

Hmm. I made a note to check with my assistant to see if I could postpone the London meetings.

The trip home was unremarkable except that KLM upgraded me to business class again. Okay, you're forgiven KLM. Pass me the champagne and another sandwich.

I was due to go back to Budapest a few weeks later. I'd be very interested to see what would happen if they did, in fact, have transcripts of our conversations. God, I hope I didn't say anything too bad.

5. A walking bible

Before I go too much further, I should tell you what I actually do for a living. Because, if you're not familiar with the world of television, it can seem a little strange.

When you watch a program on your new LED widescreen television, the show usually has a presenter who is famous in your country, and the contestants or participants are local people with whom you can identify.

Most viewers therefore believe the show they are watching must've been invented in their own country by their local television producers (or whoever else makes their local television programs). I've lost count of the number of people who have said to me, "How can this show be anything other than (fill in the country name here)? It's so specific to us and our culture."

But most of the time, that's not the case. There aren't that many good ideas in the world. What happens is this.

Twice a year, in April and October, most of world's television executives, up to 15,000 of us at a time, flock to Cannes in the south of France to very large conferences where we buy and sell our ideas for new television shows.

Why Cannes?

We aren't stupid.

We are all on generous expense accounts, so we aren't going to a small village in the Ukraine, are we?

MIPCOM and MIPTV, which is what the two conferences are called, are the place to see and be seen if you are in television. If you are not a regular at the front bar of the Carlton Hotel during MIPCOM or MIPTV, you haven't really made it. No matter how important you think you are at home.

The luxury beachside promenade in Cannes becomes packed with men and women, most of whom are dressed in black. Even though we think ourselves to be creative, for some reason we all wear the media worker's black uniform.

All of us go to Cannes twice a year, either on the lookout for the next big television hit or believing that we are selling the next big phenomenon.

In the old days, most of the big television show ideas came out of the United States. The big American producers would send their salesmen to Cannes to be feted, flattered and fed. And they would rake in the cash because the intellectual property they owned was sold into country after country.

European television executives had little choice. If their competition bought the expensive new American program, their own jobs could be in trouble.

Many Europeans found out the hard way, too, that you couldn't just steal a US idea and make the show without permission. American lawyers crawled the planet looking for production companies in obscure countries who might try to copy their great show without paying for the rights.

Jeopardy, Days of Our Lives, The Honeymoon Quiz and other enormous shows from the US went round and round Europe for years, all the time promoting the idea that the US was the only place where television shows were invented.

Shows from Europe were considered to be too hard to understand, because they usually weren't in English, or they were considered too difficult to adapt to an audience in another culture. And, to some extent that was true.

There's a reason you don't hear of many big international French or Italian television programs. French television shows have always been so French it was, with a few exceptions, too hard to adapt them to the tastes of the Japanese, the English or New Zealanders for example. The same with Italy. The same with just about every non-English speaking culture.

German shows, for example, were until recently, so specifically designed to appeal to the very large and appreciative German audience, that production houses and broadcasters didn't give much of a thought to the idea that, with a few tweaks, other cultures might enjoy them too.

Speaking broadly, European television channels were not seriously interested in selling their own shows to other cultures. They were thought to be too hard to repurpose, there was no way to protect the intellectual property without a large team of lawyers and it was all just too hard for the small returns they expected to get.

In the 1990s, however, things began to change.

6. The rise of formats

In the 1980s, television broadcasters in many countries discovered that, because of changes to the tax system in the European Union, it was suddenly cheaper and simpler to buy shows from independent production companies, than to make them in-house.

This, by the way, had long been the practice in the US, but the concept was new in other places. Broadcasters had always made their own shows, so they could completely control the content and the costs.

They were initially wary of giving up that control, but the financial advantages of outsourcing became so obvious, the idea swept the industry in a short number of years. Nowadays, most broadcasters in most countries buy in most of the shows they broadcast, rather than make them themselves. They just put their logo on the end credits to make it look like they care.

As well as making shows cheaper to produce, outsourcing the work to production companies also reduced other risks for the broadcasters.

Just like movies, television shows are expensive and there is no guarantee they'll succeed. The chances of getting a hit are just as remote as with movies. A lot more shows fail than succeed and a failure costs money and jobs. I know of one show in the US which cost a whopping $52 million to set up (I won't name it to save a few friends the embarrassment). The plan was for the show to run for a year and the big set-up cost recovered over hundreds of episodes. But the show was so unpopular with the audience, it was cancelled after six weeks. All that money went up in smoke.

Another show was made into a pilot (test episode). Everyone was enthusiastic about the concept, so $750,000 was spent on the pilot. The person at the broadcaster who was responsible for buying new shows took one look at the tape and said "no thanks". The producers had spent three quarters of a million dollars and only one person ever saw the episode. Ouch.

So outsourcing proved to be a lot cheaper for the broadcasters. They could let production companies go to the expense and trouble of hiring creative people to come up with clever ideas. The production companies also took most of the costs and risks involved in getting these clever ideas developed to the point that they became possibly good television shows.

"Develop?" I hear you ask.

"My television show idea is perfect," you insist.

"My genius idea is to put 10 beautiful people on an island and wait for them to fall in love with each other. It's brilliant. Why would it need to be developed? Just put it on television right now, damn you!"

Okay, but …

What do the beautiful people do on the island while they are waiting to fall in love?

What happens if the shy ones go to opposite ends of the island and never talk to each other?

What happens this week which will make me absolutely want to watch the show again next week?

How does it all end?

How long is each episode?

What night of the week is best for it to go to air?

What visual elements are there besides the beautiful bodies? How many cameras will you need to guarantee you capture all the intrigue and drama?

How many microphones?

Do the contestants see the cameras and camera operators?

If not, how do you hide them?

Can the contestants interact with the crew if they see them?

Do you put cameras in the toilets and showers so the contestants can't learn there are such places they can go if they want to speak to each other without the producers knowing?

How is the show promoted each week?

Do you need to have a doctor or psychologist on hand to deal with medical or mental health emergencies?

And so on and so on.

There are a million more questions your idea needs to answer before it gets anywhere near to becoming an actual TV show. The original spark you had is just the beginning. It actually takes a lot of time, money and creativity to turn your good idea into a successful TV show. Traditionally the broadcasters paid those costs themselves and took the profits or losses when the program succeeded or failed.

But by the 1990s, independent production companies had begun to invest their own money to develop their own ideas. If no one bought their show or if the idea was a failure, the production company took the hit.

So why did they do if it was so risky?

Because, in return for accepting the risk, the production companies got to keep the ownership rights to the shows they developed, just as the companies in the US were already doing.

If the show was successful, they could get very rich indeed.

If a broadcaster invents, produces and airs a successful show, it owns everything about that show and can use that success any way it likes.

Create spinoffs, print posters, produce more episodes cheaply or use the stars of the show in other network owned shows, for example.

If a production company invents the successful show, it sells to the broadcaster only the right to broadcast the finished program in its own territory. The broadcaster might get good ratings and earn the money from advertising within the show, but usually nothing else.

The production company keeps the ownership of the idea and therefore the rights to sell the show everywhere else in the world. It can choose to make action figures of the stars, commission comic books, produce board games, or make spin offs, or whatever it wants.

For a wildly successful show like *Who Wants to be a Millionaire?* it can amount to millions and millions and millions of dollars. (In one year, for example, the makers of *Who Wants to be a Millionaire?* made over UK £40 million from just the board games developed from the show.)

For a genre phenomenon like *Big Brother* it can turn a successful multi-million company into a successful multi-billion dollar company.

That was us.

Producing television shows quickly became big business because, as I said earlier, there are never enough good ideas. The production companies which harnessed the right people began making serious money and grew rapidly.

The company I joined in the mid-1990s, Endemol of the

Netherlands, was fortunate in that it had not one, but two, geniuses at the helm. Joop van den Ende and John de Mol are fifth-dan black belt masters of television and entertainment.

Part of their success was that they worked out early on how to make their shows jump cultural boundaries. Commonplace nowadays but revolutionary then.

There are only three universal themes – music, sport and sex – which can be broadcast in their original form in every country. Come up with a show with one or more of these themes and you have a better chance it will be successful, no matter where you sell it.

Some might claim there is a limit to how many of these themes you can twist into television show ideas. But, there are still many unexplored corners of each waiting to be discovered.

Masked Singer anyone?

Every other genre of show – dating, reality, quiz, etc – must be culturally specific to work successfully. It's not often you can take a show from one country and put it to air in another without first changing a lot of things. Some of the things you need to change may make it unworkable in the new land.

To give you an example, picture a brightly lit studio.

To a big musical fanfare, in comes a handsome-looking, middle-aged male host, usually with slicked-back hair. Then a sexy, young female co-presenter in a low-cut dress also enters. The sexual banter between the two suggests more might be going on between them.

The show they deliver over two hours features bad comedians, celebrities and politicians as guests.

There is lots of talk, arguments, controversy, laughter and singing and a lot of obvious in-show product placement.

The episode is recorded in the presence of a large, enthusiastic audience of middle-aged women who clap and cheer wildly throughout. An overly loud band punctuates all the pivotal moments of the show.

Sounds appalling right? Believe it or not, at one time this formula was the mainstay of most of the successful programs in Italy (and helped Silvio Berlusconi, the man who owned the channel they were broadcast on, to the Italian Prime Ministership three times).

You can still see the occasional show like this in Italy even today. But as hugely popular as this sort of old-fashioned variety pomp was in the land of pasta, few audiences anywhere else were remotely interested in either buying the idea or broadcasting the same show. It was so specific to Italy that it just wasn't possible to translate it to French, German or English.

Those of us in the creativity business learned that, as well as the three universals (sex, music and sport), there was a second layer of the human experience which would translate interculturally – emotion.

Anger, sadness, love, greed.

Come up with a show pivoting on one or more emotions and you could expect to sell your idea in a variety of places. *Who Wants to Be a Millionaire?* for example, focusses on the battle between greed and fear.

Greed and fear are universal emotions.

Almost overnight, production companies in many countries began coming up with shows based on emotions – *All You Need is Love* (love), *Fear Factor* (fear), *Make My Day* (joy and sadness), *The Chair* (fear and greed,) to name but a few.

As these secondary themes started to take off around the world, it became more financially sensible for these production companies to develop show ideas with more than just their local audiences in mind.

An independent production company obviously first tries to sell its great new show to its local broadcasters, because that is the easiest possible sale (it knows its own local market best) and it's the best chance to get its investment and risk money back quickly. But the real get-out-of-jail money is made by selling the idea to other countries (or territories as they are called in the television business).

The entire business model hinges on turning the unique idea into a saleable product, which is called a format. And fiercely protecting that format from the many people who will try to steal or copy it.

When I went to South Africa for the first time in the late 1990s, I showed a room full of South African Broadcasting Corporation executives tapes of Endemol's most successful European shows.

Afterwards, I asked, "Are there any questions?" The first question came from the back of the room: "Why would we pay you for these shows and not just copy them?"

My answer was that we would sue the people who did it and we had deeper pockets than them.

That wasn't always foolproof.

I know a producer who twice successfully copied the concepts which made *Who Wants to Be A Millionaire?* a hit – the battle in each contestant's mind between greed and fear (see my book *Making a Millionaire: My Way* for more on the secrets of this phenomenal show).

When John de Mol first invented *Big Brother*, the first thing he told us creative types who worked for him was not to wait for others to rip off the idea. He tasked us with copying the show ourselves, so we could stay ahead of the pack and dominate the genre he had just invented. Which we did.

We came up with a variety of new shows based on the same general concept, many of which have since made it onto the box. And some of which have not.

The idea of putting unemployed people in the *Big Brother* house and competing until the winner was given a dream job as a prize, was considered poor taste. As was the idea of putting people into the *Big Brother* house who were dying of various conditions or illnesses.

Some would recover, some would not.

The winner would be the one left alive at the end.

He or she would win the house and a big cash prize. For some reason, that idea didn't get a green light. Neither did another idea for contestants who needed organ transplants.

Such is the creative process.

Lots of hits.

Lots of misses.

No bad ideas.

As the format business grew, the companies with the deepest pockets, and therefore the most lawyers, became the most powerful. These big companies, of which we were the biggest, would argue that their format was unique and belonged solely to them. They had risked a lot of money to make it a successful product.

If you wanted the show, you had to pay the appropriate license fee. Or they would see you in court. If you came up with a similar show to theirs, you could expect a lawyer's letter and probably an appearance in court, unless you stopped making it.

A few years later, a small company I briefly worked with in Poland, was forced to take a great new show off the air because a big Swedish company claimed some elements of the Polish show were similar to one of its shows.

The elements were nothing alike.

It was just a lawyer's threatening letter which, as any lawyer will tell you, is just smoke and bullshit. But the Swedish company was big, the Polish company small and the weight of the legal threat was too much to ignore.

The Polish program was cancelled and the Swedish company happily added the Polish show to its own catalogue and thereafter treated it as its own.

It was a shame.

But the bigger fish always swallow the smaller fish.

7. What is a format?

So all television shows are formats, right? Well no. Some are just shows. Take a typical gardening program, as an example. There are hundreds of them and they all look pretty much the same.

The expert comes in, sees the disaster that is the backyard and garden of the contestants. He or she talks to the contestants about what they would like their backyard to be, then the expert (and his or her team) renovates the area, giving the viewers clever and useful take-home information along the way.

When all the work is done, the contestants return and say "Oh my God!" when they see their impressive new backyard. Then the viewers get to see what the place looked like before and after the renovation. And that's it.

Whether it's gardens, kitchens or cars, these shows are all the same. No element in this description is unique to any of them.

So if I want a gardening show on my television channel I can just cobble together these sort of elements, call it something clever and no one can tell me I can't. Like the Italian variety shows described earlier. They might be very popular and successful (and they definitely were and are), but its not possible to sell them anywhere else, because other producers can copy them without fear and without paying a license fee.

Broadcasters can just use the same generic elements you used in your show and off they go. They won't buy your show if they don't have to. And they won't have to because your show was not a format.

There's an old saying: you cannot sell a house you do not own. The same applies for television programs. You cannot hope to sell a show which is full of elements which you did not invent.

A format, however, is something you can sell (and more importantly – legally defend) because it contains one or more unique elements, ideally a long list of ingredients which makes the idea new (more or less).

So, if you dream of coming up with the next *Big Brother*, you have to ask yourself the following questions.

What are the main ingredients of my idea?

Are they unique?

Is my idea just a show or is it a format?

Okay, your show has a presenter in an expensive suit or a co-host in a low-cut dress. But every show since the beginning of time has had a presenter wearing something like this, so this idea is not yours to sell. I'm not buying your idea because it has a presenter, even if the presenter wears a clown suit (although, to be honest, as far as I know that particular idea has not been done, so it could be something to consider).

So your show has a big, colourful and dramatic set in a big bright studio, full of flashing lights. Again, not yours to sell, so I'm still not interested.

Your show has three contestants who answer questions and win big money as prizes. If I had a dollar for every show like this, I'd be a rich man, so I'm not paying you for that either.

And is that all you have?

Because I'm busy and have other people to see.

But then, you tell me that unlike every other show in the

history of television, your presenter is not nice and supportive of their contestants. Your presenter is a mean son of a bitch who insults the contestants at every opportunity, seems very happy when they fail and disappointed when they win.

Wait. What? This is definitely something I've never seen before, and so yes, I am now listening carefully.

What is your new idea called?

The Weakest Link?

I'll buy it!

Here is a very large cheque.

Thanks for coming in.

Having a mean and nasty host is a great hook for a show and, at the time, *The Weakest Link* was unquestionably unique. So the owners of the format could be confident that if anyone else came up with a show where the presenter was a mean son of a bitch, it would be easy for them to send a lawyer's letter and successfully defend their idea.

That show had the three elements you need to turn a program into a format – a strong hook, (at least one) unique elements and was very visuallyinteresting.

From a producer's perspective it was legally defendable and therefore saleable, so it quickly became a strong and profitable format around the world.

The biggest and most successful television formats are those which have the greatest number of unique elements (revolutionary) or those which weld a strong, unique element (hook) onto an existing familiar genre, like *The Weakest Link* (evolutionary).

The island reality show *Survivor* was revolutionary. It was the world's first reality format and took the industry by storm, because every part of the program was unique and new.

It was so revolutionary, I recall how difficult it was for the

UK production company, that developed the idea, to convince any of the normally risk-averse television broadcasters anywhere to take a chance on it. And they weren't being cowards without a reason.

Nowadays we are used to contestants on these sorts of programs being voted off. *Big Brother*, *The Bachelor* (and *Bachelorette*), *Love Island*, etc, all involve contestants being told to go home. But what many people don't remember was that the very first person voted off the very first reality show (*Survivor Sweden*), returned home and promptly threw himself under a train.

That sad event sent shock waves through the industry and was enough to put a lot of people off the new reality genre.

We at Endemol, having bought the rights to produce *Survivor* for most of Europe, promptly cancelled the deal. The Swedish producer who later picked up those rights eventually made a lot of money from them, but she had to work very hard to convince the industry they weren't going to be killing contestants on a regular basis.

So expect to work hard if your idea is revolutionary.

It's a lot easier to sell a format which is evolutionary.

It doesn't have to be the world's biggest idea. *Jeopardy* sold all round the world for years and years, and made its developers staggeringly rich, based on just one strong hook; instead of the presenter asking the questions and the contestants providing the answers, the roles were swapped. And instead of the presenter choosing which questions were asked, the contestant did.

Okay, two strong hooks.

Simple, but stupidly successful.

Few of the other elements in *Jeopardy* are unique, but they are put together in a way that makes the result unique and therefore defendable – and also, therefore, saleable.

So that is what a format is. And if you can come up with a good one, you can expect to make a lot of money if you can find a way to sell it. By the way, if you are thinking to yourself that you have the world's most brilliant television format (and I would like another dollar for every person with one of those), just ask yourself, "what will the voiceover person say about your show to get people to watch it?"

"This Friday night at 7:30, watch our great new television show, The Greatest TV Show Idea!

"It's the show where (fill a three second gap).

"Don't miss it."

If your idea is too long and complicated to fit into the three-second gap, or if your idea is not unique enough to warrant shouting about like this, then your show needs more work.

And finally, speaking of garden shows, the producer of one UK backyard renovation program, full of generic ingredients, found a simple way to turn the show into a format. It had one of the presenters, an attractive woman, work in the dirt bra-less.

That show wasn't a strong format, but sold all around the world for some reason.

8. The American way

When a television station or production company buys the rights to make or broadcast a format, they must also agree to pay for someone from the company which owns the format, to come and supervise them as they go through the production process.

The consultant is often the same person who invented the format; a producer or creative person who knows how to make the program better than anyone else in the world. In the case of Endemol, which had 300 formats to supervise in more than 20 countries, the job was allocated to two specialists – my boss, Marc (the coolest Dutchman in the world), and me.

When you were ready to begin production, Marc or I (sometimes both of us if it was big enough) would turn up to your front door – at your expense, I might add – to be your best friend and to act as your walking bible for the format. Our role was also to try and save you money, by helping you avoid production missteps experienced in other countries.

And by the way, we would also keep an eye on you to make sure you were making the format in such a way as to not jeopardise the original intellectual property. Just because the presenter of the quiz program in your country is also a famous singer, for example, it doesn't mean she is allowed to stop the game halfway through and break into song.

The Americans were the first to establish the consulting process but, because they are who they are, the countries where they sold their programs were usually mysteries to them. So, rather than assist each new production, the consultant's job devolved to become more of a policing role.

And because often they didn't identify the core concepts of their own intellectual property, they fell back on what they knew. Stick rigidly to the rules and throw lawyers with both hands if anyone tried to do anything different.

If the presenter in the original production in the US wore a light blue suit, the presenter in the Czech Republic (for example) must also wear a light blue suit, regardless of whether or not light blue suits were available in the Czech Republic (I'm sure they were), whether or not people on television in the Czech Republic ever wore blue suits (I'm sure they did), or whether or not it was in any way appropriate to wear such a suit for the program (I'm sure it was).

It didn't matter what local tastes might be.

If you bought the rights to a US show, usually your presenter had to wear this particular suit in that particular colour, with this particular haircut. Or you ran the risk of having the owners of the intellectual property taking the rights back. There was often no consideration of local preferences or culture. And no real understanding that the reason the show was successful in the US originally, probably had nothing to do with the colour of the presenter's suit.

It's changed now, thank goodness, but I actually heard of a case where an American consultant insisted the attractive female quiz show co-host in the low-cut sexy dress, could only be a blonde. No other hair colour was acceptable. It's unlikely the format's success hinged on this pointless detail.

Endemol worked out early on that we could guarantee much greater success for our formats if we did three things.

1. identify the core concepts of our format;
2. identify the cultural specifics of the country to which we had sold the format;
3. adapt our format to that culture while maintaining the integrity of the concept;

Take, for example, one of our hugely successful dating shows *All You Need is Love*. In most countries, the success of this format hinged on the laughter and fun which could be had as the presenter took a hopeful boy on a search for his intended date and to surprise her with the request.

But in some countries, it is perfectly acceptable for a girl to ask a boy out on a date.

Would the same idea still work?

What if the boy wanted a date with another boy?

Would that still be funny and fun in this show?

In some countries, before a boy can ask a girl on a date, her father must give his permission. How to incorporate that into the format? Solving problems such as these and adapting our formats accordingly, allowed our shows to jump borders more easily and be just as successful as the original.

If you had a big wall screen showing 12 versions of *Jeopardy*, you probably couldn't tell them apart. Put up the same screen with 12 versions of *All You Need is Love* and you couldn't tell they were the same show, other than the opening titles and music. But our format was hugely successful all over Europe. And audiences in each country believed the show was theirs and theirs alone.

The broadcasters came back to us again and again because we seemed to 'get' their audiences.

That, then, was my job.

When Endemol developed a show in the Netherlands or elsewhere, I had to hang around the production, driving the producers mad, absorbing every aspect about how to make it. As an experienced producer, I had already made most sorts of programs anyway, so I knew what I was looking for.

Working with the production team, I would identify the original underlying emotion and core concepts driving the format and discuss with the producers how they stayed true to the idea while ensuring each episode was different, and just as exciting, as the previous one.

I would learn the tricks and shortcuts and how to avoid costly production mistakes. Because the formats were primarily developed in the Netherlands, one of my main tasks was to strip the "dutchness" from them. Dutch programs work very well in the Netherlands, but Italians and French won't watch them in their undiluted form.

Just as an interesting aside and to give you a good example of what I'm talking about, consider *Who Wants to be a Millionaire?* A monster hit all over the world, but surprisingly not in the Netherlands. And for a surprising reason.

Part of the success of *Who Wants to be a Millionaire?* is what producers call "shoutability". Everyone in the audience must know the answer to the question, even if the contestant in the chair does not. It's an amazing concept and a key to the show's worldwide success.

But the Dutch audience felt the "shoutable" questions were too easy, and the contestants able to win the money too easily. The Calvanistic nature of most Netherlanders (hardworking, frugal and straight forward) made them feel uncomfortable with such a concept.

The contestants weren't earning the money. Unlike everywhere else in the world, the show in the Netherlands became more popular when the questions were made more difficult.

So, having learned all I could about the production of a format, I would then proceed to study the country which had bought it.

This involved lots of TV show recordings and YouTube and Wikipedia pages, concentrating on the cultural specifics of the target country's aspiring and middle classes. Europeans live so close to each other (by comparison to Australia) it's amazing to me they are so different to each other. In the same distance as I used to go to the movies in Australia, I can pass through three countries in Europe.

Not only language obviously, but social customs are different too, which is where television comes in. Using *All you Need is Love* as an example, I knew that within the original Dutch version, the producers used 43 different format techniques to make each show interesting and fun.

In Turkey, after researching the dating/love culture there, I learned we could only use about 20 of the Dutch techniques. In Portugal, we could use about 30 of them and in Scandinavia, almost all of them applied.

To adapt our formats each time, I needed a clear understanding of each culture and a clear, pure distillation of why our format worked. And, most difficult of all, I needed to be (or at least pretend to be) as good a producer as the great people who were making the shows in each country I visited.

I used to joke that the production companies paid a lot of money to transport my body from place to place, just to get access to what was in my mind. Often, I would sit in front of a production meeting and say, "I know everything you need to know about this show, but I don't know exactly what you need to know. So, first ask me your questions and we will go from there." I was able to talk comprehensively like this for most of our 300 formats.

The task became easier each time I returned to a particular country because I learned more and more about them each visit. To the point that I came to know instinctively which of our formats would work best in which place.

Sometimes I would call a local producer to suggest one of our new formats if I knew they had already successfully made a similar one and if I felt the new one would suit them too. I became a good salesman and I hate being a salesman.

Anyway, that was what I did for a living for many years.

I was one of two international format consultants for Endemol. Nothing but flights, hotels, studios and restaurants week after week, until they all blended into one.

My boss, Marc, being my boss, kept all the best countries for himself to supervise – Scandinavia and the US among them.

I got all the rest. And because I got all the "interesting" countries as part of my brief, a lot of stupid things happened to me along the way. As you are already becoming aware.

Still, it was better than having a real job, I guess.

9. A new world record

Until recently, I admitted to a certain grudging affection for Greece. One reason, I'm sure, is the fact that Greece is completely at the other end of the 'neat and tidy' scale from the Netherlands where I lived during my time with Endemol.

Residing in a country where every square millimeter is cared for, clipped and trimmed like an English garden, was quite nice and I can't argue that it made for a comfortable life for my family. But I kept getting the urge to break something.

Of course, that would be unrealistic. I know if I dropped a piece of paper on the ground in the most remote part of Holland, someone in an official uniform would spring out, give me a stern lecture and hand me several brochures explaining the importance of caring for the environment.

In the Netherlands, I swear, you can go for a hike through the most rugged part of the country, into the deepest and darkest unexplored Dutch jungle (no there isn't such a thing, really) and find the whole place has been laid out neatly – bitumen walking trails, helpful maps signposted every other kilometre, clean seats to sit on and, of course, in the middle of it all, a nice hotel with outdoor seating, umbrellas and a handy little stand selling ice creams to sooth the throat of the weary explorer.

In Greece, by contrast, the whole place appears to the casual visitor as if most buildings and road works were given up as a lost causes some time just after the fall of the Roman empire. Just about every home outside the affluent areas appears to have been abandoned midway through construction. And on the roads, cars and bikes seem happy to make their own lanes, veering around potholes which, in the Netherlands, could accommodate new housing subdivisions.

The foolish Dutch road construction foreman who allowed such a pothole to develop on his or her section of road would be put to death (or worse – given a stern lecture and handed a brochure on the importance of keeping one's road in good order).

I often keep my eye out while driving in the Netherlands (as you are supposed to when driving).

Imagine what would happen if I needed to make a statement of defiance, floored the accelerator and screamed off, leaving two long, black, rubber skid marks on the road?

In Greece, archaeologists would be able to examine the marks 2,000 years later. The Dutch solution would be to partition off the section of freeway, divert traffic and replace the bitumen – a job which would take some time but return the road to its pristine state. By God, things are neat in the Netherlands!

But I digress. My visit to Athens was, as usual, to oversee the making of a big show. It was not a world shatteringly important program. It was a game show, but one quite difficult to produce properly and in Greece they don't have the budgets to make giant, expensive, Hollywood-style shows.

Brothers, cousins and friends of the family are dragged in and expected to help. "That's cousin Costa on camera one, cousin Savvas on camera two, and my brother Panos is the presenter."

This particular show was designed to be about two hours long, so it normally should have taken no more than, say, four hours to record it.

Little did I realise as I made my way into what appeared to be the half-built studio on the outskirts of Athens, at the end of a long pot-holed road (okay, okay – nothing more about roads, I promise) that this program would give me nightmares for weeks. As is traditional, the crew began rehearsals in the morning. What was not traditional was seeing everyone drinking beer at their workplace at 4 pm, but I was told it was a normal thing in Greek TV in the hot weather.

So, hey, don't let me be the party pooper.

"Hand me a Heineken, Darryl (sorry, I mean Christos)."

The audience began arriving at 4pm in three or four overcrowded chartered buses. There were supposed to be 200 people booked for the show but only 190 had turned up, so a few friends and family members of the crew were roped in to make up the difference ("cousin Alexis, you sit over there and cousin Eleni, you sit here").

While the audience was being seated, rather than doing a final technical check, the director, who bore an uncanny resemblance to the American actor Tom Selleck, held up proceedings by posing for selfies with the famous presenter. The presenter, I might add, had a reputation himself for holding up the show – for other reasons.

One of the cameramen, Savvas, told me the presenter used to be the star of another very popular game show. On most recording days, according to Savvas, the presenter would select an attractive girl from the audience and take her into his dressing room during the lunch break, no doubt so she could take part in his own personal game show.

During rehearsals, the crew professionally tested every piece of equipment, except the main game computer and the giant video screen which stretched along one wall of the studio.

These were "computer things", I was professionally informed, so they always worked perfectly.

When the program recording finally began, neither the computer nor the video wall worked. Why was it not surprising?

It took 30 minutes to get the equipment going properly. Then another half an hour was lost because, when the show was about to start, it was discovered the crew had not put the correct props into the studio. So, we were running an hour behind even before we started.

A few minutes into the recording, the script called for a commercial break. You'd think that having lost an hour already, the production would motor on and try to catch up. But both audience and crew downed tools and headed outside for a smoke, even though we had only started a few minutes earlier.

After a while, a few of the crew wandered back in, some bringing with them food they'd taken from the staff canteen. There was no sign of the presenter. He was last seen talking to a couple of the show's dancers. Hmm.

I could see the director chatting with a few of his friends. He seemed to be in no hurry to resume. It was all very casual.

Despite the recording process going for an hour, we had recorded only about five minutes' worth of material.

Even at this early stage, some members of the audience had decided they'd had enough. One little old lady declared loudly she was going home. A mother with a couple of kids did the same. No one seemed to notice. It occurred to me – "who let kids in here?"

Half an hour after the break began, a crew member called "Five minutes!" Half an hour later, he called again "Five minutes, everyone!" Slowly people were herded back into their seats.

This was the moment the air conditioning decided it would go on strike. The studio was built in a big hole in the ground, so there was no possibility of opening a window. The dancers (all very skinny by Greek standards) were furious at being told that, because the air conditioning had broken down, they could no longer smoke on the set. One actually had a cigarette going while the cameras were rolling and no one (including me) noticed.

You just don't expect it.

The recording ploughed on slowly, hampered by the heat and the fact that the Greek Tom Selleck insisted on stopping, after each section of the game, to check his work and to redo bits that he didn't like.

In front of the Greek Tom Selleck, I warned the local producer that stopping and starting like this was going to cause a disaster. Tom looked at me like I was a piece of souvlaki he had stepped in on the way to work. He didn't speak to me again for the rest of the night. My loss.

The producer, however, was caught between a rock and a hard place. On one side was his prima donna director who could cause him headaches by arguing or storming out in a fit of anger midway through the show.

On the other hand, the man from the Netherlands who could harm his career long term by telling head office that he was such a bad producer he should not be put in charge of anything more than a program which involved people sticking their fingers in their ears. And there aren't too many of those programs these days, even in Greece.

The producer came down on the director's side in the hope he could sweet-talk me later on. (It was a bad call. I let him sweet-talk me and buy me dinner – and reported him to head office anyway). The recording process crawled on.

An astonishing six hours after the production began, just 20 minutes of the two-hour show had been recorded. By now, the audience was starting to get weary and many took the opportunity of another break to try and leave. The crew herded them back to their seats.

One group of feisty old ladies, from the back of the audience stands, stopped the show at one point by walking down to the studio floor to start an argument with the now harried-looking producer. They claimed one of the contestants in the previous quiz round had answered the questions much too fast for their liking. The general view of this group of old lady rebels, was that the contestant must have been given the answers in advance.

Several of the cameramen and a lighting technician agreed with them and joined the argument, now involving a large group of people in the middle of the studio floor. I didn't say anything but, later on, when I saw that particular contestant get a ride home on the back of the motorcycle of one of the crew members, I was inclined to think that something dodgy had taken place.

After much huffing and puffing, the producer agreed to re-run the game to demonstrate clearly that everything had been done correctly. That decision angered another group of audience members who believed the contestant in question was a nice young man and didn't look the sort of person who would cheat.

Most of this group appeared to be relatives of the contestant. One elderly lady, dressed in black, (perhaps his mum) became very angry at the idea that the nice young man would have to give his prize back. She had to be led out of the studio kicking and screaming.

When the producer tried to restart the recording, he discovered the disgruntled group of relatives had left the studio in a huff, creating a large empty space in the audience stands.

Everyone else was asked to shuffle around to cover the hole.

Then the presenter couldn't be found – again – and the audience and crew were forced to wait until he turned up (I had looked in his dressing room, but he wasn't there and it was hard to tell if any girls were missing from the audience).

By now I had started taking notes, in case someone pulled a gun and there were deaths. I wanted to be prepared to give honest evidence to the court that none of it was my fault.

People were getting very angry in the heat.

After another hour of recording, and by now half the show was in the bag, to my amazement, the crew downed tools again and headed off on their rostered meal break. Sweating audience members, most fanning themselves with bits of paper, were handed small cold drinks and sandwiches. Some of them waited until the crew was distracted and took the opportunity to slide away into what was now, undoubtedly a nice evening outside. Whispers about the location of a secret passageway to freedom circulated among them.

Those who chose to stay, sat and lay around the studio floor (and some even on pieces of the set!), like victims of a particularly nasty battle. There were food and bits of rubbish scattered around, some of which would be visible in shot, but no one in the crew paid them any notice.

Several of the little old ladies in the back of the audience stalls seemed particularly quiet.

I walked up during a break and discovered they were fast asleep. They stayed like that for the rest of the night and you can see them in all the shots, propped up like dummies, not clapping or cheering or taking any part at all. But no doubt much happier than those still awake.

I collared the producer again during the break and commented that the situation was appalling. He smiled, nodded his head and agreed with me. Then commented on my nice tie.

Sorry pal, no points.

He then suggested that to speed things up, we should delete parts of the game, like the finale where the winning contestant gets all the prizes. The look on my face made him step back quickly and drop the subject.

After another hour, the crew returned from their break.

The producer and director had obviously put their heads together and realised they'd be in this sweat-filled hole in the ground until spring unless they changed the way they did things. The producer slid up beside me, complimented me on my haircut, and asked my opinion on how the rest of the recording should go.

Relieved that he'd finally come to his senses, I repeated the things I had been telling him all evening. To my great relief, off he trotted and began to do it properly.

I raided the production liquor cabinet and poured my first whiskey of the evening. Blessedly, the recording speeded up. During a walk around the studio floor during the next break, I smelled something burning. That worried me because the studio, as I said, was in a hole in the ground and there was only one staircase out.

I had a quick look around, but couldn't see anything wrong.

Ten minutes later, still worried, I returned to the studio floor and the smell was worse.

After much searching, I traced it behind the set where I discovered that some genius crew member had laid two bits of wood, debris from one of the props, on top of one of the big studio floor lights. The wood had been smouldering for an hour or more and was just beginning to flame as I got to it. I swept the wood off the light and stamped on it before it could set the studio alight.

The set was made up of highly flammable wood, paint and canvas. It would make a highly toxic death trap. The producer, when I told him, seemed to be rapidly approaching a point where he was incapable of taking in any more information. He was up to his arms in trouble with the dancers, who were all surly and complaining and threatening not to go on.

Just then, the unjustifiably cheery props man reported to the sweating producer that all the big balloons to be used in the big finale were popping under the hot lights and he may not have enough of them left by the time they were needed.

And the floor manager called in to report that more audience members had taken an opportunity when his back was turned, to sneak out. We were down to under a hundred. If any more left, the producer would have to move the rest of them from seat to seat as we changed shots, to make it look like a full house. I poured myself another whiskey.

After a ball-tearing nine and a half hours, we finally got to the big finale in the game. The winning contestant had to pass one final test to take home all the prizes. To his credit, the presenter was still as bright and bubbly as when we began – what now seemed like days before. He cheerfully informed the winning contestant that all he, the contestant, had to do was to spin the giant wheel four times and predict if the number each time would be higher or lower than the previous one.

To the feeble cheering of the small band of shell-shocked and shattered audience members clustered together in the back of the shot, the contestant grabbed the wheel and spun it. It stopped on number seven.

"Will the next one be higher or lower than a seven?" asked the presenter dramatically.

"Higher," guessed the contestant. He grabbed the wheel and spun it again.

Uh oh! It was a seven again, so the presenter asked him to give it another spin.

It was a seven again.

Another try? asked the presenter, trying to catch the producer's eye. The producer had his head in his hands and appeared to be weeping.

It was a seven again!

What a surprise!

And again. And again, and yet more sevens.

The models sagged in their high heels and the presenter threw his hands up and disappeared into his dressing room, lighting a cigarette as he went.

The winning contestant wasn't giving up that easily, though. He was determined to win. He kept spinning the wheel, even though most of the cameras by now were turned off and the crew stood around watching him with interest. Even the remaining women from the audience came down to help him (we were all old friends by now). Almost everyone, including me, took a turn to try and get the damn wheel to stop on something other than a seven.

I had just knocked back my third whiskey and was beginning to feel all devil may care. After all, we were in this hell hole together, surely never to see daylight again.

The props man eventually wandered up and set to work to fix the wheel, a problem he later admitted he had caused. Before the show, he'd noticed the wheel didn't spin smoothly, so he'd attached a small but heavy piece of metal to one side of it which had the wheel spinning smoothly again. Of course, that bit of metal always ended up at the bottom, which meant the contestant was only ever going to get a seven at the top.

I noticed more audience members sneaking out.

"Lucky bastards," I thought.

The dancers retreated to the kitchen with their shoes kicked off, smoking and chatting to some old ladies from the audience who had decided to use what little time they had left on earth (all of it apparently to be confined in this television studio) to help clean up the kitchen. There was a group of about 10 of them sweeping, mopping, washing up and packing things away. I think they were the same ones who had been asleep in the audience for most of the night. No wonder they were so chirpy. I wondered where their husbands thought they were.

After a long time, the props man declared that he had no idea how to fix the wheel.

The producer, by now in desperate need of a shave, a shower and a good lie down, declared that the game would go on with the contestant, off screen, drawing a card from a deck to decide what number he had drawn. There were fewer than 50 people left in the audience by this point. They were grumpily clustered into a small group in the back of each shot and forced to move each time the director wanted to change it. Which was a lot of effort at this time of day.

The presenter was dragged unwillingly out of his room, the dancers told to straighten their makeup and the game continued towards its gruesome climax.

From a deck of cards held by the presenter, the contestant drew a card. Then he was asked spin the wheel. Someone off-screen quietly helped the wheel stop on the correct number and the contestant was told to leap about like it was all for real – I guess on the edited program, no one would notice. The remaining audience members were asked to jump around and cheer for the winner, but it was like herding cats. No one smiled. Not even the contestant who had won all the prizes.

Finally, the production was over, a full 10 hours after we began – a new world record for me and one I hope never to witness again.

Out of the studio at last, the remaining audience members, brave souls who should have received medals for courage in the face of the enemy, discovered their buses had left hours earlier. It was 3 am and they had no way to get home. I was well into my fourth whiskey, the producer on his third shirt.

He decided the crew would give everyone a ride home. So, in groups of one, two, three and four, the tired crew shuttled the little old ladies home in cars and on their motorbikes.

The Greek Tom Selleck roared off in a big car with no one else inside.

Bastard.

The sight of a plump older lady on the back of a big motor-cycle roaring off into the night will stay with me for a long time. At 5 am I finally retired to my hotel for a few more whiskeys and to reflect on the day. Ten bloody hours to record one game show! In some countries I'd get less jail time than that for actually killing the producer.

Now there's an idea …

10. Travelling isn't always fun

Most people dream of a job which comes with lots of travel. I was one of them. Not anymore. My admittedly perfect job came with a spinning hamster wheel of grinding short flights, in and out of all sorts of airports and anonymous hotels, in all sorts of weather.

It's not as much fun as it looks in the brochure. Often, I would kiss the family goodbye too early on Monday morning, then struggle to get home in time to watch my son's Saturday morning soccer game.

Here was a typical two-week jaunt. The first step was a car trip to Cologne in Germany for a meeting with a German colleague. There's a lot to be said for being able to drive to a meeting in an Alfa Romeo at 200 kph. I loved it. Okay that bit of the travel wasn't so bad.

After my meeting, my colleague invited me to a big night-club in the city where Celine Dion was to launch a new album. Turns out she wasn't there in person. She appeared via a video satellite hook-up. We were disappointed to have been Dion-less and so left the launch to have dinner in a nice Turkish restaurant down the road instead.

Sure, sure, that bit wasn't bad either. And afterwards, I had a fantastic 200 kph two-hour drive home. Amazing to be able to travel at that speed legally.

Yes, I realise I'm not really painting my grinding travel schedule as being so bad, am I? Bear with me. By the way, enroute home that night, I passed a truck with a slogan painted in giant letters on the side: 'Who the fuck is AWA? Holland's biggest distributor of gaming equipment, that's who!'

I didn't think you were allowed to use swear words on signs. I also saw a German car with the personalised number plate OBEY 666. Very scary, but 200 kph gets you past most scary things quite quickly.

I spent one full day at The Hague getting new visas for Hungary and Poland. These two countries were not then members of the European Union and it was a burden to get them.

You may recall the trouble when I went to Hungary the first time without a visa. And in the pages ahead, you will read about a similar hilarious Polish experience. But don't let me get ahead of myself. This journey was to include my first travel to Poland.

It got off to the usual bad start. At Schiphol Airport, where I had arrived on time (for a change), I discovered the travel company had not sent my ticket from its city office. I had to wait a nail-biting 40 minutes for it to be brought through heavy traffic to the airport.

I had already decided not to wait outside and had, surprisingly really, managed to talk my way through the customs, passport and security desks, and the gate check-in counter, right to the door of the plane without being stopped.

I knew the airport procedures that well. I probably could have been able to talk my way onto the plane, but fortunately the person from the travel company, clutching my ticket in her sweaty hand, screamed to a halt in front of me at the last moment, having also talked her way through all the checkpoints.

That was also the moment I discovered the travel company

had booked me onto a Polish Airways (LOT) flight, not KLM.

I had assumed KLM and had been ready to talk my way on board a KLM aircraft which was heading the same way about the same time. Instead, I made a quick sprint to the gate where the LOT plane was about leave.

Turns out LOT was quite good, even though the planes looked a bit old and ratty. The Poles pride themselves on making good pilots and I couldn't argue with that during my first journey with them. I later had some issues but we will save that.

I had expectations of Warsaw being a low grey city, with giant blocks of grey concrete apartments, bad roads and dirty old cars. It turned out I was right on the money.

While it may have thrown off the yolk of communism, the Warsaw local government hadn't yet listened to the marketing consultants about the advantage of making your city an attractive tourist location. Maybe the marketing consultants were too scared to go there.

I would not have liked a job selling house paint in Warsaw in the 1990s. You couldn't give it away free on street corners by the look of the buildings.

According to my map, the old section of the city was destroyed in World War 2 and had been rebuilt quite nicely. I didn't get to see much during this first visit. I was told the area of the former Jewish ghetto, while interesting to see, was too rough to travel around without a security guard.

I decided I didn't need to see it.

I was also told to be careful where I parked my car. Car stealing had become the fastest growing sport for young and old alike in Warsaw. Most of the stolen cars ended up in Russia.

The Polish language is a scrabble player's fantasy come true. Every word is sprinkled liberally with c's, s's, z's, and y's, in what looks to the casual viewer, like random order.

Polish scrabble players can score more than the magic 300 points just by putting down the words for 'cat', 'tree' or 'house'.

Endemol had set up a subsidiary in Warsaw shortly before and had put three Dutch people in charge. After only a short time, they already hated Poland with a passion and were fighting among themselves like cats in a bag.

As soon as I arrived, each of them was in my ear about how badly the other two were performing and how well they, individually, were doing by comparison. This was despite the fact that, according to them, Poland was hell on earth.

It was part of my job to make the people in our outposts feel like headquarters was sympathetic to their problems. In fact, headquarters only cared that they kept bringing in the money. But you never say that out loud.

Part of my job was to nod sympathetically at all the complaints and, just like Cybil Fawlty, say "Oooh yes, I know" and act as if I cared, too.

Our salesperson had already sold two of our formats in that first month, so I thought he might be doing a good job, despite what the other two told me.

Another part of my visit was to check on the production of one of these two formats, which was in full swing. Also, I was asked by the boss of the office to help sell a few more to the local television network. At a meeting with the head people from the network, I managed to convince them to buy three more. God only knew where we would get the staff to make them.

We had already soaked up anyone in Poland who knew anything about television. The problem for us was the attitude of many of the local producers.

Everyone you interviewed for a job had a university degree

in film production. Most thought it was humiliating to work on cheap dating shows, quiz shows or music competitions. And didn't hesitate to let you know they had been a second, second, second assistant to the assistant of Steven Spielberg when he went to Poland to make *Schindler's List*.

Having said all that, the program I saw in production was, surprisingly, made well. The unending complaints from my three Dutch colleagues, had led me to expect the Polish workforce to be a bunch of amateurs. But I was pleasantly surprised.

The local staff obviously hated the Dutch people in return. One day, while talking with several people in the office, one asked about my accent.

I informed them I was Australian.

"So, you're not Dutch?" asked one.

"No, Australians generally come from Australia," I replied.

"I knew you weren't Dutch," she said mysteriously.

And off she went round the office to the other staff, informing them that she had been right guessing I wasn't Dutch – because I was nice.

On the flight back to Holland the next day, I was very embarrassed by one of my Dutch colleagues, who was coming back with me to spend the weekend in the Netherlands with his family.

He spoke at the top of his voice the entire trip and never missed a chance to loudly rubbish Poland and its people.

He was so loud, the customs people at the airport decided to search our luggage to give us a hard time.

I don't know why we send some people from head office. No wonder the Poles hate them. I did learn my first bit of the Polish language from a local he spoke to – yarp-ya-dollar (that's what it sounded like) – it means "go fuck yourself".

I should also say I learned "Gin-dobra" means "hello", "Gin-koo-ya" means "thank you", and "tak" means "yes". These other phrases might be as useful to me as yarp-ya-dollar. The Polish visit put that country at number 40 on my travel list (I've been to well over 60 now).

I briefly held the record at work for total number of countries visited (thank goodness for small Pacific islands), but not for total number of flights in a year. I made about 60 return flights my first year in the Netherlands but in the office that year, there were two or three people ahead of me.

The big boss had taken more than 80. We had a competition going. The prize was the joke, a return flight to London. It was a joke because you wouldn't want to win that prize, even on your day off. The Amsterdam to London flight was one of the most torturous journeys in Europe.

By the time you got to Schiphol Airport through the traffic, waited at the airport for the inevitable delay, sat like a brick in the crowded 45-minute flight to Heathrow and then spent two or three hours getting into the centre of London, it was often faster to walk there. None of us wanted to do it.

Anyway, I was only back in the office for one day when it was time for me to return to Hungary. Our sales people had sold one of our formats there and I was to supervise its production.

During the flight, someone in business class had a heart attack. The chief steward got on the intercom and asked for anyone with any medical experience to make themselves known to the staff.

A man next to me looked around, motioned to the steward closest to us and told her that he was not a doctor, but he had studied medicine.

She grabbed him and disappeared with him towards the

front of the plane. I didn't see him again.

As he strode up the aisle with a serious look on his face, you could see other passengers thinking, "thank God he's a doctor".

It made me long for the day when the steward would get on the intercom and declare, "Will anyone with television production experience please make themselves known". I would bravely signal to the nearest steward and modestly explain that yes, indeed, I was a television producer.

"Thank God," she would say. "There's a passenger in business class who's suddenly gone terribly over budget and is in danger of not completing his post-production before we land."

"Perhaps I can help him," I would modestly offer. And we would stride up the aisle to the grateful glances of other passengers whispering to each other, "Thank God he's a television producer!" It puts it all in perspective, doesn't it?

Despite the troubles on my first flight to Budapest, this arrival was painless and the airport minibus to the hotel presented no problem. I asked reception for a room away from the road and was given a room, not only away from the road, but one that was also well away from the hotel.

It was at least a one kilometre walk from the elevators to my room. They should really have put a sign on the inside of my door which stated, "In case of fire, try to die quietly and with dignity, because you're not going to make it to the stairs before the place burns down." Maybe put a smiley face on the sign to lighten the bad news.

The production I had come to watch went well and was as professional as any I'd seen. Two executives from the production company and the show's producer asked me to dinner afterwards.

We went to a traditional Hungarian restaurant near the river. It was lovely. The menu was traditional too. And I really mean

92

traditional. The friendly waiter advised me to try the 'Disznoto-ros orjaleves husoscsonttal es tormaval', which apparently was a famous Hungarian traditional meal.

It sounded intriguing.

"What is it?" I inquired eagerly.

"Pig spine soup with meat bone and grated horse radish."

"Ah, horse radish?" I politely commented, hoping no one noticed I had gone green.

"Damn, horse radish is no good for my belly, I'm afraid."

"What about trying the 'Fokhagymas baranygerinc parott parajjal, another well-known Hungarian specialty?" suggested the waiter, not suspecting a thing.

"And what might that be?" I inquired, now on alert.

"Lamb spine with garlic and stewed spinach."

I appeared to give that a lot of thought.

"Well, I've had lamb spine a couple of times this week already and, although it is a classic, perhaps I should try something different tonight."

The waiter then suggested I try a basic stuffed cabbage.

I was on my guard by now.

"What's it stuffed with?"

"Pig's hooves, ears and tail. It another traditional dish and very popular."

"It's just so hard to choose," I declared. "Everything sounds just so delightful. Maybe I'll just have fries?"

"We do have pork sausages," he declared hopefully.

I wasn't fooling him after all. I gratefully accepted. And that's what I had. Pork sausages and potatoes. It was tasty. The other stuff sounded appalling.

I did later try all of them at various times, but can confidently state they won't catch on with the non-pig or lamb spine-loving public. They were as their names suggested.

Just as in Poland, I learned some Hungarian words.

The word for thanks is "kiss-en-em". I couldn't bring myself to say it to the burly, unshaven taxi driver who dropped me back at the hotel at midnight. He might have taken it the wrong way.

I had a 6:30 am plane out the next morning. I called for the airport bus to pick me up at 5:30 am to give myself plenty of time. But there was only one airport bus for the whole city! After collecting me, the bastard went all over town, picking up other people whose planes left well after mine. It was only with a fast sprint that I got to the gate with moments to spare.

When I arrived back in the Netherlands I went home, changed my clothes and immediately headed back to the airport for a flight to Finland. The damn travel people had left my ticket in Amsterdam again, but this time it didn't take too long to get it to the airport. This trip was my third to Helsinki.

Unfortunately, I often only went to places where our programs had production problems and the poor Finns were struggling with one of our dating shows.

I know it sounds ridiculous, doesn't it? But it's true.

Finns are often very Russian in their outlook and, for many of them, expressing emotions on television is not really an easy thing to do.

So, the show turned out to be rather somber and depressing, rather than a madcap and zany dating game for modern teenagers. Anyway, the flight to Helsinki was murder. Storms all the way there. Heavy fog and snow on arrival.

The pilot fought the plane all the way to the runway, then obviously thought "fuck it" and dropped the aircraft the last 100 meters onto the ground. We bounced and bounced before he got it going straight. Even the stewards were terrified.

I discovered the travel office had booked me into the grandly named 'Ramada Hotel Presidentti'. It sounded great, but turned out the hotel was really just an annex for Finland's only legal casino. The one company had held the exclusive rights for slot machines and casino games in Finland since 1938.

Before the marketing consultants got it changed in 2004 to the "Grand Casino Helsinki", it was called by the delightfully friendly name of "Casino Ray".

No doubt it was just along the road from "Restaurant Russell" and "Art Gallery Betty".

Hundreds of people were throwing their life savings onto the roulette wheel table – it made me quite homesick. I had a couple of lever pulls on the poker machines for old times' sake.

They were old fashioned, three-reel machines with cherries, where the player got back about 50 cents on the dollar and you could go through $50 before you'd finished your first gin and tonic. Which I did. So I didn't stay long.

The weather hovered around freezing the entire three days I was in Helsinki. Not too bad. At that time of year, the worst feature was the darkness – only four hours or so of sunlight each day. If sunlight is really the correct word.

Just a lighter shade of murky grey would be more accurate. More snow was predicted, but it didn't happen. I had dinner out twice with the people from the TV station.

Dinner in Finland is not so much a multi-course meal as it is a small range of nibblies to go with a constant stream of vodka. My colleagues tried to get me to drink something called a Salmari, which tasted like liquified liquorice. I took one sip and my lips tried to curl themselves up my nose. About 40 proof.

No thanks. Apparently, it's a popular drink with the kids. Cheap and quick way to get drunk. We've all been there.

At one of the dinners, I sat with the presenter of the dating program they were making. He was very nice all evening and laughed at all my jokes. The program hadn't been terribly successful so far, and I suspect he thought I had come to Finland to fire him.

I didn't. I didn't have such authority. But I think he was quite relieved when he found that out. Also no doubt relieved he didn't have to look interested or laugh at any more of my stories.

From Finland I went directly back to Poland, which meant a visit to the Polish consulate in Helsinki for yet another visa (thank goodness those days are over). Because of the visa, I needed yet another passport-sized photo of myself. I was told there was a booth at the main Helsinki railway station.

Outside the station, a beggar tried, in Finnish, to get money from me. I told him cheerfully that if he couldn't beg from me in a language I understood, I wouldn't give him any money.

"Okay," he said in perfect English.

"Can I have 5 marks for a cup of coffee then?"

Damn! I handed over the cash grudgingly. Only later did I discover that coffee there only costs 2 marks. I hope the poor man didn't overdose on coffee. So, after a short hop on Lufthansa to Sweden, a long wait in the terminal there for the connecting flight and a LOT plane to Warsaw, I was back in Poland and getting mighty sick of travelling.

At Warsaw airport, my driver was late to collect me. The delay allowed me time to get to know a few of the pirate taxi drivers who made a good living ripping off tourists at the arrivals gate. When you come through the door, you always think there are a lot of people there waiting for their relatives, but it's actually a crowd of men offering black market rides into the city.

They charge unsuspecting tourists up to four times the normal amount, so you should avoid them.

The problem was, as I looked around the arrival area for my driver, I looked like a lost tourist and the sharks pestered the hell out of me. I had to be quite rude to turn them away. Fortunately, most didn't appear to speak English, so they pretended not to understand most of the words I used.

I even tried a few of the new less-than-polite Polish phrases I had picked up last time I was there, but they didn't seem to understand them either. Maybe it was my pronunciation.

By the way, over the years I learned how to say "Go fuck yourself" in 20 languages, which was very useful. I also learned how to say "sorry" in the same number of languages, which also turned out to be handy.

The reason I went back to Poland was to get started on a music program we were scheduled to start producing in Krakow, Poland's second city. The three Dutch colleagues from the Warsaw office and I rode three hours on the train there.

It was a nice modern train and, no doubt just to amuse me, the conductor was dressed just like a World War 2 soldier. Or maybe that was his normal uniform. As is usual in my travels, I didn't get to see much of Krakow.

We took a taxi directly to the studio and had a quick tour around the facilities. Then one of my colleagues and I spent several hours interviewing about 20 people who wanted to work for us there.

We saw one or two who might have been prospects ("We worked on *Schindler's List* you know") and organised for them to start a trial with us the following month.

Then we went back to the train station and the long trip back to Warsaw. On our arrival, at my insistence, the four of us went for dinner at Poland's only Japanese restaurant.

I was hungry and wanted some sushi.

It was a risk, but I had memories of being offered the ghastly sounding traditional Hungarian fare and didn't want a repeat.

Where better to eat raw fish, I thought, than Poland's capital city, which was only 250 km from the nearest sea and only barely out of communist starvation rations.

There were no Japanese people in the restaurant. In fact, there were no people in the restaurant at all – not even waiters or kitchen staff. Was it even open?

We found a 100-year-old man in a cheap suit on guard near the front door. So we asked him if he had a table free.

Hilariously, he asked if we had a reservation. We said no, and he looked around the vast empty room as if trying desperately to spot a spare table. He then let loose a stream of Polish which was probably "maybe I can squeeze you in. Wait here a moment."

And off he walked. He didn't come back.

Five minutes later, he still hadn't reappeared, so we just sat down at the nearest table and, when a waitress magically appeared from the kitchen a few moments later, we ordered drinks and food.

Even more magically, it was passable sushi. Not great, but it was relatively cheap and I didn't get sick. My Dutch colleagues admitted they had no idea what the local traditional Polish cuisine might be and, after I described the Hungarian version, they didn't want to find out. I have no idea where the old man from the front desk ended up. Or if he was ever seen again.

Maybe he didn't even work there.

The next day I headed back to the airport.

I'd been away from home so much, I wanted to buy a gift for my children. Guilty father syndrome. However, the marketing consultants hadn't yet made it to Warsaw airport either.

The single duty-free shop offered a choice of half a dozen crappy plastic toys, or ancient chocolates which looked like they were still covered in dust from the last bombing missions of the war. My children wouldn't touch either, so I saved my money.

I have to say, after two solid weeks away, I was happy to get home, sit still for a moment and nibble on a simple cheese sandwich, rather than face another full restaurant experience.

Even if the restaurant offered cabbage stuffed with pigs ears, hooves and tail. Yum.

11. It's how you sell it

It's a little-known phenomenon, but dating and romance-type television shows can attract a big gay audience. I've seen figures which indicate that at least 5 per cent, and maybe as much as 20 per cent, of the people watching the lovers kiss at the end of the big finale, are not looking at that particular couple in the same way as you might think. It's an audience segment that no professional producer can afford to ignore.

I was first made aware of this when I made a program called *Man O Man,* for the Grundy Organisation in Australia many years ago. This was a show designed to appeal to physics professors, astronauts and international business executives.

It involved finding 10 good looking men and getting them to perform silly games and cute stunts in the studio, in front of a big and boisterous crowd of women.

The men would wear less and less clothing as the show progressed. The women in the audience, using hand-held voting machines, would choose which of the men they preferred.
During the course of the show, the losers of each round would be pushed into a pool of cold water by one of 10 beautiful female models. The only dry man at the end of the program was the winner.

As I said, a high-level program for intellectuals, addressing man's basic inability to deal with his own mortality and his rightful place in the natural world. Ahem.

And can I be brutal here?

The women usually kept the cute, funny or intriguing men in the game as long as possible. But when it came to the final vote, when it was a choice between the eye candy or the 'interesting' man, they always went for the eye candy.

Always.

Every single time.

Sorry guys.

We used to have all sorts of trouble getting contestants for *Man O Man*, even though it was a top-rating program.

The men we approached to be contestants weren't stupid (well, actually, many were), but even the most avid gym junkies could work out there were nine chances in 10 they'd end up in the water as a wet loser. Most weren't prepared to risk that sort of damage to their over-exercised egos.

To get around their reluctance, someone (not me, I swear), had hired a couple of very attractive researchers to do the contestant recruitment. These researchers would visit the gyms and the nightclubs every day, approaching men they thought might be good looking and, er, brave enough to be on the show.

The researchers would dress appropriately (wink wink), push forward their assets and start a conversation about how handsome / well-built / tall / Italian/ whatever the man was (swoon).

The gym junkie and nightclub-hugging types often have the delusion that all women are naturally hot for them. So, it was usually not much of a shove for the researcher to get them to agree. I was told that sometimes, if there was a reluctant man who the researcher really wanted on the show (usually because we were short of numbers that week and would accept almost anyone to fill the cast), the researcher might gently imply that, if the victim agreed to come onto the show as a contestant (wink wink), she could all but guarantee (wink wink) that he, being the best looking man she'd ever seen, would be almost certain to win the main prize, a luxury holiday for two.

"Who knows," she might ask, "maybe you could even convince me to go on the holiday with you?" (Wink wink, shove the cleavage forward, try not to gasp at the body odour or the deodorant spray mist.) As well as developing superb eyelid muscles from all the winking, these poor women quickly became very cynical about the male of the species.

For some reason, from a young age, women believe that men must, just must, have more complex personalities than is first apparent. After all, women do have complex personalities, so men must also have them, right?

It's crushing when a woman gets to the age when she realises that, sadly, men are just what they appear to be – simple creatures driven by sex, and sometimes sport – and that there's nothing, absolutely nothing, more complex than that going on behind the eyes.

Eyes, by the way, which rarely move north of the untied buttons on a woman's tight shirt. This is true even of physics professors, astronauts and international business executives.

Trust me.

This appalling research approach (if it can even be called that) was always effective, which should tell you a lot. It gave us lots of good-looking and mostly willing contestants. But it also gave us an obvious problem.

Nine out of the 10 men who agreed to be contestants eventually discovered, shockingly, when they were pushed into the cold water of the pool, that they'd been misled.

Many of them got angry. Some even threatened the program with violence or a lawsuit.

"Your honour, my client's superbly defined physique, as illustrated in these beautiful photographs numbered 1 through 250 which I tender to the court, is a thing of beauty and not to be trifled with in such a manner. By the way, your honour, the photos are available for sale in the court foyer."

We had a second big problem, too.

Each recording session attracted a large number of women to be in our studio audience. It was women's only event and you could only get in if you made a booking in advance.

We were full every week.

To get the audience all worked up and excited, so they delivered the screaming, shouting and laughing ambiance we needed for the recording, we doled out lots of bottles of cheap champagne-like sparkling wine to them.

Not strictly ethical maybe, but the show had been sold to management on the premise that it was meant to be like a girl's big night out – so sparkling wine was appropriate. And we obviously adhered to all relevant liquor licensing laws. Ahem.

Every week, the audience was full with groups of women taking part in what in English are called 'hen's parties', a bride-to-be's final night out with her friends as a single person before her marriage. These girls were determined to have a good time, even if it killed them. Many were already well on the way to being drunk when they arrived, so our fizzy booze just made things ... more dramatic.

There were girl-on-girl fights in the waiting room and reports of women vomiting and passing out. The studio cleaners complained bitterly after our recordings about the disgusting condition of the women's toilets.

I thought they were exaggerating, until one morning I went to see for myself and nearly gagged. Vomit and waste were strewn over the floors and walls. Women can be disgusting. Not like men at all.

In the layout of the studio, we had an audience seating area by the inground-pool (the pool into which the losing contestants were pushed) which was a dead spot for the cameras. It never appeared on any of the finished recordings. Our warm-up guy, whose job it was to allocate seats for audience members, would place the drunks, the ugly and the more offensive women into this section where they wouldn't been seen or risk ruining the recording.

Before you start hitting me on the head about fat shaming or whatever, take a moment and look at most television shows which have an audience in view. There are only ever good-looking, middle-class people on-screen. The uglies are always kept well out of shot.

The rule in television is that the audience reflects the show, the show reflects the audience. It's just like the fake laugh track encourages a viewer to laugh at the jokes in a show, even though he or she might be sitting at home alone. A good-looking audience in the background makes a viewer feel they are a good-looking part of the show, too. And most television programs are designed to appeal to a middle-class audience because those people are the ones the advertisers want to reach with their products. It's worked like that since television was invented, so stop looking at me like that.

But, in our case the warm-up guy made the mistake one night by admitting to the audience that the seats near the pool were the cheap ones for the uglies. Oops.

No one in that section smiled for the rest of the night.

They just sat there, arms folded and glaring.

Luckily, we couldn't see them on-screen, I guess.

But their sour mood dragged down other audience members nearby and I wasn't happy they didn't have a good time like everyone else.

I discussed the issue with the warm-up guy and the following week he instead made a big performance of moving some of the drunk, or less attractive-looking audience members, to our "special, exclusive VIP poolside seats." There they were "guaranteed to get wet, ladies! Woo, hoo!"

This time, the uglies he put there had a great time, jumping up and cheering and telling everyone how great their "special" poolside seats had been. We still didn't see them on camera (fortunately), but you know. Same seats, different result.

It's only how you sell it.

The third and biggest problem we faced was that, at the end of each recording, we couldn't get the damn women to leave. They were all full of alcohol, horny from having been up close and personal with 10 good looking, near-naked men and the night was still young as far as they were concerned.

They didn't want it to end.

The studio security people reported that it often took ages to get our audience out of the building.

Several times, they'd found drunk women asleep in a back room or under the hedge on the street outside the studio. We would have faced a public relations nightmare if one of them ever came to harm. So, I had a number of related problems which I solved by coming up with what I still regard as one of my most spectacular brainstorms (he says, as if that list is several pages long).

I gave the researchers some money and told them to drag

the nine wet and angry losing contestants and the one dry, happy winner to a nearby bar to help them commiserate on their shocking and unexpected loss. Buy them each a drink or two, I said, and keep them there. Don't let them leave.

I then asked the warm-up guy in the studio to announce to the drunk and rowdy audience that all the near-naked men they had just drooled over, were now in the bar a short walk up the road. The men were waiting, if the ladies wanted to go and say hello to them.

The studio was empty in 60 seconds. And, when I went to the bar to check how things were going there, I found each of the contestants surrounded by a dozen or more women, all sweating pheromones. Someone, if not everyone, was going to get lucky that night.

As a result, not only were none of the contestants angry with us anymore, but the researchers started getting calls from them in the days afterwards, reporting about the fun experience the entire thing had been. If we ever wanted them on the program again, we should just call.

They'd be happy to help out.

Several also reported that they had good-looking friends who, once they'd heard about the great experience it was, wanted to volunteer to be contestants, too.

Again – same problem, but different result.

All that detail was to lead you back to the gay vote. As part of helping prepare the contestants in *Man O Man* for their silly costume stunts or their (usually appalling) attempts at singing or dancing in tiny swimwear, I, as the producer, would sometimes be forced to get hands-on with them.

It was important for the program that they all look as beautiful and as sexy as we could make them.

I went as far down that path as I needed to.

"The Indian chief needs much more body oil on his chest," I'd shout to the associate producers backstage, running my hands over the man's body to redistribute the oil already there to the more obvious places, before he would go on stage.

"Look, see how the Lone Ranger's ass-less chaps are showing his testicles," I'd complain to the clothing designer, trying to tug the offending pants back into place.

"Little Red Riding Hood here needs to wear underwear under his dress. Everyone in the front row will see his package when he lifts up his arms," I'd complain.

You get the idea.

As a result of my close attention, several of the contestants came to an obvious conclusion about the red-headed producer who, to be honest, it wouldn't have hurt to spend an hour or two in the gym himself.

Maybe he was inclined towards the male side of things, they'd wonder? I was flattered by the attention, of course (he says, fluttering his weak eyelids) but remained on my side of the road. Fully professional.

"Just doing my job, sir."

I was several times propositioned while making that show because, having been told of the big secret gay audience available to me, I put two, and sometimes three gays into the 10 man line-up each episode. The girls would gush over all of them.

The boys knew which were their favourites.

And we were a big hit with all viewers throughout the run of the show.

Many years later, and sadly demonstrating how little some of us progress in life, I was asked to make another near-naked man show, this time in Poland.

The premise of the show, a weekly reality series, was simple. We would scour the country to find six beautiful men, then over several months, teach them to dance and strip off their clothes in a suggestive manner. The cameras would follow their progress each week.

At the end of the series, we would stage a big, live performance in front of 1,000 well-lubricated women, to show how well the men had learned their skills.

"Television reaches new heights of intellectual achievement," headlines in the science journals would read. "Wish I'd done something that important," Spacex and Tesla billionaire boss, Elon Musk, would comment.

To direct the show, I hired an Australian Polish documentary director called Roman and asked him to relocate to Poland.

Roman spoke perfect Polish, obviously, and was a camera operator as well as a director, so he was perfect for the reality side of things. I wouldn't need two or three crew members in each scene making everyone feel nervous.

Just Roman and his camera.

He also turned out to be great company during the months we spent together making this piece of modern art.

Finding the six contestants was easier than expected.

Polish gym junkies can be just as egotistically misled as their brothers in Australia. Actually, it was the lure of becoming famous and rich (which was how the researchers sold it to them – you should never trust a television show researcher is the lesson here) which was enough to get many Polish farmers' sons out of bed early and along to the auditions, in their smallest, tightest pairs of shorts.

Once we had chosen all six, including two gay ones, we put them in a house in Warsaw and director Roman followed them with his camera, as they came to terms with the fact they were to be trained as strippers and soon to become famous and, no doubt, rich (most of their conversations were about the money and fame, not really about the parts which involved them taking off their pants, which tells you something).

One problem emerged early.

I had to sculpt these already gorgeous men so that they were god-like for the program. But one of them, despite having the face of an Adonis, was as hairy as a silverback gorilla.

After much discussion, I determined the fur would have to be removed. So, the poor bastard was dragged kicking to a women's hair clinic and given a wax treatment.

Full body hair removal. It took most of a day. You could have filled a queen-sized mattress with the amount of hair they removed from him. His screams drew a crowd to the front of the shop.

When I saw him afterwards, the poor man looked like he'd been dipped in hot water. His whole body was bright red, his skin puffy and splotchy and he kept scratching around his groin.

Turns out the staff at the clinic had taken me literally when I'd asked for "full body hair removal". They'd been very thorough, even removing it from places we'd never be able to show on Polish television, even late at night.

Roman shot a lot of reality scenes over the next few days which were unusable because, in the background, this poor man had his hands down his pants, scratching furiously.

The problem got worse several days later when the same contestant, and the rest of us, learned that, surprisingly, he was allergic to the wax treatment.

His entire body came up in a mass of angry red hives, all of it, apparently just as incredibly itchy as his reproductive organs.

The prognosis was that his skin, even with treatment, would take weeks to repair. I was sympathetic, obviously, and immediately gave instructions for the contestant to be kicked out of the show and replaced by a less chimp-like reserve contestant.

A good producer always has back-ups.

Roman talked me out of it.

He told me the contestant had been great in the reality scenes he'd already filmed, and it would be a waste of talent, as well as money to throw that footage away. Roman knew the way to my heart was to talk about wasting money. And he was right. We kept the lobster in the show. Fortunately, he recovered and looked great again in the big finale.

The network caused us a problem when the boss insisted, at the last minute, that we include someone's cousin as a contestant. I couldn't dissuade the boss by pointing out that having seven men, in a dance group called a sextet, did not add up.

Alexander, when he arrived at our filming location, at least didn't look like the network boss' pimply teenage son, as I had depressingly expected.

Not at all.

Wow!

He actually looked more like the legendary Italian cover model, Fabio. Alexander was a tall, strapping, barrel-chested handsome man with long, flowing brown hair who had all the girls in the office sitting up straight in their seats.

Top-level Polish eye candy.

I could live with that in the program. However, Alexander was a full 10 years older than the other men we had chosen.

You wouldn't think it would matter, but it did.

The rule I mentioned earlier about the audience reflecting the viewers, also applies to the contestants.

If you want 20-year-old girls to watch your show, you need to have 20-year-old men as contestants. And vice versa. If you have 30 or 35-year-old contestants, the younger viewers won't watch. People only like to see themselves or their aspirational idols on television. And we didn't want 35-year-old viewers.

The network wanted 20 year olds. But we had no choice in the matter, and it was their call, so on we charged. As had happened before, I was forced to get up close and personal with the boys, which got me the same sideways looks from a couple of them. I flicked my hair, pouted and shrugged it off.

Old Alexander (which is what we called him good naturedly) was very competitive in the more intellectual and complex segments of the program, such as 'chopping wood in the snow with no shirt on', 'abseiling down a rock wall with no shirt on' and 'jogging through the beautiful snow-covered forest with no shirt on'. And he absolutely stood out from the crowd in the more technically challenging segment 'looking wistfully into the snow-capped distance, while leaning against a tree with no shirt on, patting a large dog'.

But Alexander came undone in the most unlikely of places.

Someone (not me, as usual) came up with the idea of having all seven of our sextet sit in a small sauna, with just small towels preventing their plumbing from bumping into one another.

Director Roman, fully clothed and me, (also fully clothed, I will only go so far), squeezed in there to film them all hot, sweaty and alluring. Our beautiful female presenter (who, by the by, was also a qualified doctor I'll have you know) glided into the sauna, draped only in her small towel, to interview the boys while they glistened. All very sexy.

But I have to tell you filming is hard in a hot sauna and the poor men were stuck in there for ages.

It got very warm and stuffy very quickly.

Everyone ended up skin wrinkly and wrung out, especially fully dressed Roman and me. In hindsight, we should have filmed the entire segment without the heat turned on. With the 10 of us in there and the door closed, we generated more than enough heat and carbon dioxide to bring up a sweat.

The lens on Roman's camera kept fogging, so it took a long time until he and I were satisfied we had recorded enough footage. I'm not sure what the recommended maximum time is for someone in a sauna, but we kept everyone in there well past the point the health and safety people (if we'd had any) would have called an ambulance.

We didn't have any, of course.

I was saving money.

The younger men took the extended sauna session in their stride and flounced out with their tiny towels hardly limp. But Alexander sagged and sagged again in the heat and, by the end of the recording, he looked like a well-used mop and bucket.

Roman and I also eventually staggered out to breathe some non-testosterone-laden air, looking pretty bedraggled ourselves. While cooling down, we looked at each other and said quietly, "Did you see Alexander?

"Oh my God, he looked dreadful, didn't he?"

"That heat did him no favours at all, poor dear."

"He'll be so sad."

We gave each other a cat's bum face – you know it – purse your lips and look disappointed. We harrumphed at each other in a manly fashion, spat into the snow and walked away in as manly a manner as we could, nodding sternly to each other.

We weren't wrong about Alexander though.

He dropped out of the program soon afterwards.

A shame. He was a nice person.

The girls in the office were all devastated.

Another problem with choosing beautiful men for a show like this, was that, as well as looking good, they were also expected to dance. And nature is often very cruel like that. If you get lots of one skill or ability, such as a beautiful face, you often miss out completely on other things, such as brain cells or a sense of rhythm. Quite frankly, for some of our contestants, walking and breathing were two things they struggled to do at the same time.

Dancing proved to be a serious challenge. We were lucky in a couple of ways. One of the men had a fantastic dance-like routine already worked out before he got to us. It was no doubt his party piece to impress the ladies in his local nightclub. He would drop to the ground and spin his legs above his head, like an 80's street rapper.

The first time I saw him do it, I was impressed. It looked great. It was the only move he had, though, and his act involved merely repeating the same move over and over again.

During a three- or four-minute song, it proved to be a lot of legs spinning in the air. Seriously quite a lot. Sigh. But, it was more than the others could do and a place to start.

The other way we got lucky was our choice of choreographer. I won't name her in case she gets embarrassed, but she was a pocket battleship and, like a sheep dog, she hunted the contestants in the gym for weeks and weeks, until they could do their simple dance routines in their sleep.

She kept the choreography simple (for obvious reasons) and the contestants applied themselves diligently. By this stage, they were starting to feel the weight of being famous and, to their credit, they applied themselves.

Aside from the odd glass of vodka (this was Poland after all) and small amounts of other substances, there was little risk they'd sneak out of the house at night to get trashed.

They were all perfect physical specimens (and knew it), very disciplined about their diets and getting their beauty sleep. They were usually too exhausted from their six-hour daily dance rehearsals to even think about going out for fast food or to find company. I also had a security guard stationed at the front door. I'm not that silly.

It all led to the big day, several months down the track, of our gala finale, a performance to be recorded in a Warsaw auditorium and broadcast to the nation a few days later. The network promoted the event and, because the program had rated well during the series, tickets had sold out. The group would be performing in a large hall, full of screaming girls.

There is a photograph somewhere of Roman and me sitting in the first row of seats before the stage, putting the contestants through their rehearsals. It was where I faced my final hurdle, the biggest I had yet faced in this extremely difficult-to-produce program. It concerned the big dance number which would end the show.

The plan was for the group to dance around the stage sexily for a while (or as sexily as they could manage) and with one of the six on the floor spinning his legs in the air over and over again (sigh). They were dressed only in glittery tight long pants.

At a predetermined point in the music, they would all come to the front of the stage and turn their backs to the crowd, legs slightly apart. To the beat of the music, they would bend forward and grab their glittering, tight pants, which were held together only by Velcro. Using two hands, they would savagely rip the pants off, all at the same time, revealing six perfectly formed asses to the screaming audience.

It was the big finale, common to all these sorts of shows, and one guaranteed to get a big reaction from the crowd. The important question I had to answer was one I had never faced in decades of television production.

What was under the Velcro? I had two choices. Boxer shorts or G-strings. It was of vital moment for the success of the show, but I really didn't know what to do. I had no previous experience with this sort of thing. I mean, how could you? Roman looked at me blankly and was no help either.

The only way to find an answer was to have them practice both ways. First, I had them rehearse the move wearing G-strings under their pants. Dance, dance, dance, turn, rip revealing five perfect hairless bottoms (and one covered in stubble).

Roman and I, sitting right up against the stage, were confronted with a way-too-close view of a narrow piece of shiny G-string cloth being the only thing between six male anuses and those of us in the auditorium's front row seats.

Roman and I gave each other cat's bum faces and our heads wobbled side to side like a Pakistani trying not to say no. Possibly, possibly.

Then I got the contestants to do it all again – dance, dance, dance, turn, rip – but this time the reveal was a collection of colourful and tastefully tight boxer shorts. Roman and I gave each other cat's bum faces again, accompanied by a repeat of our Pakistani-style shaking of the heads. Maybe, maybe.

Certainly the boxer shorts were nowhere near as exciting or erotic as the almost full anus reveal. They were meant to be strippers, after all. And strippers take off their clothes so we can see their private bits, don't they? But which would the crowd of screaming girls prefer?

I made them try the G-strings again. Anuses. Then the box-er shorts again. No anuses. But as many times as they did it, I got no closer to finding an answer.

G-strings again. Boxers again. Over and over until we start-ed running out of time to get the G-strings washed and ready for the show (No, I don't like to think about it, either).

I just couldn't decide.

Finally, noticing that all the girls from the production office had somehow found the time to come and sit with us to watch this impromptu show, I turned to them for the answer. And watching their reaction, it was simple from there.

It was a moment I should have recognised from *Man O Man* many years before. You see, the show was designed to appeal to 20-year-old Polish girls, not to two older Australian men who, appeared to be in danger of perhaps turning gay if they did too many more beautiful man shows and ended up with permanent cat's bum faces.

I went with the boxer shorts and, in the big show finale, when the boys surprisingly carried out a near flawless – dance, dance, dance, turn and rip – the crowd went wild at the sight of their tastefully covered bottoms.

The show was a big success.

As I told Roman afterwards, men and women are different in so many ways, but never more so than when it comes to sex-ual allure. That's why the boxer shorts were the way to go for the big reveal. Women, it turns out, like to be stimulated by a feather. It's we men who prefer the whole chicken.

It's all just how you sell it.

12. Courting La Diva

Escaping a desk full of paperwork, I went back to Finland for a couple of days. On a previous trip there, I had helped sell a really old-fashioned game show called *The Honeymoon Quiz* to a local television station.

Couples who have just been married, allow us to make them look silly by getting them to compete, dressed in their wedding clothes, in a series of whacky and zany studio games for the chance to win a dream honeymoon and lots of products for their new home. It was a very old idea.

It had been years since any other television station in Europe had expressed an interest in such a show. But the Finns took one look at it and said, "Yep, that's for us." What does that tell you?

After the sale, I had to go back there and teach them how to make it. That first required me learning how to make it.

It was not one of my regular formats. The process involved asking the people in our company who had made the Dutch version when it was last broadcast a few years ago (just after television was invented). Our people who made these shows are generally happy to share their knowledge thankfully and were most helpful to me. *Honeymoon Quiz* is a show with lots of big props, a big rowdy audience and a presenter and contestants who know how to have a good time. Everything has to be big, bright, colourful and fun.

The first problem facing the Finns was that they were going to try and make the program in a studio the size of a food storage cupboard (with the food still in it). And for me, another problem was the show's reliance on young, attractive couples to play the game. Young attractive couples who would, by the way, be required to act whackily and zanily (which are two words I just made up).

I love them dearly, but the Finns, I can tell you, are not attractive as couples. It's the men. Many, many Finnish men look like they were hit face first by a city bus when they were young. Most of them look as ugly as a bag full of hammers. Fortunately, the women make up for it.

Finland was ruled by Sweden for 700 years, so a lot of beautiful Scandinavian-looking blondes inhabit the country. Unfortunately, the country was also ruled by Russia for a long period, so there is a sizeable chunk of the female population who would not look out of place in a Russian men's shotput team.

Finland has one of the world's highest per capita consumption of vodka, which obviously helps them keep their reproduction rate at a reasonable level. Another problem for a television program which requires outrageous behaviour was that, culturally, Finns are about as whacky and zany as a division of Russian Red Army infantry. They are lovely, but a very serious people. I've seen exceptions, but not many.

The biggest problem of all for a television program which is based on marriage is that Finland's relationship with marriage, is a bit out of step with the rest of the world. The country has a roughly 55 per cent divorce rate (quite high, but a way behind world champion divorcees Portugal, at 71 per cent). So a show which makes marriage and honeymoons look like never-ending fun and games is obviously unrealistic.

A better idea would be a show called 'You will piss me off eventually'. Because of its fierce Nordic culture, Christianity didn't bite Finland until well after everyone else in the region. It's obvious the idea hasn't quite sunk in as deeply as in other places.

Finnish women are noticeably more equal in society, much more so than in countries where Christianity put women in their place very early on. I discovered it is culturally acceptable in Finland for a woman to ask a man out on a date, with the intention to get him drunk, take him home and have sex with him.

Really.

Then, no doubt, refuse to call him afterwards.

(I'm still waiting Helen!)

I'm no oil painting (yes, yes, spare me the smart comments please) but I have found myself nursing a beer in a bar in Helsinki and been shocked to my socks when a woman approached me and asked if I was there with someone.

If not, could she buy me a drink?

If I looked up and saw it was a Russian shot-putter, I'd usually dredge up one of the many excuses women have given me over the years.

"Oh thanks, but I'm just waiting for a friend to arrive."

"No thanks. I'm only having this one, then I have to leave."

But if I looked up and it was a Scandinavian goddess, my answer was more likely to be, "Well, I guess I could have just the one", and bat my eyelids coyly.

I love Finland.

And Finnish women love big, flashy weddings.

They will obviously get a man home, have sex with him and eventually, all going well, plan and carry out a big white wedding with a bus full of bridesmaids.

Then, sometime later, many of them will be unfaithful to

their husbands, get divorced, find another man and set up for another big, white wedding with another bus full of bridesmaids.

Or maybe the same bridesmaids they used the first time. Who knows?

They love the idea of the big wedding, but obviously are not as keen on the full-time job that comes with it. However, the Finns are nothing, if not earnest, and they try so hard to do things right. I can't help but love them. I always try very hard to help them make their programs successful.

The day I arrived in Helsinki, I was wandering around the television station and found myself invited by the general manager to attend an award ceremony due to take place in the company boardroom on the top floor.

The boardroom resembled what I imagine KGB headquarters in Moscow looked like in the 1950s. Heavy, dark timber beams lined the ceiling; there was thick, dark, wall-to-wall carpet underfoot and the walls were completely covered with giant oil portraits in heavy wooden frames of the television station's founding fathers. Enough to give you nightmares.

The station, I learned, sponsored a nationally important cultural award every year. A citizen who had advanced Finnish culture (no jokes please) that year was awarded a nice trophy and 50,000 Finnish marks, the local currency at the time.

So, all the very well-dressed board members and staff (and one not so well-dressed Australian) stood knee deep in the carpet, nibbling on culturally Finnish nibblies, for long minutes waiting for the star of the show, a famous female opera singer, to arrive. For a while, I found it hard to keep anyone's attention in a conversation. They were smiling and nodding politely at me, but I felt I was alone in the room.

At one stage I was tempted to yell "I have a large penis!"to see at reaction I would get. I'm sure they wouldn't have reacted ll. Sigh. Same as in Helsinki bars. Then I realised there was a elevision set in the corner tuned to an ice hockey game.

Finland is a madly enthusiastic ice hockey nation.

On this day, its favourite sons were playing Russia in the Winter Olympics for a place in the final. The game was a close one and every red-blooded Finn, even those rare ones who didn't like ice hockey, was rooting for the home team to beat the accursed Russians, their most hated ice hockey enemy.

I was told that while the game was on, I could have laid down in the main street of Helsinki and not get run over by a car, because the entire country was inside watching the game.

Not that you would have wanted to lie down in Helsinki's main street at that time, because even as the rest of Europe basked in an early spring, it was five degrees below zero in Finland and the country was covered in a thick blanket of snow.

Flying in, it had looked like winter wonderland. The previous week it had been -20°C. I was told -5°C, was the local version of early spring.

Anyway, I gave up trying to make conversation and joined in to watch the loyal and courageous Finns battle the Russian antichrists. Just as the game reached half time (it was tied at three goals each and no one in the boardroom was moving), in walked the opera singer to receive her award.

What appalling timing!

And what irony!

The very people who wanted everyone in the world to know they were big promoters of culture, were forced to tear themselves away from sport on the television.

It was quite delicious.

The star was unlike any other Finn I have ever met. She was

an opera singer, apparently very famous, not only in Finla[n]
but in London and New York as well. I had never heard of .
and I don't remember what her name was.

And, while everyone else in the room was in sober suits or
pearls (but generally not both at the same time), La Diva had
on a bright yellow jump suit, cut low to reveal her large opera
-trained bosom, knee-length brown cowboy boots and a brown
leather jacket with cowboy fringes.

She had piled her long, blond hair on top of her head in a
stylishly, messy manner. Totally beautiful. Totally outrageous.
Her demeanour and outfit set the sober Finns in the boardroom
all atwitter. They beamed teeth at her and shook her hand soberly and vigorously (the Finnish way of swooning).

By the way, I learned an unusual thing about the Finnish
language from this amazing woman, who was so famous she
only needed one name. Like Madonna (no, I still can't remember it). Her name was about 20 letters long and didn't seem to
have any vowels in it. I did notice in the media release about
her, however, that her name was spelt three different ways. In
Finnish, apparently, you attach prepositions to a name when
talking, so it is spelt differently depending on where you use it
in a sentence.

Something like this.

Instead of "I am going to visit Brian Bigg", they say "I am
going visit Brian Biggto" or "Let's buy a gift Brian Biggfor" or
"My God, isn't Brian Biggsuchahandsomeman that."

It must make it difficult for tourists to find someone's name
in the phone book. Under the stern gaze of the founding fathers, the singer's award was applauded.

The chairman made a nice speech. La Diva replied with an
exceptionally long speech about the state of Finnish opera and

while cried a few times to demonstrate how deeply touched she at aas by the whole event.

It would have been a lot more emotional and moving, had not the television in the corner, unbeknownst to La Diva, been left switched on (with the sound muted).

Every time the singer turned her head away to make a strong point to the people on this side of the room, all heads on the other side of the room swivelled to the screen where the score showed the Russians had gone ahead by one goal.

When she turned to look at the other side of the room, eyes and smiles there returned quickly to her face. At the same time, the heads on this side all swivelled to the television. It was like watching the crowd at a tennis match, but they were so very good that La Diva didn't notice it at all.

This little pantomime went on for 15 minutes and ended, not when La Diva finally stopped talking, but when the final siren sounded in the game, revealing that the Russians had won the game and Finland was out of medal contention.

A deep sigh reverberated around the room and La Diva nodded her head at this obviously strong reaction to her wonderful speech. She finally accepted her cheque and trophy and went around shaking hands soberly and vigorously. We all then retired for more Finnish delicacies and chat in quiet tones.

I escaped as soon as it seemed polite to do so.

The following night, I was free of commitments, so I decided to go to the cinema. It was only a kilometre or two from my hotel into the city. Before the movie began, I wandered through Helsinki's biggest department store, which was open for late night shopping. The only customers were a few Russian prostitutes (or girlfriends as their gangster boyfriends no doubt call them) in their big fur coats, each accompanied by several dangerous-looking bodyguards. I avoided going near them. I'm told they are often unstable.

I was hard pressed not to laugh, though, watching all the Russian tough guys looking embarrassed wandering around the women's lingerie section in the wake of their beautiful, skinny, highly strung wards.

I saw several varieties of Australian wine for sale in the store bottle shop, but I resisted the temptation. The price of the wine helped me say no. I could have bought a small vineyard in Australia for the same money.

The movie, which was in English with Finnish subtitles, ended about midnight and, despite the temperature being about -15°C, I decided to stroll home. Finland has a crime rate as low as Japan's.

The only muggings and robberies are between Russian gangsters and other Russians, so I wasn't concerned.

Singing 'Waltzing Mathilda' and 'Advance Australia Fair' quite loudly to make sure they wouldn't mistake me for a Russian, I strolled home, a bit more quickly than I had planned because -20°C turned out to be very damned cold and I thought my toes would freeze and fall off.

The Honeymoon Quiz show gets made soon. I'll let you know if it turns out to be whacky and zany, but I have a feeling it will be more stern faces and handshakes.

That's more Finnish.

13. Getting belted

I got smacked across the face by a prostitute the other night. She just hauled back and slapped me as hard as she could right upside my head. My ears rang. My glasses flew across the room and made a smashing sound when they hit the tiles.

It hurt a lot. She was a big girl.

Now don't get me wrong.

I have occasionally said things which might have justified getting a belting from a hooker. But in this instance, I was innocent (that's my story, your honour, and I'm sticking to it). Give me a chance to explain.

One of the not too wonderful consequences of working in television is that we often labour well into the night. In many countries, we rehearse all day then go for our dinner break as the audience starts to file in and take their places. The recording of the show usually starts about 7 or 8 pm and, if all goes well, the director usually calls a wrap by 10 or 11 pm.

The exceptions are Portugal, where things often don't end until 1 or even 2 in the morning, and France, where a recording can go all night if you haven't been careful and hired a director determined to make Fellini look like an amateur.

But even if everything does end on schedule at 11 pm, we don't leave immediately. By the time we send the audience off home, clean up the studio and conduct a quick after-show meeting with the staff to discuss how it all went, it can be very late before the taxi returns me to my hotel. And television is a stressful game. It's usually a waste of time trying to go to sleep with litres of adrenaline still coursing through me. Sometimes I need a drink to settle down.

The other consequence of finishing late is that there are very few places to go if a beer is required to cap off a bad night or celebrate a good show.

The international hotels we television types stay in usually have a ground floor bar which stays open late at night, serviced by a surly bartender, who often doubles as the night clerk. They encourage us to go to bed, they charge big money for the alcohol, but most of us are on expense accounts, so that doesn't work.

Usually the only other customers in the bar at that time of the morning are the prostitutes who have been at work in the hotel during the evening. They usually look more worn out than we do, but it's a hard life for all of us.

In Eastern Europe, the prostitutes are often not your drug-addicted, skinny, tattooed vampires we get in the west (although there are those as well – I'm looking at you, Hungary).

When the wall came down and the uneconomical factory jobs in the glorious socialist republics dried up, a lot of men found themselves at home with a wife and kids and no income. Some of them came up with a plan to send mum out to work at nights. She would get dinner ready for the family, then put on her best Sunday dress and head out for a few hours to try and snare a drunken German businessman in the bar of the nearest 3-star hotel. I'm not kidding.

I've talked to a lot of them and that was their story. Surprisingly, even the ones who looked like my aunt Gladys reported they made good money.

You wouldn't have sex with them, though.

Not in a million years. For a start, the ones who didn't look like your aunt Gladys, looked like your mother in her best going-to-church dress. They were not supermodels. Few looked sexually appealing, except to those few freaks who should be in jail.

Worse still was to consider that many of the women didn't have much education and often knew nothing about AIDS or how it was transmitted. I read that in some former Soviet countries, the AIDS rate among prostitutes could be up around 60 per cent. No thanks. The drunken German businessmen deserve bravery medals.

For a while I travelled with an English man representing a British show we were making in a few countries (best not to name it). He shrugged off my fears about sex with the locals and dived in at every opportunity – at almost every hotel we stayed in.

He told me the prostitutes were as cheap as chips compared to those in England. And there were so many of them, he told me, he could usually haggle them down in price, which apparently he couldn't do at home.

He would spend hours trawling for the cheapest deal he could get and boast over breakfast the next morning about how much of a discount he'd haggled. He always put the experiences down in his expenses claims as 'laundry'. He just shrugged when I mentioned the AIDS rate. Why was I the only one paying attention? I must be the freak.

In Budapest, at the hotel where we usually stayed, the prostitutes were ranked according to which of the three bars in the hotel they worked.

The Aunt Gladys types were restricted to the ground floor.

The drugged-up vampires lurked in the dark, loud music bar on the second floor. The real stunners were to be found on the top floor where the alcohol cost the most. So naturally, that's where we drank each night, too.

We television types were often to be found having a quiet, after-work beer surrounded by a bevy of temptingly beautiful, expensive women who apparently thought we were the most interesting men they'd ever met. The English bloke would get himself all worked up over them, then head downstairs to hire a cheap one from the basement bargain, rather than pay the top price upstairs.

In Bucharest, I stayed in a big, international hotel and was nearly mobbed by a gang of prostitutes as I made my way to the elevator late one night. I'd made the mistake of deciding not to go out to eat.

I was tired after a long day in the studio and not convinced the Romanian capital was a safe place for a stupid foreigner late at night. Earlier, I was in the back of a taxi stopped at a red light in the city, when a man with an AK-47 casually slung over one shoulder, had wandered across the pedestrian crossing and stopped to glare in at me. I gave him a big 'please don't shoot me' smile and, fortunately, he stalked off.

Rather than risk a mystery Bucharest dining experience, I decided to gamble on the hotel restaurant. Bucharest is still the only city in the world where I have seen tuxedo-dressed security staff vetting people trying to get into a McDonalds restaurant.

I kid you not.

Out front, they even had a carpet, a velvet rope and a long queue of hopeful diners in their evening finest. I felt the restaurant in my international hotel had to be a step up from that. But honestly, I wasn't expecting an amazing culinary journey.

In the grand ballroom of the hotel, I discovered the only customers this evening were to be me and a bevy of prostitutes. And, while they were all smoking, they weren't eating (I should have taken that as a warning).

As the only non-prostitute customer, I turned out to be popular with the girls. Who knew I was so handsome and funny?

The food was unsurprisingly terrible. The best thing you could say about the menu was that it was neatly typed. After shovelling down what was supposed to be chicken, I wandered into the hotel casino looking for a drink.

The sign outside described the place as a casino, but it was really only a converted conference room next door to the restaurant. The staff on the front desk had mentioned that drinks would be free. Always a good selling point with me. But as a casino? James Bond would have taken one look inside and reached for a large martini, shaking and stirred.

It was a small airless room, filled with worn-out gaming tables. There was a bar at one end, way too many surly staff staring at me and a similar gaggle of prostitutes all smoking. As with the restaurant, I was the only non-prostitute customer.

Perhaps all the other guests knew it was better to go out and risk the AK-47s than stay in the hotel and risk the chicken.

On arrival at the casino bar, I was handed a generously large (free) whiskey and invited to play roulette. Which I did. I assumed the whiskey wouldn't stay free if I didn't gamble a few shekels. I'm so glad I did.

Amazingly – astonishingly really – the first number I chose on the roulette wheel came up a winner. I had won! How lucky was that? The staff and girls cheered for me.

The dealer handed me a pile of chips. Then even more amazingly, the second number I chose also came up as a winner.

Wow! Everyone was amazed. And cheered even louder as more chips were pushed towards me. I was less amazed.

Two in a row?

Never seen it happen. Hmmm.

Then I must have been the luckiest man in the world, because the third number I chose also came up.

Astonishing.

I never heard of such a thing happening before.

What were the odds of picking three numbers in a row on a roulette table? (Actually about 46,000:1. I looked it up).

Maybe I should have rung the Guinness World Records people to see if I had qualified for an entry. By this stage even the prostitutes were starting to giggle at my 'amazing' good fortune.

Did they really think I would believe the game was not rigged? And that my growing pile of chips was making the girls laugh even more loudly at my jokes?

Did I really look like a German businessman?

That was the saddest thought.

Of course, there was always a chance it was my natural boyish charm and devilishly handsome good looks. In any case, the booze was free. I was handed another large whiskey.

I was only betting small, but in about an hour I found myself US$150 in profit.

I couldn't lose. The secret to winning when gambling, I realised, was not to lose. I debated having a third whiskey, but then disappointed everyone who had put so much effort into making me feel so special, by standing up and announcing to all that I was off to bed.

I handed all my profits to the pit boss and asked him to distribute them to the staff to say thank you for looking after me so well.

He would not have understood the sarcasm in my voice. The grateful reaction of the staff made me feel like I was Gandhi handing food to the starving. They obviously didn't earn very much.

It also made me think the drunken German businessmen who make up their usual clientele, didn't usually give back their 'winnings' until later in the night and not to the staff.

The prostitutes certainly all looked disappointed as I waved on my way out the door.

A few minutes later, I opened the door to my room. The phone was ringing. It was the night clerk manning the front desk downstairs. "Would I require company this evening?" I replied "no, thanks" and hung up.

Soon afterwards, there was a knock on the door. An aunt Gladys look-a-like stood there. Would I like her to come in?

"No thanks," I said and closed my door. A few minutes later, the phone rang again. This time a sexy female voice asked me if I would like some company this evening. "No, thanks," I replied and hung up.

Thereafter, every half hour or so the phone would ring, or someone would knock on my door. It looked like the front desk guy was making a lot of money charging the girls a few bucks to contact me. I guess they were hoping that, at some point after a few whiskies, I would change my mind and develop an over-whelming desire to contract AIDS.

I unplugged my phone just after 1 am, when it became clear they just wouldn't take "fuck off and leave me alone" for an answer. I slept badly that night. The next morning at breakfast, it was a competition to see who looked the most worn out, me or the prostitutes. I reckon I did.

The hotel was far from being full with Germans.

Anyhow, back to my story.

Very late one night in Warsaw, we had finally wrapped up a production of a big show which had involved a whole group of us from the west. We were all staying in the same hotel, so to burn off the excess adrenaline from the night's stress, we ended up in the downstairs bar with a small posse of the hotel's prostitutes, all being served by the surly night clerk.

I was on my third drink and chatting with the director of the program we'd just made, when one of the Aunt Gladys' came up behind me, hit me in the head as hard as she could and started mouthing off to me in loud Polish.

My glasses were recovered, bent but luckily not broken, and several people dragged the angry woman away from me. She was still slagging me off as she got to the other side of the room. I was mystified. I knew who she was, I'd often seen her in the bar late at night, but I had not talked to her. Nor had I done anything to deserve a belting and berating from her.

Then, across the room, I noticed the group of men from our lighting department were laughing like drains at my predicament. Their boss, Michael, the Belgian lighting expert I hired for a lot of my shows, could hardly stand up he was laughing so hard.

Under questioning, he admitted he had been chatting to the prostitutes and learning the Polish words for some of the vulgar practices they get asked by clients to perform. He'd been very pleased to memorise one particularly nasty phrase.

When Aunt Gladys came into the bar, he'd tried out his new phrase on her, implying that it was her speciality. She had been horrified and demanded to know where he'd learned such a thing.

Michael had pointed to me and told her, "He told me."

132

She'd just stormed over and cracked me one, much to everyone's amusement. Ha ha! Now everyone calls me the man who got beaten up by a prostitute.

Very funny.

I should go back to Romania. At least there, the prostitutes there know I'm the most handsome, funny and lucky man they've ever met.

14. Killer robots

By golly, I've seen some wild animals in my time. At one point I was asked to go to South Africa to help our salespeople sell some of our formats. I'd never been to Africa before, but in some ways it was very similar to Australia. Lots of big sky which, after the permanently low skies of Europe, was a welcome change. Millions of eucalypt trees everywhere, too. More than in Australia apparently. But that was where the similarities ended.

South Africa was one of the most violent places in the world. So, before we left the Netherlands, our group undertook special security classes to make sure when we got to Africa we didn't do anything stupid or risky, such as walk in the street, speak to anyone or buy something in a shop.

The classes successfully made us more afraid.

The first thing I learned on this trip was that the Dutch airline KLM, thoughtfully timed the arrival of its daily flight to Johannesburg to coincide with the arrival of five other airlines.

There were thousands of people walking through the terminal at precisely the same time as we began to try to get off our plane. What a nightmare. What made the nightmare worse was that the other flights had all come from Saudi Arabia.

Every person in the terminal, other than me, was dressed in white Arabic style clothing, and sporting white fez style caps.

We were told they were Muslims returning from the Hajj, the holy pilgrimage to Mecca. I don't really know what the pilgrims do each day in Mecca other than pray, but as soon as I stepped off the aeroplane, I learned that, while on the Hajj, no one showered or wiped their bottoms.

The stench of body odour and human excrement in this herd of white clad pilgrims was so overpowering that people from our flight started gagging and covering their faces with their shirts and coats.

The terminal was so crowded, no one from our flight could get more than 2 or 3 metres from our aeroplane door. We stood on the air stair for an hour, jammed in with this massive, sweating pile of stinking humanity, until people started to get sick and collapse.

Fortunately for us, the Dutch steward in charge of our flight got fed up waiting. She said the Dutch equivalent of "fuck this for a joke" and opened the emergency door in the air stair which led down to the tarmac (pre-9/11 things were so much simpler) and led a couple of hundred of us, all following like little ducklings, across the tarmac past bemused airport workers, to another door nearer the customs and immigration counters.

Once back inside with the noxious stench, she pushed her way forward to the counters and harangued a border official until he agreed to immediately process the passengers from the KLM flight. God bless her. I mean Allah bless her I suppose.

Our security briefings had made us apprehensive about what to expect in South Africa and to be fair, the country lived up to its reputation as a scary place.

At night, in our luxury tourist compound, it was difficult to get to sleep over the sounds of the security guards and their Alsatian dogs patrolling the perimeter.

In the newspaper the first morning, I read that a local white farmer and his family had been pushed into a grain silo by a group of robbers the previous day. The entire contents of the silo were dumped onto them, suffocating them. We Dutchies were as nervous as hummingbirds the first few days. So many threatening looking people, black, white and coloured.

One morning on our way to work I got a first-hand lesson. There were three of us and our driver in a Land Rover. We had stopped to get fuel at a large petrol station. While our driver was inside paying for the fuel, my boss, who was in the front seat, suddenly muttered the Dutch equivalent of "fuck this for a joke". I remembered the same phrase from the KLM steward at the airport.

Outside his window, a large man had appeared. He was armed with a large rifle. The man glared in the car window at us. I looked out my own window and could see two other men, one armed with a shotgun, the other with a pistol. Oh my. Then, as if from nowhere, 10 more heavily armed men appeared around us. We all thought our number was up – that we'd inadvertently wandered into South Africa's largest-ever armed robbery.

Just as my bowels began to clench, an armoured van roared loudly into the petrol station. From inside, six more heavily armed men jumped out. There were now more armed men in this one petrol station than served in the Australian army.

Rather than gun us down, as we confidently expected, several of the men proceeded to the cash machine attached to the wall of the petrol station and refilled it with new banknotes. Then they re-locked the machine, jumped back into the armoured van and drove off.

The other armed men around us jumped into other cars and

disappeared as well. So, I learned a valuable lesson. When you need to refill your local ATM with cash in Johannesburg, you need at least 10 – and up to 16 – heavily armed men to do it. And one other small lesson I learned. You don't need to go to the Hajj to make yourself smell of body odour and human excrement. Just be a tourist in a car when an armed man comes up to your window.

Speaking of wild animals, I also learned during this trip that snails can be dangerous and disgusting. It was a local delicacy at our hotel and apparently "everyone tries them". Snails done in a mushroom and garlic sauce. While the rest of my group was umming and ahh-ing about whether or not to try them (and most wisely deciding against it), I was the stupid one who said "I will try anything".

As you will have read in some of my other stories, volunteering to taste the local wildlife is rarely a sensible idea. And it wasn't here either. The snails were awful. I know many people love to eat them, but my mind couldn't wrap my head around the fact that they were snails. And I knew in my youth I had actually vomited up more appealing things.

In fact, I vomited up this delicacy too, but blamed it on large amount of red wine consumed both before and after the main course. To drown the taste. Never again. Snails are one of the few South African animals safe from me. I later ate crocodile, water buffalo, antelope and even ostrich without repercussions.

On a much brighter note, I got to put my hands on the remains of a leopard's dinner.

It started with a conversation with the producer of a popular South African soap opera. We were thinking of buying the company he worked for, and my job was to make friends with the man so his company would think kindly towards us.

The producer turned out to be a good guy.

During one conversation, I mentioned to him my interest in anthropology and the fact that I had read extensively about the amazing discoveries made in South Africa. In fact, just a year or two earlier, archaeologists had found a complete skeleton of an Australopithecus called Little Foot at a famous location called Sterkfontein, near Johannesburg.

What a stroke of luck.

The producer was friends with one of South Africa's leading archaeologists. He was sure his friend would be happy to show us around the dig site. A phone call or two later and the following weekend, the archaeologist picked us up from my hotel in his Land Rover and drove us to Sterkfontein. The entrance to the caves was locked up tight because it was a Saturday, but he had the keys. We spent hours clambering over the dig as the archaeologist breathlessly described to me the discoveries there.

Sterkfontein is a limestone cave system where evidence of the first human ancestors was found. Apparently in prehistoric times, a hill above the caves hosted a grove of trees which was home to prides of prehistoric lions and leopards. Over uncountable years, rain had eaten into the limestone and created a sinkhole which eventually formed a large cave system underneath the grove. Whenever the lions and leopards dragged their food up to the top of the hill to eat, rain would wash the remains down the sinkhole into the cave.

The limestone preserved them in good condition for the millennia to come. In the 1930s archaeologists dug up the world's first evidence of an Australopithecus there. Another group, 20 years later, found the skull of an adult female Australopithecus which was given the nickname Mrs Ples. I was in heaven all morning and, to my delight, my fantastic day wasn't over.

The archaeologist suggested we drive to South Africa's capital, Pretoria, for lunch. Which we did. Afterwards, he revealed he also had the keys to the Natural History Museum there.

So, we drove there and had the museum to ourselves for several hours. While looking at the display of the Australopithecus discoveries, my new best friend revealed that the bone displays in the public areas were just copies. For security purposes, the real fossils were downstairs, locked up. Down the stairs we trooped, and he had more keys which unlocked a variety of storage cabinets.

Did I mention he had a whole bunch of keys with him? He delicately held out to me the skull, the real skull, of Mrs Ples. The actual real Australopithecus skull of one of the earliest humans. Mind blowing. Seriously one of the most amazing things I have ever experienced.

While down in the bowels of the museum, I was allowed to handle the skull of another human ancestor found at a place called Swartkrans. This was of an adolescent pre-human boy who was killed by a leopard 1.5 million years ago.

The skull had two puncture wounds in it. Apparently, the leopard had grabbed its victim by the head and dragged it to the top of a small hill to feed. Just like at Sterkfontein, the remains had washed into a limestone cave where they had been preserved. And here I was, more than a million years later, running my fingers around the fang holes.

Awesome. I wondered if South Africa might have actually been less dangerous back then.

On the way back from Pretoria, I met more South African wildlife. And learned a new lesson. Never wind down your car window when driving through the African bush. Along the highway, we were forced to come to a halt as a large troop of baboons (a congress of baboons? A flange of baboons maybe?) ran across the road in front of us.

I wound down my window to get a better look until my friend told me, rather urgently, to wind it back up. "The baboons only run when something is chasing them," he explained. And sure enough, just seconds later, a large cheetah ran across the road, just metres from the front of our car.

I had my window up by then, but the cheetah stopped and stared at me. Perhaps it was attracted by the smell of body odour and human excrement which had suddenly emerged from the passenger side of the car.

I'd say the most important lesson I learned from my South African journey came on our final night. Several of the actors in the soap opera offered to take us Dutchies out for a drink as a farewell gesture.

My colleagues begged off, saying they were tired and needed to get ready for the trip home the following day.

Me, being me, said "sure, let's go".

My company's local representative graciously allowed me to use her beautiful new white BMW. She also spent some time explaining to me the local road rules. As you might expect, this was mainly to do with avoiding violent death.

Apparently one of the most popular sports in Johannesburg was carjacking. The bad guys drive up behind you at the traffic lights, then gently bump you. If you were silly enough to get out to investigate, you'd be shot, and your car taken. The car was usually on a plane to somewhere else in Africa within the hour.

Carjacking at this time was so popular they were thinking of signing up sponsors and televising it. Never, ever – ever – I was told, was I to stop at a red light in the city at night. Law-abiding drivers who did so were either stupid or obviously tourists and, either way, that was how the bad guys knew how to find the best victims.

I was also told not to stop if I saw an accident by the side of the road. This was also a scam, another way the gangs got you to stop so they could steal your car (and shoot you). To be honest, the whole night out was starting to sound a bit too much like a war movie. But I had promised. I arranged to first go home to shower and change clothes, then I would meet the others in the city.

Several hours later I found myself at a bar where, for the first time in my life, I was the only white person in sight. In the days of apartheid, the blacks were not allowed to drink where the whites drank and instead established illegal bars called speak-easies. Despite the law having since being abolished, the locals still preferred to drink in their normal watering holes.

People kept looking at me and I felt very uncomfortable. It made me realise how it might feel when the shoe was on the other foot. You got the feeling you were constantly under in-spection. I was with a very well-known soap actor called Peter. He introduced me to a lot of people who were apparently very famous in South Africa, from movies and television. I had no clue who any of them were.

When it came time to go home, Peter advised me to follow him closely and he would lead me back to my hotel. Off we went, me in my colleague's shiny white BMW, closely tailing Peter's shiny blue BMW.

The German cars were very popular in South Africa at this time. Unfortunately, Peter drove like a maniac and I struggled to keep up with him. I guessed it must be safer to drive like a maniac, so the bad guys know you are a local.

At one point Peter drew ahead of me, just as the traffic light in front of me changed to red.

I wasn't going to be a silly victim.

I understood my instructions well.

I charged on through the intersection, first looking left and right to make sure no one was going to sideswipe me. Just then, a police car came around the corner and, with lights and sirens, ordered me to pull me over. I hesitated. Part of me wondered if this was another scam. But the siren and lights were insistent. I came to a stop and could see Peter's car roar off into the distance. The police officer, a small black man in a brown uniform, gestured for me to get out of my car. He asked to see my driver's license, which I handed over. Then he asked, "Would you like to tell me, sir, why you ignored the robot at the intersection?"

That sentence didn't make much sense to me. I tried to process it, but then admitted to him that I didn't understand.

He merely repeated himself.

"Can you tell me, sir, why you ignored the robot?"

Robot? I looked back at the intersection, which, at this time of night, was deserted. There was no robot there. No obvious robot anyway. Maybe it a very small one?

I turned back to the police officer and shrugged.

"There's a robot?" The policeman started to get irritated at my obvious stupidity.

"Sir, you just ignored the robot right in front of me. I saw you."

I turned and examined the intersection yet again, looking for a robot of some description. The officer was quite adamant about it, so there must have been something.

I had in my mind the robot from the American TV show of the 1960s, *Lost in Space*. A large humanlike machine with waving arms shouting "Danger, Will Robinson!" Maybe, I thought, they ran scientific experiments in the streets at night in Johannesburg? God only knew, but I needed to say something.

I put on my stupidest tourist smile.

"I'm sorry officer. I certainly didn't see any robots and I apologise if I almost hit it. I am a visitor here and this is my first time driving through the city. I'm not used to robots on the streets."

All these things were true. He wasn't mollified.

"Where are you from?"

"I live in the Netherlands," I explained.

"I know they have robots in the Netherlands," the policeman insisted.

The puzzled look never left my face. I thought to myself, "Well yes, the Netherlands is a modern state and I guess there must be robots of all sorts in the various scientific institutions. But on the street?"

"I guess they do have robots in the Netherlands, officer, but you never see them on the roads. At least I never have. I'm actually from Australia," I replied, hoping by now for the sympathy vote.

"I absolutely know they have robots in Australia, so what are you playing at?"

By now he was getting angry at me and I was getting more and more confused. I kept looking at the road expecting to see some sort of robot roll or walk along it, no doubt followed by a team of scientists in white coats. Why the hell would they conduct scientific work in Johannesburg in the middle of the night on a potentially busy street where stupid Australian tourists could almost run over them?

Shouldn't they at least put a notice in the newspaper advising everyone about which roads are to be used for their experiments? It would be safer. The officer was losing patience with me.

Just then Peter roared back towards us in the other BMW.

He had known something had gone wrong when my headlights disappeared from his rear vision mirror. He had made the decision to come back to find me, thank goodness.

When he pulled up behind the policeman, you could see what the policeman was thinking. The stupid Australian was obviously just pretending to be a total moron to distract him from the real robbers who were sneaking up behind him in a shiny blue BMW. He put his hand on his gun.

Peter slowly climbed out of his car. He began talking to him in the local language.

After a few moments of chat between them, Peter suddenly burst out laughing. The officer started laughing too, thank goodness. That just left me – a complete dork standing on the side of a road in the middle of the night, not having a bloody clue what was going on. I explained to Peter that the officer had accused me of almost running over a robot, but that I hadn't seen one, honestly, I hadn't seen any mechanical equipment of any sort on the road.

Peter explained with a big grin on his face.

"Robots are what South Africans call traffic lights."

Oh! Bloody hell.

The two of them found it so hilarious, they laughed with abandon for several minutes, the tears rolling down their faces. I had a pained smile pasted on my face.

Eventually, because the officer recognised Peter from the soap opera, he settled for an autograph and bid us on our way, still smiling. I stuck like a barnacle to Peter's tail the rest of the way home.

The next morning, I was back at the airport and there wasn't a smelly Hajj pilgrim or rampaging robot in sight. Leopards, baboons, Alsatian dogs, hummingbirds, snails. All valuable lessons learned in the one trip.

15. Addressing the conference

I've learned the hard way I should not get too blasé when asked to do public speaking. In my job I do so much blathering to crowds, I've grown into the habit of rarely giving it a serious thought until the actual moment I'm called on to perform my song and dance routine.

One time I was asked to address a major European television and film conference in Amsterdam on the subject of 'multicultural adaption of program formats', which is a fancy title for what I do for a living. But before you start thinking that the invitation was a long overdue recognition of how great I am at my job, the invitation was actually offered to Endemol.

Endemol was a co-sponsor of the conference, so someone from the company was invited to make a speech every year.

My boss, John de Mol, had been asked to do it but, being the smarter one, he handballed it to me. He instructed me to use the speech to promote a successful dating show we made in eight countries called *All You Need Is Love*.

Here is how it works. On video, a boy admits he likes a particular girl. She might be from the same high school. She might be a work or sport colleague. Picking up his courage and looking directly at the camera, the boy records a message asking the girl if she would go on a date with him.

In the studio, the presenter invites the boy to join him, talks with him about his life and the girl he likes, then shows the audience the video the boy has made. The presenter then asks the boy if he would like to see what happened when he, the presenter, took the video to the girl and showed it to her. Of course he does. That's why we are all watching.

The presenter then plays a video of the girl looking at the boy's tape – and her reaction. On the girl's video, the presenter asks if she would go on a date with the boy, as requested.

If she agrees, the presenter surprises the boy in the studio by bringing in the girl and there is a warm and embarrassing moment as they meet each other. The presenter then announces the program will pay for their first date and they go off happily.

If, on the tape, the girl says no, the boy slides out of the studio, totally embarrassed and regretting his rash decision to go public with his secret affection.

All You Need Is Love is not something I might watch on my days off, but it's very successful with the *Neighbours* audience.

I had given similar presentations about this format before, so wasn't overly stressed about doing it at the conference. The secret, I had learned, was to show a few clips of the funniest segments of the program and tell a few anecdotes about how crazy it is to make *All You Need Is Love* in places where you sometimes first have to ask the father of the girl if it is okay for the boy to ask her on a date. My spiel had always worked well before.

Because I was busy in the days leading to the conference, I didn't think about it further or read anything about it until the day my diary told me it was happening. Then things started to go bad very quickly.

Amsterdam traffic is appalling at the best of times, so I got there late. On arrival, I discovered the organisers had been in a panic, thinking I wasn't going to turn up. I had been travelling a lot and had not returned their calls.

I told the woman who was the liaison, to calm down. I assured her I would be entertaining and have the crowd laughing in no time. She gave me a funny look, which should have been a clue, but I paid it no mind because just then one of the conference technicians discovered the videotapes I wanted to show wouldn't play on their system for some reason.

So, instead of spending the remaining moments before the conference began finding out more about what was due to happen there, I was kept busy trying to fix my videotapes, which I did with seconds to spare.

As the audience of several hundred people began to file into the vast auditorium to take their seats, I was introduced to the four other people who, I was told, were to be on the panel with me and who would also make presentations.

Wait. Panel? Other speakers?

Well, okay, I thought.

I guess I should have read the brochure.

"Would I like to speak first?" asked the organiser, looking at me worriedly.

"No," I said. "Let someone else go first."

It was to be the only good decision I made all day. It turns out the people on the panel with me weren't like me – television producers having a laugh about a light-hearted and fun game show. Oh, no.

The chairman of the panel was the General Secretary of the International Federation of Journalists, who was slated to talk about the rise of racism in European media. My head went up suddenly – what the hell?

Then there was a professor from the University of Zurich, who was to talk about the death of European culture under the onslaught of cheap mindless television (that cut close to the bone). Next to him was a person who was head of a group called 'Multicultural European Broadcasting', who was to speak about the rise of fascism in the New Europe (c'mon, seriously?).

The fourth was the Director of the South Slavic Language Service of Radio Free Europe, who would speak about how the media had permitted and abetted the mass murder of thousands of innocent people during the war in the former Yugoslavia.

And after these undoubtedly worthy speakers, next up would be me – Brian 'dating show' Bigg – planning to give everyone a good chuckle over a zany new show for the whole family, a whacky, crazy half hour where boys will go to any lengths to ask that special girl out on a date.

Thank God I didn't agree to speak first.

So, we panelists all took our places at the front of the auditorium on the raised platform, where everyone could stare at us. I nearly passed out in terror as, one after the other my fellow speakers made their speeches, talking about all these worthy subjects, some of them near to tears, others rousing the audience to anger over the level of injustice in the world.

The deep frown, which everyone in the auditorium could clearly see on my face, was not my concern at the apparent indifference of European governments to the inexorable rise of racism and neo-fascism, but a desperate bid to think of something to say which would prevent the hundreds of people in the room from realising that the only Australian in the place was a complete dickhead.

What made things worse was that, because I had been late arriving, I hadn't collected a translation earpiece which was available for everyone at the door on the way in.

Stupidly, I had assumed the conference was to be in English.

But as soon as someone started speaking French or German, everyone in the room just slipped their earpiece on and a real-time translation was played for them. I didn't have one. And I didn't realise I needed one, until the chairman said something like, "Now here's the very important speech you've all been waiting for by this famous Swiss professor", and everyone in the room reached for their earpieces.

The man talked for half an hour in Swiss German, a language understood by only about a million people in a small part of Switzerland. There was no way a boy from New South Wales would know a word of it. There I sat, everyone in the conference following the speech rapturously – except for me.

I felt hundreds of sets of eyes staring at me. So, forgive me, but I did the only thing I could think to do under the circumstances. As the professor spoke, I listened to the tone and modulation he used and, when he seemed to make a very strong point, I nodded in agreement, shook my head wisely or raised my eyebrows at what sounded like a controversial opinion.

To the crowd, it was as if I could understand every Swiss German word he said. I even took notes, as if the things he was saying were so startling, I just had to write them down. But really I didn't have the first clue. But no matter. When he finished his speech, I led the applause strongly and I challenge anyone in the room to pick that I didn't have the foggiest idea what had just gone on. He could have been talking about monkeys for all I knew.

Fortunately for me, the chairman said immediately in English: "I'm sure we all agree with the professor that the death of European culture under the onslaught of television advertising is a bad thing." I wrote that down too, in case there was a question about it later.

Then, inevitably and painfully, it was my turn. But by now, for better or worse, I was ready.

I turned my internal bullshit meter up to thermo-nuclear and stood up in front of the microphone.

"Good afternoon," I began and gave a wry, worldly smile. "As these wonderful speakers have all correctly pointed out, Europe is changing and changing rapidly, perhaps too rapidly for many people. The old ways are disappearing and not everyone likes the new ways which are replacing them.

"The rise of the so-called 'New Europe' is nowhere more obvious than in the decreasing relevance of formerly important national borders as well as the growing fear among populations about the potential loss of their once proud and dominant national cultures.

"I have discovered in my travels," I told them, "that the rapid shrinking of historical cultural differences was leading, counterintuitively, to an increase in demand from people in most countries for a restatement of their cultural identities.

"The more people were forced to think of themselves as Europeans first and Germans or French second," I said, "the more strongly did the Germans feel about being German, the French about being French and so on." (Grave nodding of heads around the room).

"This trend was becoming very evident in television, where audiences in most of Europe, under pressure to give up regional identities, were actually demanding to see their own much-loved cultures reflected more strongly in the programs they watched.

"The television companies which were most successful doing business in the new European landscape, recognised this trend and tailored their sales products accordingly." Much scribbling of notes in the crowd. "We at Endemol were leading the way in reinforcing and reinvigorating national cultural traditions through the unique way we regionally differentiated our international program formats."

I had already worked out that my worthy and serious audience would never publicly admit to watching a light-hearted dating show – they were all public servant types, fans of government broadcasters like the BBC – so I waxed on about "how public broadcasting had a responsibility to lead public opinion throughout Europe."

"But if governments and European Union committees wanted to see into the heart of the new landscape – into what ordinary people were really thinking – then they needed to see what the people were watching on commercial television, which was where the actual centre of the new European cultural identity could be found."

You should have heard me go on like that for 20 minutes – complete and utter drivel – without notes I might add – just driven by fear. At the end, I showed my videotapes of *All You Need Is Love*.

("You must remember that for better or worse, cultural diversity in Europe, along with the support of multiculturalism and the repression of racism and intolerance, can only be done through the mass media and the support given by commercial television through culturally interesting programs like this one.")

Because I had managed to make the program appear ideologically correct, we all had a good laugh at my funny clip highlight videotape and then I sat the hell down before my legs gave way under me. But I wasn't out of the woods just yet.

The chairman called for questions and, for over an hour, I got all but two of them. You'd think the serious bastards would want to know more about mass murder in Bosnia or find out who the new Nazis were. But no.

"Was there racism in the selection of contestants for *All You Need is Love*?"

(No – the producers of the program in each country were instructed by Endemol to reflect racial tolerance in the selection of contestants at all times – ahem).

"Was Endemol deliberately encouraging multi-culturalism in the segment where the Portuguese man asked the African girl on a date? Or was it just a coincidence?"

(Big smile. "What do you think? Of course, it's no coincidence. We have to show how we can lead as well as reflect racial harmony in all our programs.")

And, God help me, a French woman even asked very seriously, if I had considered it worrying that, on my videotapes, women weren't shown to be asking the men out.

"Wasn't this encouraging sexism?"

("An excellent point, but these shows, for better or worse, reflect the culture as it now is, not how we might like it to be.")

More grave nodding of heads.

These professional conference-goers were taking a zany game show as a serious proposition! I had hit a nerve. And, what was worse, I had entertained them – a dangerous thing to do at a conference where everyone has spent endless hours listening to reports of mass murder, racism and intolerance.

Afterwards, I was surrounded by eager fans and invited to go to dinner with some of them on a cruise around Amsterdam's canals, so I could explain my theories to them in greater detail.

I ain't that dumb.

Face to face, they would have seen through me in about 10 seconds, so I made up a story about having to catch an early plane to South Africa and raced home, grateful to escape.

But. The woman who organised the event rang me later and told me I had been the hit of the conference. She would love it if I could give a similar address to other planned conferences.

"I don't know if I can," I said.

"I understand," she said.

But I don't think she did, really.

16. The most handsome man I know

It's inevitable, I guess, but working in a high-profile industry behind the former iron curtain has brought me into contact with a colourful variety of the very dodgy characters. And here I must make a distinction between the small 'c' criminals, who have their hands out for the odd favour or bribe, and the large 'c' criminals, who would shoot you without a backward glance if you pissed them off. I don't mind telling you, I've had a fair bit to do with both sorts. I've also pretended to be friends with a few people who I won't be inviting over for tea and biscuits any time soon.

Criminals of the small 'c' variety aren't so bad.

For example, the man in the blue uniform who turned up to our studio one day in an eastern European country which shouldn't be named.

We had just begun to record episodes of one of our hot new quiz program formats.

To call where we worked a "studio" was me being particularly generous. Yes, I was officially paying for what was described on the invoice as a television recording studio. But in any other country of the world, it would be more correctly called an abandoned warehouse in an industrial park in a run-down area on the outskirts of the city.

To call the show 'hot' however, was not any sort of exaggeration. We were recording in the middle of summer and the building had no air conditioning. We had loaded truckfuls of computers, dozens of powerful lights and several hundred people into the small, corrugated iron garage and were trying to make our magic.

The temperature on the set was over 50°C all day, which the humans barely tolerated but it was so stifling, the computers constantly broke down. Each day about midday we were forced to throw open the doors to let some air in, so the computers would cool down enough to start working again. Oh, and also so the audience members wouldn't die. I shouldn't forget to say that. It was not fit for man nor beast in there.

One of the clever members of the staff had begged, borrowed or stolen an industrial air conditioner from somewhere, and large silver coils of air conditioning piping snaked across every floor in every direction. But for the most part, the noise and heat this dodgy-looking machine gave off made conditions worse, not better.

So, on this particular day, right into the middle of our sweaty entertainment show sauna, strode the aforementioned man in a blue uniform. He was on the older side of 50 and imperiously told the staff who approached him that he was the fire warden assigned to the building.

He was, he announced, shutting us down for numerous breaches of the fire safety code. Who knew there was such a thing in this place? But fair enough, it was hotter than the surface of the sun in there, so we were obviously guilty.

Hearing this, the senior local producer nodded wisely to me and, taking the 'fire warden' by the elbow, guided him out of the room for a chat. We went on with the recording of the show.

That was going very slowly, because not only were the computers not coping in the heat, we had to stop after each question and answer section to allow our presenter to change out of his soaking wet shirt into a new, freshly dried and ironed one.

Sometime later, I noticed the 'fire warden' sitting peacefully in a chair in a corner of the studio, a small fire extinguisher at his feet, reading a book and drinking a beer. For the several weeks our recordings lasted, the man turned up most days (not every day, mind you) and never said a word. Just took up his post in the corner, read books and drank beer, while our production continued to swelter and our presenter and contestants (oh, and the audience) melted in the heat.

We had a number of people from the audience who swooned with dehydration and needed to be carried outside, but our new fire warden never batted an eyelid in their direction.

The senior local producer informed me I was now paying the man a small wage every week to ensure we wouldn't be shut down. He also revealed the man was not really a fire warden (oh really? Surprise, surprise) but a relative of a crew member.

"We must have a fire warden and a first aid nurse," my colleague told me, completely overlooking the fact that when we were doing up the budget for the show, he'd told me not to bother budgeting for either because no one would ever check if we had them.

"This man is cheaper than a real fire warden and won't shut us down, which a real fire warden would do because of the heat. He can be trusted," my colleague told me.

Wait. First aid nurse?

We ended up with one of them, too.

A woman in a sort of nurse's outfit turned up two days later (obviously once I had proven I was a gullible fool). The 'nurse' sat with the 'fire warden' every day and also drank lots of beer to stay hydrated.

I was told the nurse was the fire warden's wife. I suspected the two of them were slipping my colleague a few shekels out of their pay packet every week to thank him for the jobs I was paying them for. God help us if we ever had a fire or a real medical emergency. No doubt, I would have had to bribe another of the producer's relatives to drive the ambulance.

On another occasion, for another program, I sent a camera crew and two presenters around an eastern European country to record segments on location for a new reality show. They spent a long and tiring week recording videos with potential contestants. They assured me by phone late on Friday night, they had great material on tape which would edit into a fantastic episode. After traveling all week, the crew found themselves in the north of the country and decided to stay overnight in a nice hotel before returning to the capital.

The next morning, they came out to find the car, containing all the camera gear and the precious recordings, had been stolen from the hotel's secure car park, with nary an alarm to be heard. So efficient was the theft, it was almost as if the thieves had a key.

Fortunately, before the trip began, the senior local producer had insisted we fully insure the crew and car. At the time I thought it was strange, considering this same producer was always trying to save us money by using his relatives and friends for jobs, rather than costly professionals. But, as he pointed out to me after the theft was reported to the police, we were lucky he'd been so thorough as to insist on the insurance.

So, no harm, eh?

But I wasn't happy. The car and camera equipment were one thing (or several things actually), I told him, but the weeks' worth of recordings we had lost were a different kettle of fish

(Europeans always look at me strangely when I use expressions like that, because they just don't get the literal meaning – I don't have the heart to tell them no one does).

"Those lost recordings," I berated my colleague, "would cost us thousands of dollars to re-shoot. And trying to recapture the mood and excitement of the original performances was never possible. It was a disaster."

"I wish," I told him, "there was some way we could get the tapes back. It didn't matter about the car or the camera equipment, but if it was possible to recover the recordings, it would be worth my while to pay some sort of reward."

At that news my colleague told me, "let me see what I can do" and left the room.

Several days later, he burst into my office with the great news that he'd made a breakthrough.

"Really," I asked innocently? "What sort of breakthrough?"

He had somehow managed to make contact, he said, with people, who knew people, who knew people, who could get us the tapes back for US$5,000.

"Amazing work," I told him. "Tell them US$1,000 or no deal." He slouched out. Almost surprisingly fast, he returned to say his new contact would accept no less than US$3,500 for the priceless tapes.

Again, I told him no deal and had to endure 10 minutes of arguments from him about why I was being too stubborn. I hinted to him that I'd found another crew who would reshoot the entire week for us for US$2,000, so I could afford to play tough with the thieves.

Luckily for me, he soon came back with the news that the thieves would accept US$2,000 for the tapes, after all. I accepted. A few days later we got the tapes back by courier.

I even made a profit on the deal. My colleague informed me he had insured the car and its gear for much more than their real worth and the insurance company would pay us out in full. Would I consider giving him a bonus for being clever?

"Of course," I said. "You've been too clever by half." (As I say, they don't understand most English expressions).

Small 'c' criminals I can live with.

Further up the scale are the would-be big 'c' criminals. These aren't the really dangerous men, but the ones who would like you to think are dangerous. Into this category I put all the former KGB people I was forced to shake hands with in a number of countries, concerning dodgy deals which never ever happened.

I knew when my local partners or colleagues were setting me up for a dinner or lunch with a former KGB person, because the restaurant was always the most expensive in town and my colleagues offered to pay – which rarely happened in these money scarce countries.

And my colleagues always promised me the deal we were to discuss was the biggest ever – a sure thing. It was clear they were deathly afraid of these ex-KGB types, even though, with the fall of the wall, the KGB wasn't supposed to officially exist.

When I met them, the KGB Gollums (and they were usually slimy, untrustworthy-looking individuals in cheap, shiny suits), all went through the same dance. They would hand me a business card, which told me they were the Managing Director of a company which appeared to have been in existence for an hour. Their handshakes were moist and limp-wristed (even with the bigger men which was always surprising), and they never ever looked at me in the eye – from the first handshake to the end of the meal and saying goodbye. Their body language was always revealing.

They inevitably ordered the most expensive items on the menu, regardless what sort of food it might be and they always made a point of saying to my colleague at the end, "you are paying" as if to show me they were imperious and my colleague was wise to be scared of them.

The deal was always something enormous and a guaranteed sure thing because of their contacts – "people from the old days". Wink, wink.

My role was almost insignificant they would tell me. At my own expense, I merely needed to write and print a large, glossy and expensive-looking pitch document about their fantastic idea. Then I should write/shoot/edit and pay for a half hour video about the idea ("should it be an hour, Mr Brian, rather than half-hour? You are the expert here, Mr Brian, you tell me"), then fly at my own expense to their country where I would go along with them to several meetings, show their contact in the bank or financing organisation that I was firmly on board with the project; I should sing and dance about how great the idea was and how the whole thing would be a done deal ("because someone high in the bank owes my new friend favours from the old days". Wink, wink). For this tiny amount of work, I would always be told, millions of dollars would float to the ground around me – tax free naturally, in the country of my choosing, as if I was a Swiss banker's son.

The first couple of times it happened, I got really excited. I had seen first-hand that many of the former KGB types had grabbed lots of state assets in many of the former iron curtain countries. I knew some of the people who had grabbed formerly state owned TV stations and media companies and they were doing very well indeed.

I thought, at first, there was a real chance of earning some serious dollars. But, having spent my money and watched as the deals sailed off over the horizon without me, I realised I had been the fish. It's a term used in poker for the person at the table who is the sucker. The saying goes that if you look around the poker table and cannot tell who the fish is – then you, my friend, are the fish.

After the first few times, I treated the meetings only as a favour to my local colleagues and a bit of fun. When introduced to the Gollum, I looked deeply into his eyes, which put him off right from the start. I would grip his hand in a fierce handshake from which he couldn't escape and then hug him Russian style, which also put him off (they aren't the touchy types).

I would also order the most expensive meal on the menu before he could, so it looked like he was copying me. I would rave about how great his idea was (even if it was a shit idea) and enthuse about how much money we were sure to make. At the end of the lunch, I would give him the same warm stare, firm handshake and attempt a hug. Then, with the Gollum and my local colleagues beaming big smiles at me, I would promptly forget about the whole thing.

The colleagues were usually grateful I got them off the hook with the KGB man. Only once did one of them follow up the meeting with a phone call. And then it was only half-heartedly. I fobbed him off. It was a hairbrained scheme to put television screens, showing TV commercials, on the top of all the fuel bowsers in petrol stations in Eastern Europe.

The thing is, those screens are everywhere now and I am too scared to research it and find out which company owns them. I may, to quote myself, have been too clever by half.

At the deep, dark end of the criminal pool are the men in Eastern Europe you really don't want to muck around with.

The first time I had to go to Romania to make a show, I was asked by the Romanian man who owned the company to meet him in Madrid before travelling on to Bucharest. A strange request, I thought. Even stranger was where his office was. At the top of one of Madrid's tallest buildings.

A proper suite it was, very posh and very expensive. The man turned out to be very nice. He was the director who invented the look and feel of Italian commercial television, which, if you've seen it, is unmistakable. I described it in an earlier chapter.

The director who came up with the idea, made lots of money and invested some of it in a media company in Romania, his home country. So why, I inquired when I was ushered into his office, was that office in Madrid?

It was much safer, he explained to me. He hinted that there'd been threats against his family, a pastime which is still surprisingly popular in Europe, and that he couldn't safely live and work in Bucharest. He conducted all his Romanian work in Madrid, snug in his secure building.

That should have put me off Romania for a start.

What did put me off, was getting to Bucharest via Madrid. From Amsterdam, it would have been a simple one-hour flight. From the Netherlands via Madrid, it took a full day.

Leaving Madrid, I first had to fly to Milan, wait in the terminal for way too many hours, then clamber aboard a small 10-seater twin turbo prop aircraft for the last leg.

On the ground in Milan, I was the only passenger through the gate and optimistically thought I'd have the plane to myself. After a long wait on the tarmac, though, a van pulled up to the aircraft. Eight big Italian men piled out of the van and up the aircraft's small stairs. Wait just a minute, I thought indignantly. I had been forced to go through security. Had these guys just

162

bypassed the normal passenger gates? How dare they?

The new passengers were all wearing suits, despite the heat, and were all suspiciously large men. They piled in, with the younger men in the front and two older men in the back row – all of them staring daggers at me for no reason that I could tell.

Just as I was working myself into an 'it's not fair, you made me late' indignation, my mind recalled the Romanian director's warning to me about the prevalence of organised crime in Bucharest. He'd warned me that there was effectively no law and order there. Staring at the other passengers, the word 'mafia' occurred to me in capital letters. I had been planning to round on them and declare "look here, you damned fellows, it's just not right that I did the right thing and you fellows didn't bother. What's more, you kept us all waiting!" Instead I buried my indignation and then my head in a book and pretended not to notice anything.

The two flight stewards on board also adopted the same attitude. Despite the numerous and clear signs in English and other languages declaring it to be a non-smoking flight, the stewards apparently didn't hear, smell or see anything unusual when all eight of the men lit up cigarettes on take-off and smoked continually the entire flight. I must admit I didn't notice anything either, even though my eyes watered and I coughed continually the whole way. Lovely chaps I'm sure they were, but we didn't get to know each other.

On arrival in Bucharest, another van met the plane once we landed. The Italian men filed off, no doubt so they could be spared the indignity of having to go through security like the rest of us. Or just me, actually. I was happy to see them go. I thought to myself "I survived that brush with Italian mafia easily enough".

Until the next day when my local Romanian producer colleagues offered to take me out for dinner. As we walked into the restaurant, the eyes of a large group of men at a nearby table all stared daggers at me. It was my friends from the plane.

They were having dinner with another large dangerous-looking men and about six or seven women. The women were all young and pretty and done up like prostitutes. (They probably were prostitutes, but who am I to judge?) I went cold. I realised my new friends would remember me from my distinctively loud hacking cough on the plane. And hell, would they would think I was following them? What to do? I took advantage of the fact they were all smoking (despite the many 'No Smoking' signs), to ask the waiter for a table in another room. I smiled at the men and went next door where we had a nice meal.

The unexpected advantage of our move to the restaurant's other room was that we could hardly hear the terrible gypsy band which was moving around the tables, entertaining the guests in exchange for money. My Italian friends at the big table kept sticking local Romanian dollar notes in the pockets of the band, so the boys with the violins and piano accordions never moved an inch from them the entire evening. My loss.

I actually began dreading the chance of seeing the good old fellows again on the flight home the next day. They were already suspicious of me. For them it would be too much of a co-incidence to see me a third time (I've seen all the movies). Just in case, I didn't go to the restaurant toilet all night. I was about to explode by the time I got home.

The next day the boys weren't on the flight, luckily.

I had another brush with really bad guys when asked to make a silly reality program in Poland about male strippers, which you will have read about elsewhere here.

The concept of the show, as I explained already, was simple enough. Scour the country for six beautiful, sexy men and turn them into a stripping group, with a big finale performance before a crowd of screaming girls.

Straightforward enough, except that for some reason, the broadcast network boss decided he wanted a man called Tomasz (not his real name) to present the program.

In photos, Tomasz looked perfect – over 185cms (six-feet) tall, long dark hair and gorgeously built. Plus, he was a male model and stripper himself, so he should know what he was talking about as a presenter. Ideal for the program and handy for me that he was the one the network wanted. Finding the best presenter for a show is always one of the biggest dramas.

The problem was that Tomasz currently lived in Las Vegas, not Warsaw. And the reason he lived in Las Vegas was because there was a contract out on his life in Poland. Seriously, the word was out that he was to be murdered if he came back.

Tomasz' crime was being too good at his job. As one of Warsaw's top male strippers, he'd been hired by a local mobster to entertain ladies at a birthday party for the mobster's pretty wife. Tomasz had done his bit and got the women and the mobster's wife all hot and bothered by taking off his trousers to music. But then he'd later stepped over the line completely by starting an affair with the wife. Never a clever play.

The mobster found out and, as you'd expect, was not happy. Tomasz discovered the mobster was not happy one morning when he went out onto the balcony of his apartment and found that a large explosive device had been placed there. Fortunately for Tomasz, it had failed to detonate.

Tomasz and his glittering Velcro trousers decamped to America that same day.

Now the network and I wanted him to come back.

The first problem would be to work out with the mobster if that would be possible. As with all such delicate matters, my Polish colleague told me "let me see what I can do".

Several days later he reported a breakthrough. The mobster, he said, would temporarily suspend the contract on Tomasz if I paid a fee of USD$5,000 and abided by several conditions - that Tomasz stay in the accommodation we would rent for him and not, under any circumstance, go out at night to clubs or bars.

If Tomasz was seen out and about, the deal was off because there were a lot of people who would recognise him and think the contract was still up for grabs. I agreed. Tomasz agreed because he wanted to see his family in Poland again. And one day soon afterwards, he quietly flew into Warsaw.

Tomasz turned out to be perfect for the program, as expected, and a great guy to boot. We got on very well together.

The day after the big finale concert, I was sitting with Tomasz, other Polish colleagues and the show's directors, Adrian and Roman from Australia, at an outdoor restaurant in Warsaw recuperating and enjoying the cooler weather.

During the lunch, Tomasz mentioned that he would be more comfortable sitting inside. Why, I asked? Too cold for you? That's when I found out there had been another condition on Tomasz' return to Warsaw. He had promised to leave the country again the minute the show ended, because the contract on him would be reinstated. And here we were sitting at an outdoor restaurant in a busy part of the city, in direct contravention of that condition.

We all hurried inside. Tomasz went straight to the airport after lunch. The rest of us got drunk with relief. I mulled on how easily and quickly my Polish colleague had managed to get up close to a major gangster to organise the deal in the first place. How much of my USD$5,000 had found its way to the mobster's pockets, I wondered?

Soon afterwards, I ended up getting up close to a gangster on my own.

In another country which needs to remain nameless, the studio complex where we produced that country's top rating game show, was owned by a man who looked and acted like a very bad person.

But looks can be deceiving, can't they?

He was a huge, barrel-chested man with close cropped hair. He never went anywhere without two just-as-big bodyguards beside him. These monsters, I was reliably assured by the local producers I worked with, were always armed. As far as I could tell, everyone in this country carried a gun. So, you know. Meh.

At the time, and ever since the fall of the Berlin wall, this particular country had produced 90 per cent of the world's pornography. Organised crime was so bad, the FBI had set up an office in the capital to try and get on top of the crime before it got to America's shores.

The big, newly built complex on the edge of the city where we worked, had a studio, restaurant and hotel-style accommodation available. The local producers had worked out a deal on all of it to save money. I stayed in my international luxury hotel in a different part of town, because I've never been keen on paying for my bed by the hour (which people appeared to be doing at this place).

Anyway, the local producers were obviously terrified of the studio owner, who was sometimes to be seen hanging around the studio to watch the show being produced. One day they reported that he had asked to meet me. There'd been several news stories about me in the local media and he was curious. They suggested I should say hello to him, so they could stay on his good side. They were getting a good deal on the studio rental and didn't want to lose it by being rude.

Oh great. Was I free for lunch the next day? We met in the restaurant attached to the complex. I'd never noticed anyone dining at any of the tables. I suspected it was merely a front business, possibly to account for unexplained cash flow.

But there we all were, at a large round table in the middle of the room, attended by 10 uniformed staff, including chefs. There were six of us dining. Me, the two local producers in their best suits, the owner and, surprisingly, his two bodyguards, who'd somehow been given permission to sit at the main table. I should have complained about having to dine with the help. But I didn't.

I avoided the range of traditional national dishes on offer (fool me once) and chose grilled fish. It was delicious. Only the boss and I spoke for the two hours of the lunch. The bodyguards glowered at the producers and ate in silence. The producers kept their eyes down and ate in silence, other than when I needed something translated.

The boss turned out to be a terrific lunch companion. Intelligent, worldly-wise and able to tell a great story. The conversation between us was actually light and cheerful. We turned out to have a common interest in poker, which kept the chat going for a long time. Of course, I avoided more controversial subjects (killed many people lately?) so I had a surprisingly good time. At the end of the meal, I reached into my wallet as a gesture to pay, which of course, my host refused with a big pantomime show. As I knew he would.

Afterwards, the producers gushed about how well it had

gone. I was pretty pleased about it too. I had survived my first brush with the local underworld easily enough.

Until a few days later, when the producers told me we had been invited back to the restaurant to play poker with the boss and the goons. Oh great. Was Friday night okay for me? Absolutely fantastic.

We ended up back in the restaurant at the appointed time, the same six of us. Again, we were the only patrons. I'm not sure if the place was closed so we could play poker in peace, or whether my initial assumption of the restaurant merely being a front was correct (I never met anyone who ate there, except me and the two producers and we didn't pay).

The big table was laid out for a poker game. The entire staff, including chefs, were lined at attention along one wall – all 10 of them. They stayed there all night like that, apparently just in case we wanted something to eat. They were a credit to the level of professionalism among restaurant staff in Eastern Europe.

As usual, I expected to be expertly robbed by the locals, so I had only bought a couple of hundred U.S dollars to play with. The boss explained we couldn't play with the local currency because it was valueless and no one used it, even in the local shops. We all nodded our heads at that and exchanged US $100 notes for poker chips.

Just as with the lunch, the game was fun. Of course, I wasn't one of the people standing to attention along the wall the entire night. About midnight I ordered a steak sandwich, more to give the staff an excuse to leave off standing along the wall, than because I was hungry. They showed their gratitude by making it the world's largest and most complex steak sandwich.

The boss was great company again. His bodyguards were both fish (see above) and the producers tried to pretend it wasn't agony for them to lose their $100, which it no doubt was. About 2 am, when we called it quits, I was in front by about $150 and the boss about $300. The others were down a lot – I think they all lost deliberately. Not me.

I was actually quite grateful not to have been robbed. So, recalling my earlier gesture to the staff in Bucharest, I asked the boss to distribute all my winnings to the poor chefs and waiters who were still lining the wall, wilting like flowers.

It was as if I had suddenly turned into Mother Theresa. The staff gushed at me gratefully when the boss distributed the cash to them. By the extent of their gratitude, I think I gave them a week's pay. I was just happy to get out of the place without a bleeding wound. The boss and I parted as new best friends.

There is a final note to this story.

Some weeks later, when I made a return trip to oversee the progress of the show, the two producers urged me to go with them after work one night to a new casino which had just opened in the city. Rather than spend the night in my sad and lonely expensive, luxury hotel room, I dressed in my best clothes and pasted on my cheeriest smile.

At the casino front desk, the first thing I noticed was a photocopied picture of me pinned up on the wall. Uh oh. What's this? When they recognised me, the reception staff snapped to attention. One dived onto the phone, the other started waving his arms and rabbiting away at me in the local language. I turned to go, thinking he was telling me to leave. Had I been banned from the casino for some reason? Wouldn't be the first time, I thought.

As I turned to leave, I came face to face with one of the most beautiful women I have ever seen in my life. Norwegian stock, if I was to guess. Tall, stunning, platinum blonde and dressed in some wispy thing that left my imagination storming the barricades and charging headlong into the guns. Rather than brush past me without noticing that I existed (which is how my relationships with women like this usually go), the goddess stopped and held out her hand to me. She gave me the sexiest smile I have ever received from a woman in my life and said what I assume was her name. I missed it completely. My eyes and my mind were singing Tchaikovsky's 1812 overture to the accompaniment of a 50-piece big brass band. Holy Mary. The staff behind the desk were all smiling broadly, rabbiting at me in the local language and gesturing to the goddess.

I smiled broadly back at them, not having the first foggiest clue about what was going on. The goddess solved the impasse by looping her arm into mine and escorting me past the grinning staff into the casino. Ok, I thought, I will play along. She smelled like heaven in long grass.

Inside, we were the centre of attention. Everyone was looking at her, she was that gorgeous. At least, I assumed they were looking at her. Could they have been looking at me? Am I that good looking in Eastern Europe? No, probably not. It was probably her.

The goddess directed me to the cashier's cage and held out her hand for money. I gave her one of the same USD$100 notes I had used for the poker game. She gave it to the cashier and was handed a pile of chips in return. Then she took my arm again and steered me across the room to the craps table, where the crowd parted before her like the Red Sea.

No doubt they were all wondering why such a magnificent example of the human species bothered to tow around her handicapped elder brother – that's him, the fat, red-headed moron with the goofy smile.

Someone handed us a couple of glasses of champagne.

I don't know how to play craps. All I know is that one player gets to throw the dice and everyone bets on the outcome. Never done it and never had much of an interest in the game until this night. The goddess put some of my chips (I guess they were "our" chips now) onto some numbers and someone else threw the dice. Then people cheered. I had won. The dealer pushed a lot of chips our way.

The goddess gave me a big hug and a lingering slow kiss, then grabbed our chips and bet on other numbers. Someone threw the dice again and we won again! Two in a row. There was more cheering.

Wait just a minute. I had been here before, right? My alarm bells began ringing. A little more loudly than my lust bells were ringing. Which was pretty loud.

Just like in the Bucharest casino, had I somehow become the luckiest man in the room again? I still had no idea what was going on at the table, but the goddess was clinging to me like she was in danger of drowning.

She kept putting down chips and we kept winning. The crowd around the table stopped betting on anything else and just plonked their chips down onto the same numbers chosen by the goddess each time. The cheers got louder. We were all winners. I was getting quite sad that these people didn't realise the game was so rigged.

Then, from across the room, the boss of the studio complex strode towards me, followed by his two goons. He greeted me like a long-lost relative and hugged me like we were brothers. He kissed the goddess like he was her randy elder brother and they swapped "How's it all going?" stories in the local language.

It dawned on me. This was his casino. And I was his special

guest because, since our lunch and poker game, I was his new best friend.

It explained the goddess. She was bought and paid for. It explained why I was winning at craps even though I had no idea how to play the game.

My first instinct was to wallow in my good fortune. Dump the wife and kids and make a new life with the goddess (who really appeared to love me – really. What are you implying?), take my craps winnings to buy a flashy car and new shiny suit. I'd spend my life hanging out with my new pal, who was making a ton of money by the look of his own shiny suit. I would be the centre of attention like I had never been before.

But I didn't.

Sigh.

As soon as I realised what was happening, I knew I couldn't. Was it integrity? Who knows what integrity is? But I knew if I spent the night with the goddess (as was expected of me by the wolfish smiles from everyone around me) and kept my gambling winnings, the boss would own me.

Who knows what favours he would ask of me in return? I held the keys to a lot of television money at the time and the idea that, if I went further down this road, he would be able to leverage me, took the fizz out of my champagne.

Sadly, I piled up our winnings and left the craps table, to the loud groans of all the other winners who were sorry to see us go. The goddess and I found a table in a quiet corner and sat and stared silently at each other for 15 minutes over our champagne glasses. A large part of my mind (and other parts of the rest of me, to be honest), was reluctant to let this ship sail. Wasn't there some solution which would allow me to bask in her sunlight for a while longer?

We sat in silence, not because of our admiration for each other's beauty (ahem), but because she had no English, German or Dutch and I had no Norwegian or whatever other language came out like honey from between her perfect lips. I felt I should just sweep her up and marry her before she woke up to herself.

But that led to a disturbing thought. If we were to be married, how would we communicate? Conversation over breakfast would undoubtedly put a strain on our new love.

Me (peering over the newspaper to where she buttered my toast): "I see the prime minister's still running the country into the ground, dear."

Goddess (handing me my toast):

"Du er den mest kjekke mannen jeg noen gang har møtt." *

You are the most handsome man I have ever met (Norwegian).

Me (taking the toast and nibbling some of it):

"Exactly, dear. I blame the damned liberals!"

Sigh.

I knew the boss would have paid her a small fortune to go with me for the night, and I was grateful to him, but I just couldn't think of a way out of my sticky corner if I gave in to my baser instincts. Not to mention that I was already married and had kids, of course. Of course. Not to mention that. What are you saying?

I gathered up our pile of chips and went to the cashier's cage, where I changed them for a reasonably large pile of American dollars. I handed them all to the goddess who, to her credit, managed to look surprised (and if I'm being honest, it was the first true emotional response from her to anything so far).

I looked deep into her stunning grey eyes, thanked her for being perfect and walked out before I could change my mind. My bottom was black and blue by the time I got home, from kicking myself for being such a stupid, stupid bastard.

Way too clever for my own good.

17. Body language

One of the things you develop, when working in countries where few people speak English, is a good appreciation of non-verbal communication. When you aren't distracted by the noise coming out someone's mouth, you start paying attention to all the other things they are telling you. I first noticed it when producing *Who Wants to be a Millionaire?*

During the taping of the program, I usually had no idea what the Danish/Swedish/French presenter and contestant were talking about to each other. I knew the presenter was asking the contestant about his family or his hopes and dreams. That was part of the process. But I didn't know specifically what they were saying. But I would see the presenter leaning forward eagerly to engage the contestant.

Early in the game, that's a good thing. We want the contestant to feel that the presenter is on their side. But I made a mental note to myself to tell the presenter, during the next editing break, to make sure they leaned back during the big money questions, to physically disengage with the contestant, so the contestant felt alone and anxious.

That was also part of the game.

It was easier to see what the contestant was telling me.

Usually they would sweat (in one country which shall remain nameless, a small two-bar heater was positioned at their feet to make sure they heated up – a warm body is a nervous mind. See my book *Making A Millionaire: My Way* for more on these dirty tricks).

But most of the non-verbal information from a contestant would be beamed from his or her eyes. When a question was being asked, contestants would stare pleadingly at the presenter as if to say, "Please let me get out of here – I'm trapped."

Then the contestant would glance down at the screen in front where the question and the four possible answers were written. Had the correct answer somehow magically appeared there?

Then the contestant's eyes would go back up to the face of the presenter, as if the correct answer could be sucked from his face. You would see the contestant's eyes unfocus, as he drove down into his memories looking for a clue to the right answer. This pattern happened invariably, across all contestants and all countries. Eyes to the presenter, then down to the screen, then back to the presenter, then to some unfocused place in the sky, then back to the presenter.

If the contestant happened to look anywhere else than these limited number of places – and remember the camera is always close on them – if his eyes went in any other direction, for example towards the audience stands behind the presenter's head, we immediately went on alert for cheating. Several pairs of eyes belonging to the production staff would carefully scan the audience section where the contestant was looking, to see if someone there was giving him the answer.

More than once, we saw an audience member holding up one, two, three or four fingers to give an answer to the contestant. Sometimes it was a random audience member caught up in the moment.

Once, we had a woman at the top of the audience stands,

so caught up in the tension, she screamed the answer at the top of her voice. One time, in a country which shall also remain nameless, we saw three people lift their right hands to their heads in unison just as the contestant looked at them. Obviously, a pre-arranged signal.

Unfortunately for all the contestants who had brought along a secret brains trust in the hope of cheating the game, we had a system to deal with it. Before the contestant could deliver his or her answer, the director would suddenly announce over the intercom there had been a technical problem with the microphones. We would have to stop taping, he would announce, to fix it. The current question, unfortunately, would not be valid. Sorry everyone.

The audience would get a 15-minute break to go outside for a drink of water and the chance to go to the toilet. When they returned, after the 'technical problem' had been resolved, the contestant's group of friends would find themselves relocated to the second set of audience stands, those behind the contestant's head not the presenter's, where he or she could no longer see them. And we remained on the alert for any coughing noises or stamping of feet, which was also common with friends trying to help.

And while on the subject of cheating in *Millionaire*. In another eastern European country, the production on this particular day was interrupted several times by staff in charge of audio production. They reported there was a buzzing noise in the microphones we were using. It was intermittent and difficult to pin down, they reported. And it continued to cause problems for our taping.

We tried everything to fix the problem.

Eventually one of the producers realised the noise was a series of buzzes, either one, two, three or four, which happened only after the presenter had revealed the question and possible answers. We didn't need to be Einsteins to work out what the problem was.

We surmised the contestant must have had a buzzer set up in their shoe or on their body and someone in the stands was activating it. We didn't bother to find out or accuse the contestant.

Without letting on to the contestant that we were on to him, he was given several questions no one in their right mind would know the answers to.

These questions are commonly referred in the industry as "CKs" or contestant killers. Usually about 14th century poetry or some obscure branch of science. These questions sit in a special file on the computer and can be dropped into the game at a moment's notice. The contestant's friends were unlikely to be able to help. And, in this case, they couldn't. The contestant was forced to make a guess, chose a wrong answer, and went home with no money. As we intended. He didn't profit from his scheme, and we avoided the bad publicity of a cheating scandal like had happened in another country (ahem).

It had been just lucky for us the frequency he chose for his buzzer was close to the one we used for the microphones. Otherwise, he could have taken a lot of money from us.

But enough about *Millionaire.*

Non-verbal became my primary means of communication as I travelled around non-English speaking countries teaching people how to make our formats.

When I arrived in a country for the first time, it was common that the producer of the program would himself, or herself, collect me from the airport.

No doubt it was to size me up and put me in my place.

The local producers were often only told that some idiot from the Netherlands would come to teach them how to make the new show. And each of them felt they were already the world's best television producer, so usually felt outraged they were to be taught how to suck eggs.

When they met me for the first time, their defensive walls were sky high – arms crossed, fierce scowl on their face, shoulders hunched. When they found out I wasn't Dutch, that I was Australian, a little part of that scowl lifted. But not much.

The producer usually had a cousin who lived in Australia or they had themselves visited Australia sometime earlier, or they had secretly dreamed of one day going there to see the whales. Anyway, at least I wasn't Dutch.

No one in Europe likes the Dutch.

I might add that no one in Europe likes the French, Germans, Swiss, Italians or Spanish either. It's like a squabbling family. They all complain about each other, which makes my boss' decision to hire an outsider like me for the job very prescient. But the fact remained that the particular producer still felt he or she was the world's best television producer, and therefore didn't need any help from the not-Dutch consultant, thanks very much.

The program looked simple enough.

I knew the producer was usually afraid I would make him or her look less than god-like to their own staff. Television production is full of oversized egos. They waited, crouched angrily, for me to utter the fateful words "ok, this is how you must do it," so they could gleefully pounce. Usually it was with phrases like "We don't do it like this in my country," or "that definitely won't work here" or "we've already tried that, but it won't work in this market." All accompanied by a condescending smile.

What each was busting to say was: "I've determined before you got here, that we will do it differently than you have in mind, primarily so I can put my own stamp on the format and prove that I am, indeed, the world's best producer."

And then they planned to sit back, with a smirk, and let me splutter and complain. Their reputation before their staff would be enhanced, not damaged. I suspected they had already warned their staff that "if the bastard from Holland tells you to do something, just ignore him and come and tell me". But few of these local heroes realised that, while this program might have been the highlight of their career so far, this sort of interaction is what I did for a living each day, and I was good at it.

Meeting the world's best producer wasn't a unique event for me. I did it three times a week. I kept looking at their body language for signs of when to proceed and it rarely let me down.

After my arrival, I would avoid mentioning anything about the format, for hours and hours, if need be, until they couldn't stand the suspense. I would complement them on the enormous number of beautiful women in their country (see *Doing Backflips* elsewhere in this book) and ask their opinion on the local political situation, which I would have researched on the internet the previous day. And the success or otherwise of their local football team, which I had also researched.

I made it sound like I had always had a deep and abiding interest in their country and would ask a long list of questions about it. And I would also ask them questions about themselves. I would make it almost impossible for them not to quietly boast about how experienced they were, the great shows they had made and their own hopes and dreams.

I would make up stories about my own life which matched theirs so they could see how similar we were to each other.

I would hint that if he was as good as he said he was, I could perhaps help launch him on the international market.

Lies, lies, lies. But all to deliberately avoid the very subject they were busting to get to.

Eventually, if I kept it up long enough, they would unwind their bodies, distracted by my obvious deep interest in their country and their career. By the time we got to the studio, even if was the next day, we had begun to become friends.

When I felt the time was finally right, I would open my account by asking them what they thought of the format and their opinion about the best way to make it in their country. After all, they were the local expert and obviously a world class producer. Wait, you could see them ask themselves. The consultant was asking me? They never expected that, and it helped to unwind them further. Maybe, I could see them thinking, this person from Holland wasn't such a loser after all.

At the end of our first interactions, when they realised I wasn't going to stand in front of their staff and declare myself dictator, their jaw would unclench, their thrusting chin would retreat, their arms and legs unwind. When I saw all this happen, I could finally get on with the job of making them do the things I wanted them to do the way I wanted to do them.

Of course, I found it effective to always follow the rules laid out in the *How to win friends* books.

I let them be the alpha in the relationship. I kept the level of my eyes below theirs at all times and constantly mirrored their posture – if they crossed their legs, I would do the same moments later; I kept a slight smile on my face and always looked them firmly in the eyes.

The books say you do this while consciously thinking to them "I want to fuck you" – both to men and women.

A lot of times, I couldn't bring myself to think that, but my smile, steady gaze and slow graceful movements remained.

In the movies, the bad guys always move fast while the good guys move in slow motion. Moving quickly gives off an air of panic, of uncertainty, while moving slowly conveys the impression of confidence. I always moved slowly, which in a busy TV studio during a recording, is amazingly effective.

I kept my hands open, to show I had no secrets. If it was appropriate, I never missed an opportunity to touch them reassuredly on the arm or shoulder. According to the books, breaking a person's personal space like this is something only a friend would do. I was telling them with my body, even if we couldn't really communicate in words, that I was his friend first, colleague second, overlord a distant third. It was usually enough.

Oh, and I never directed their staff to do anything at all, ever. If I wanted something changed about the production, I wouldn't stand in front of the staff and dictate. I would quietly take the producer aside when no one was watching and ask him, if he was "absolutely sure" what he was planning was the correct way? I would remind him that earlier, he'd come up with a brilliant way to do it better (the way I had suggested him).

The producer usually came to appreciate me allowing him to have all the glory and letting him remain the hero in the eyes of his staff. And how everything I "suggested" to him was only directed towards making a better program, not at making him look silly. He usually took my advice. After all, we were now best friends.

Because he made all the announcements and his staff took directions only from him, he usually came to believe that all the decisions he made were his, not mine. I was apparently just sitting around drinking coffee.

This was important.

The old-fashioned American way, "Do it this way or else" usually meant that, as soon as the consultant left for the airport, the local producer changed everything back to the often-misguided ways they had wanted to do it in the first place. After all, they were still the world's best television producer, right?

If I successfully got the producer to believe the way he was making the program was a reflection of his own amazing genius, he would be more likely to keep doing it the way I wanted, even after I got onto the plane.

So, I worked constantly to reassure him, usually in front of his staff, that the way he was making the show was "amazing" and "fantastic," even if earlier in the day I had struggled to get him to do it in the first place.

A few days later, as I prepared to leave, I usually found a way to address the staff for the first time. I wanted to lock the producer in, so I would tell his staff, in front of him, that he had "grasped a concept which even great producers in other countries had found incredibly difficult to grasp" and how the producer had really made the program his own work of art.

It was a guaranteed hit, I told them.

I knew he would have trouble changing anything without his staff wondering why he would alter his own genius.

When he dropped me back at the airport, now beaming at me full of teeth, we were friends. I was always happy to see episodes of the program months later, which looked pretty much the same as I had set them up originally. That was the way I judged how successfully I did my job.

It didn't happen perfectly all the time, of course, because television producers are nothing if not contrary thinkers (again see *Doing Backflips* elsewhere in this book).

In one country, a junior person on the production, whose job was only to interpret for me while I was there, decided he knew better how to make the show. I found out later that, after I left, he had started issuing changes and told the producer they had been my instructions. Clever plan.

But usually the show stayed the way I wanted. In Bucharest, during a visit there for a music program, I noticed something in the show I didn't like. When I pointed it out to the producer, she told me, "Mr Brian that's what you told us to do."

I replied "Really? I don't think I did."

The producer then chatted in the local language to her assistant who ran off and returned moments later with a printed book. The producer opened it to a page and showed it to me.

"See?"

When I had been there to set up the show, apparently someone had followed me around and written down every stupid word I'd said. Then they had printed it all in a book so the staff would know the rules to follow. Gulp.

Turns out I had definitely said it. I could only smile and silently vow to be more careful about what I said in future.

18. Hiring staff

Becoming proficient in reading body language taught me a few things about hiring staff, too. You may not always like it, but the way you appear and act tells someone like me a lot about you, even before you open your mouth. If you arrive for a job interview, nine times out of 10 I will have made up my mind whether or not I will hire you, before your bottom has reached the seat.

Television production is a hard game. You never get paid enough, you always work longer hours than you expect, on shifts that even an all-night petrol station attendant would refuse to consider. And, as terrible as it is to accept, in television you can be the best at what you do, do everything perfectly, yet still get fired if something goes wrong, even if that thing is not your fault. It's a job with constant stress, constant disappointments and constant highlights.

One mistake and the ship sinks with you in it. It's not a job for every personality type, no matter how glamourous it looks from the outside.

So, when I hire staff for a production, body language plays a big role. If you read my other book *Making a Millionaire: My Way*, (Okay okay, no more plugs for it from now on, I promise). My editor also says I need to warn you about what follows. She says "advise people not to read it". Tell them to skip to the next chapter if they are easily offended. So I have. These are only my opinions, based only on my experiences and are not meant to be scientifically replicable.

So, if you are still with me, who do I hire? Let's start with who I don't. Obese people and other extremely overweight people have next to no chance of being hired by me. Other than in a few rare cases, people become obese (as Ricky Gervais famously stated) because they take in more calories per day than they burn off. It's entirely a lifestyle choice. I'm no skinny Minnie, but, with all the information around these days about how unhealthy it is to be overweight; an obese person declares themselves by their appearance to be either really stupid or really lazy. Or both. Either way, they declare they have no self-discipline.

Someone with no self-discipline will never be the sort of staff member I need who will work a non-stop, 30-hour shift editing a program when it absolutely needs to be done to meet a deadline. This happens more than you think. They are more likely to find a reason not to be there or look for a shortcut. Many obese employees do provide colour, movement and drama around the office, but you can usually do without those.

Strangely enough, human nature gives a beautiful woman or handsome man less of a chance of getting a job with me too. Life is always good for the beautiful. Everything is given to them from an early age. A beautiful woman doesn't have to worry about money, getting a boyfriend or finding the perfect job, things for which other women constantly worry about and fight for. A handsome man always finds rose petals thrown into his path. You can see where I'm heading with this. Nature is often cruel.

The beautiful don't need to be hugely intelligent or determined to succeed.

They will win in life anyway. So, they rarely develop the drive it will take to work as hard and as creatively as I would need them to. They, too, can find reasons to go home early and look for a challenge more suited to their obvious talents.

Too often, beautiful women are disruptive around an office environment because the other sex tends to peacock and prance around them rather than get their heads down and work.

The beautiful often don't develop attractive personalities either, because, quite frankly, they don't need to.

Damn them.

Stress and fear can make them panic (and, what's worse, cause frown lines on their perfectly smooth foreheads) which is something you don't want, especially if a show is to be broadcast live. A live show has as much stress as a space launch.

Tall men sometimes fit into this broad category, too. Because they are physically dominating, they get everything handed to them in life and usually don't need to develop the determination to break through the fear barrier. This isn't always the case, though, and we've had a number of tall men who were good producers. A tall man with a beard is usually trying to hide something about himself. I'm wary of them.

Tall women are different.

They stand out in ways that society doesn't always appreciate. They often struggle to get what they want from men, who feel insecure around women they are forced to look up to.

In business and life, tall women often must prove themselves over and over again. They usually develop the bravery they need to succeed. I will hire them.

You would think short men would fall into the same category as tall women, but they don't. Men of shorter stature certainly develop the determination and bravery needed to do well and many do. But it's a brittle sort of strength. Because they go through life trying to get their revenge on the bigger kids who pushed them around at school, small men are unstoppable, in business and government, as well as in television – up until the point they are not.

As soon as you question one of their decisions, they get defensive and angry, as if you are questioning their very manliness.

They'd rather be wrong and go out in a blaze of glory, than be seen to be weak. Unless I have a difficult and thankless task no one else will touch, I prefer not to take small men.

Short women are my go-to recruits.

Short women get nothing in life handed to them.

They must fight every step of the way for mates, careers and money. They learn early that, if they want something, they must go after it and beat everyone else to get it. As a result, they are usually very self-disciplined. You can see it in the neat, quiet, way they often carry themselves. When you get a short woman as a producer, everything gets done perfectly and on time.

Nothing unsettles them.

Small women are invariably a formidable package and naturally conservative. They won't go over budget without checking with you first and you don't have to micromanage them. They are often willing slaves for small salaries but are just as likely to walk into your office as the worst possible time to announce they are leaving because their husband or boyfriend has a new job in America. And they won't be talked out of going.

They scare me. But I want them for staff every time.

So, that then is my view on body language as it relates to hiring and firing.

I know there is a lot of debate about it, but I can tell you from having earned a living in countries where the beauty of my words was totally lost on people, it is real, useful and important. Believe me.

Look into my eyes and notice my slight smile.

Can you tell what I'm thinking?

19. Finland fish

What is it about Finland and fish? I went back to Finland to produce a music show for a big network. The local producer I worked with was the same colleague who produced a couple of other shows for us in Helsinki. We got on very well. She is a great producer. During the rehearsals, she reminded me that two years earlier she had visited the Netherlands with a colleague of hers, a producer called Heikki.

"Did I remember him?"

"Of course," I replied dismissively, as if the question was unnecessary. As you may have guessed, I had no memory of him. Or their visit to the Netherlands. My short-term memory is not what it should be. I saw a joke recently which said, "If alcohol is the cause of short-term memory problems, imagine what damage alcohol would do."

My colleague then told me Heikki was now the producer of a big show for the broadcaster, and he remembered me fondly.

"Would I like to go and see him in production?"

"I would love to," I replied, not having a clue quite what that might involve. I wish I was the sort of person who said "no" more often.

It turns out Heikki was the producer of the network's main breakfast program, which went to air every day at 7 am. He started work god-awfully early which meant, dammit, that I would have to start god-awfully early, too, if I was to go and watch him in production.

The next day's broadcast was to happen, of all places, on an island in Helsinki harbour. In the middle of winter. Before dawn. Oh, thank you.

I arose at 6:15 am. It was still dark and outside the temperature hovered around freezing. Bleary-eyed, I took a taxi to the harbour. I was surprisingly early and, when the taxi dumped me by the side of the road, I was left standing near an old boat shed in the cold, freezing Helsinki darkness. Then it started to rain. I huddled under a tree, tucked deeply into my jacket. Thankfully before I froze to death, the television crew turned up.

Heikki (who, not unexpectedly, I still didn't remember at all) greeted me warmly and took me into the boat shed, which turned out to be a depot for the Helsinki Coast Guard. It had been unlocked. I could have gone inside at any time to get out of the freezing rain and cold. Dammit. There was a heater in there. And people. Heikki introduced me to some of them.

They were from the Finnish Navy. They showed me to their locker room, where I stripped off most of my nice warm clothes and struggled into an insulated arctic survival suit. The wrists and neck of these suits are watertight to keep freezing water from getting onto your skin. They are also tight enough to choke a baby. My head swelled up as the blood got trapped up there. The boots were sewn into the legs and the entire suit was made of a hard nylon. Basically, from a distance I looked like a short, fat, red-headed lollipop.

The navy men helpfully showed me where on the suit I could find the emergency beacon and whistle. They helpfully informed me that, without the suit, I would be dead in less than five minutes in the water.

With the suit, I could last up to two days.

Oh, great.

A large group of us, all dressed in the same ungainly lollipop suits, waddled out to where two low powerboats were tied up alongside the boathouse. We jumped in, the boats were started up and we headed out into the harbour. The water was choppy and very cold in the pre-dawn darkness. A fierce bitter wind ensured all of us kept our heads down. None of us got too warm.

I was drenched within seconds, but thankfully the survival suit kept all but my head and hands warm and dry. It may have been true that most of my body could have survived two days in the water, but I would not have been able to scratch my ass afterwards. My hands were solid blocks of ice.

We motored for about 15 minutes into the bay until we reached a small, featureless, low-lying island, where a few television technical staff had already arrived and had lit a small fire. They were busy getting the equipment ready for the live segment to be broadcast into the morning show in an hour or so.

The fire was nice, but it completely failed to make any impact on my body temperature. The howling, freezing, pre-dawn wind swept over the edge of the island where we were huddled.

The breakfast show segment, I was told, would involve the presenters in the nice, warm, air-conditioned studio, crossing live to us on the island. One of the other red-faced lollipops in the boat with me was, in fact, the local weather presenter. He would chat to the studio presenters, tell everyone what fish were biting in the harbour and where to catch them, and what the weather would be like for the day. Of course, in Finland in winter, that's a relatively easy prediction.

Cold. Damned cold.

The weather presenter, I was told, would also interview a celebrity around the campfire. Celebrity? What celebrity? And, more importantly, did that mean I would have to move away from the fire?

It turned out another of the red-faced lollipops in the boat with me was Finland's most famous male opera singer (no, don't ask me his name). A third lollipop was the singer's piano accordion player. I kid you not. As I watched incredulously, they peeled off their lollipop survival suits to reveal expensive tuxedos. Tuxedos! One of the bags we had brought to the island contained, not television gear as I had expected, but a full piano accordion. My God.

Picture the scene as I stood there, freezing cold and with my mouth open in disbelief. The sun nowhere near ready to threaten the horizon on a wet and cloudy, freezing cold morning. On a windswept and small island in the middle of Helsinki harbour, the existence of which I had never before this morning considered or cared about.

At the appointed time, the breakfast show presenters crossed live to our location and there was the singer and his piano accordion player, silhouetted against the dark sky in their tuxedos.

Braced against the howling wind, they bravely belted out an aria for the television audience. At that time of day, there could only have been a few people watching. Was it worth all that effort? It was a combination of *Apocalypse Now* and *Dante's Inferno*. We just needed helicopter gunships going over our heads. Totally surreal. Madness.

Luckily, the camera couldn't see me off to one side, staring amazed, a large part of me wondering if I had accidentally taken bad drugs the night before. Most of me freezing because I was away from the fire. Was this even happening or was I in a coma somewhere and just dreaming it?

Heikki told me later that everyone competed to appear on his show. He'd had every famous person in Finland make an appearance, including the Prime Minister.

After their performance, the singer, along with the accordion player, joined the weather presenter around the fire for a long on-air chat about opera. Then the subject turned to fishing and eventually onto the subject of the particular fish the presenter had caught that morning. When did he get time to do that?

The catch of the day wiggling in the bottom of the bucket turned out to be a thing that wasn't really a fish at all. It was a lamprey sucking fish. Looked like a type of eel. If you've seen pictures of sharks with long, thin fish stuck around their mouths, those are remora, which look just like the lamprey.

The presenter told the television audience that the lampreys were not only a tasty meal when grilled, but they kept the harbour clean by eating all the garbage in the water, including the bodies of suicide or drowning victims. Mmmm, tasty. Just the sort of information a television audience wants over breakfast.

"Here," he told the opera singer and his piano accordion friend. "We've cooked a few. Try one."

The three of them munched away happily for the rest of the segment, apparently not put off by my gagging noises they could no doubt hear in the background.

Afterwards, Heikki thrust one of the disgusting things at me. "Don't eat the head," he advised. "It's not nice."

I smiled at him sickly. As he watched me, I nibbled at the other end of the horrid thing. He had a bucketful of them and I could see myself being invited to breakfast if I wasn't careful.

"Mmm," I said, filling out my cheeks to try and make it look like I'd taken a big mouthful. He didn't seem to notice.

When no one was looking I threw the rest of it into the fire, wiped my tongue on my rubber sleeve 50 times and spat until my mouth was completely dry. Fortunately for me, the navy men jumped in and munched the rest of the bucketful, so I escaped having to eat any more. Hours later I could still taste it in my mouth. Yuck.

To wrap up the live segment a little while later, the presenter delivered the weather forecast.

"Well, Mary, it's going to be another cold and rainy day in Helsinki."

And he told everyone the best places to try if they wanted to catch some juicy lamprey. Then the segment was over. The mountain of gear was packed into the boats and we headed back to dry land.

My new best friend, the opera singer, invited me to come to the premiere of his new show in Helsinki the following week (no, I don't remember the name of it).

The navy guys invited me to come back and go scuba diving with them in the summer. There are dozens of wrecks in and around the harbour. Their favourite dive spot, they told me, was the wreck of a World War 2 German U-boat. They told me the submarine still had the bodies of the crew in it. I suggested we could use them as bait to catch some lamprey. We all had a good laugh. Ha, ha, ha. I think they were just trying to wind me up.

Back at the Coast Guard depot, I discovered the survival suit had welded itself solidly to my frozen wrists and neck. It hadn't been a problem in the cold outside, but in the warmth inside the depot, the suit began to strangle me, much to the amusement of the navy men. With the assistance of three or four of the biggest and strongest of them, we managed to peel me panting and raw, out of the suit.

I came over all faint as the blood rushed back into my vital areas. My half-naked body, with bloated red face and hands, was topped off with a dishevelled Einstein hairdo. It was apparently a very funny sight to these fellows who wear these suits every day of the year.

Even the damn piano accordion player smiled condescendingly at me. Luckily no one had a camera. In an attempt to get some warmth back into my bones, Heikki suggested we head to the warmest and richest-looking hotel in the centre of the city for a big buffet breakfast. I almost knocked him down hobbling to the door. Yes please.

Bacon, eggs, toast, jam, fruit, sausages and several large cups of coffee. But no fish.

I was back in bed and asleep an hour later.

20. The National Anthem

You have to pity the poor man or woman given the enormous privilege of writing a national anthem for the newly independent republic of Lithuania when it finally broke away from the Soviet Union in 1990.

Okay the music, that's no problem. The whole area is rich in folk musical history. A local should be able to dredge up a tune to which everyone can slurp vodka and dance. But the words. What a nightmare!

"Oh Lithuania, my Lithuania
"Whose people are insania
"And travel to work by trainia."

Seriously. The only word I can think of which rhymes with Lithuania is 'mania' and I guarantee you they don't want that word in their song. It's a little too close to home. And the same goes for Poland. What the hell rhymes with Poland?

"What a glorious land is my Poland
"Did you know a Pope came from Poland?
"Everyone kicks the crap out of Poland
"Did we tell you the Pope came from Poland?
"What a glorious land is my Poland."

(All sung to the tune of *Ooh La Paloma Blanca*, or such like). I know it won't sound the same in Polish, but the reason I was mulling on these things was recalling the pleasure of visiting

198

both places in the same week.

And I was thinking about how much they had to catch up on after the Soviet Union fell over.

First, a Polish guessing competition. What happened next? I went to the Polish consulate in the Netherlands to collect a multiple-entry visa for my passport. At that time, Australians had no automatic right of entry.

The bloody visas were so big, and I collected so many of them, that at football matches I could stand on my passport and peer over the crowd. And the visa needed several stamps. In Poland, stamps are the law. It doesn't matter if you have something signed 15 times. It is not legal until it has at least one stamp on it.

The Polish consulate in the Hague looked like a school class-room from the 1960s, except for the ever-present surveillance cameras in each corner of each room. It featured attractive un-finished concrete corridors and flaking, baby shit-coloured walls.

The same woman was always behind the counter. Every time I went there. Because of the number of times I went there, she recognised me. I could tell by the fierce glare she gave me each time I came through the door. I knew her, too. I always pasted on my toothiest smile because I knew it was part of the ritual dance we always performed together.

I began the dance the same way each time – by telling her I needed a same-day, multi-entry visa and I would wait for it, because I needed to travel to Poland the next day.

She pointed out, every single time mind you, that same-day visas were only available to collect the next day. If I required a next-day visa, I could collect it a week later. I kept looking for the smile which indicated she knew she was making a joke, but this woman hadn't smiled for at least eight generations.

So as part of the dance, I poured on the charm.

199

I pointed out to her that in English, something called a same-day visa was traditionally called that because it was issued the same day. I also pointed out, quite reasonably, I thought, that a visa available the next day should rightly be called a next-day visa and be available the next day.

We would end up staring at each other. This time, as was the case every other time, our dance concluded with neither side conceding defeat. But she would grudgingly stride away to find someone with a brain to see if a same day-visa could – just this once, mind you – be issued the same day.

She always came back with the surly news that – just this once – her supervisor said I could have my same-day visa the same day. Sadly, we performed the identical routine about once a month.

Having danced with her many times before, I made the mistake, of course, of not looking at the visa they stuck in my passport this time. I assumed, as always, that my charm had won her over.

I used the visa once – no problem. Then the next time I arrived at Warsaw … you've already guessed what happened. She'd given me a single-entry visa not a multi-entry visa, no doubt just to see the look on my face the next time I went back to the consulate.

Damn! She had bested me. I dreaded the smirk she would give me. It took me two hours of singing and dancing and smiling and being charming to get through Warsaw Chopin Airport.

"I was only having lunch with your President the other day and he told me . . . and as a matter of fact, I am a very good friend of hers and have been filming a television show with her. I'm sure autographed T-shirts for your wife and the children would be no problem."

200

Finally, I managed to convince the sour-faced airport security guards that I represented less of a threat to Polish national security than the thousands of former Soviet KGB agents who strolled past them every day with a friendly wink, a jaunty step and a tip of their pointy hats.

It was during this visit to Poland, that I finally got to visit the former concentration camp at Auschwitz, which is near the city of Krakow. I'd been trying to get there for ages, having been told by many people that it was one of those places you really should visit. The problem was always its distance from Warsaw, where all my business was done.

This trip I had a spare day, but it would be an overly long drive. The local manager of our company suggested I travel by train to Krakow, the nearest big city.

"But how would I get back?" I asked him.

He looked at me strangely.

"Oh, they have a train back these days, do they?"

For some reason he didn't laugh. By the way, Krakow is a much better-looking city than Warsaw. I don't know what Warsaw looked like in the old days, but because of the combined efforts of the demolition companies, 'Adolph Hitler and Sons' and 'Joseph Stalin and Associates', a guided tour of the historical parts of Warsaw lasts about four minutes.

I've done the tour without leaving the main bar of my hotel or putting down my drink. Krakow, on the other hand, has an appropriately large number of historical buildings. The Nazis made the city the centre of government for their greater German Reich and had big plans for it until the Russians spoiled everything by not being defeated.

The city was established by the Vislans in the year 800 or thereabouts, but the first high point of Krakow's power came in 1138 when it was chosen as Poland's capital during the reign of Boleslaw the Wry-Mouthed (I kid you not) and one of his successors in 1241, King Boleslaw the Shy.

I scoured the guidebook for other great names of their rulers and found some beauties. Wladyslaw the Elbow-High (obviously a really short man rather than someone who walked around all day with his arms up), Boleslaw the Curly and the less funny, Mieszko the Old (poor man. Don't keep reminding him).

But why doesn't Boleslaw the Passive Aggressive get a mention? Or Boleslaw the Grumpy in the Mornings but Cheers Up in the Afternoon?

The book made it plain that after these classic names, the royal public relations department got its act together and from then on, the royals were called sensible things like Casimir the Great and Darryl the Wise. Much more sensible, but not nearly as much fun.

The visit to the Auschwitz/Birkenow camps was much too awesome to make jokes about. And I mean that in the old-fashioned sense of the word. Terrifying, amazing, shocking would also suit. Everyone needs to see it.

Back at the Krakow railway station, where I was to board the train back to Warsaw, some of the modern-day descendants of King Boleslaus the Untrustworthy went through the carriages moments before the train was due to depart and robbed the passengers at gunpoint. It was actually quite a clever plan. Robbing everyone just as the train departed meant the victims couldn't do anything about it until they got to Warsaw four hours later and the Krakow cops had no victims left in their jurisdiction.

Fortunately for me, I was late getting to the station and only just jumped onto the train as it began to move. Which meant I also missed getting robbed. Three of the big burly robbers pushed past me as I climbed on board the carriage, just as the train started to pick up speed, and they were obviously in too much of a hurry to get off the train to bother trying to grab my thin and dusty wallet. I didn't, of course, realise until later that they were robbers.

I merely thought they were rude Polish train passengers, of which there is an abundance. But even though I still had my money, I still suffered badly.

An obnoxiously loud English couple in the carriage complained bitterly about the robbery all the way back to Warsaw.

The Polish Airlines flight from Warsaw to Vilnius, the capital of Lithuania, ended safely, despite the best attempts of the Burt Reynolds lookalike in the pilot's seat. The idiot threw the plane around so much, those of us in Row 20 got to know each other much more intimately than we ever expected for such a short flight.

Vilnius and the Lithuanians (wasn't that the name of a rock group in the 1950s?) turned out to be quite lovely. No, let me rephrase that. Vilnius is lovely. Lithuanians are invariably lovely people but a bit strange.

I guess they've needed to adapt in strange ways over the centuries, considering how much their bigger neighbours kicked them around. They've been invaded a few times over the years, I can tell you.

Lithuania was one of the last places in Europe to be converted to Christianity. The religious thing only happened there 600 years ago. And, like nearby Finland, it hadn't really had time to stick. Their sense of right and wrong appeared to shift, depending on who was invading their country at the time.

Even before the Nazis came through in 1941, the Lithuanians had spotted there was fun to be had persecuting Jews.

Without anyone prompting them, they killed quite a few of their own population – friends and neighbours among them – purely because they were guilty of being Jewish. People they'd lived peacefully beside for hundreds of years.

When the Germans came through on their way to Moscow, the Lithuanians became enthusiastic Nazis. That's when the Germans discovered Lithuanians also had a natural talent as concentration camp guards.

When, a relatively short time later, the Russians came through the country chasing the Germans out, the Lithuanians immediately turned into good Communists. "Help you kill a few non-communists, sir?" (with no Jews remaining anywhere in the region.)

The Lithuanians took to being KGB agents like a priest to a primary school. I was told that in the years after World War 2, the local Lithuanian KGB, with the backing of head office in Moscow, killed half a million people and sent another half a million to Siberia, where apparently there were attractive job opportunities available in the salt mines. That was a million people killed or exiled, in a country which, at the time, only had a total population of two million.

Nowadays Lithuanians are all committed capitalists, but the old ways linger. They happily boasted to me that you won't see any black or Asian faces on local television.

"Lithuanians don't like that sort of thing," I was told more than once. One can surmise that being part of the Soviet Union and living so close to the mad bear of Russia, cannot have been good for their general mental state. But it must also be said I got on very well with the television people in Lithuania and made some great friends there.

On my first afternoon in Vilnius, three of us – the local

television station owner, the producer of the program I was supervising and me – were sitting in a classy restaurant, chatting while snacking on a local delicacy, the potato sausage.

The potato sausage, as you have no doubt already guessed, is a potato stuffed into a piece of animal stomach lining and grilled, much as you would do with a meat sausage. It was surprisingly tasty. Other Lithuanian yummie things we ate included a potato stuffed into some meat and a potato stuffed into other potatoes. Did I mention that the national dish of Lithuania is the potato? Well it is.

During our conversation, I found myself complaining about how tough it was for me living in the Netherlands, because I didn't get to see my parents in Australia very often.

My two new friends nodded sagely. The producer agreed it must be tough for me. His own father, he said, had not been seen or heard from since driving a truck load of spare car parts into Russia two years earlier. His body had never been found and the Russian police hadn't even bothered to investigate his disappearance because he was Lithuanian. Mortified by my own inadvertent crassness and trying to hold my face together, I turned to the network owner to get me out of trouble.

Yes, he agreed, my father probably had it rough living by the beach in Australia and only able to play golf four days a week. His own father, he reported, had never really been the same since being released from the gulag in 1990 after serving 20 years for speaking disloyally about the Soviet Union.

Yes, we all agreed, nodding wisely, life could be tough for our fathers.

Inside, I felt like a complete potato sausage.

For the rest of my visit, I avoided all mention of personal things. I know in my stomach lining that any bad story I could dredge up, would be topped by a true horror story from one of the locals.

Me: "My sister arrived late and almost missed her train."

Him: "Yes, I know how you feel. A train smashed into a bus carrying 14 of my relatives, including my sister, killing them all and another 35 of my relatives who were waiting by the side of the road."

My work in Lithuania was made more difficult by the fact that not many people there spoke English and my Lithuanian – well, let's just say that it's not as good as my Polish.

But as you no doubt read a little elsewhere, I learned to communicate primarily non-verbally with people from 15 or 16 different language and cultural groups. When I did need to explain something verbally I did it by slowing my speech down, speaking very clearly, using short sentences and small words.

I said things three and four times until I was sure the message had gone in. I mimed a lot of the actions I was trying to describe.

Sometimes in Lithuania, I ended up talking in one-syllable words and dancing round like clown, waving my arms wildly and describing how the show was to be made.

"I . . . ah . . . we . . . jump . . . no . . . why . . . ha, ha . . . you . . . we . . . stay . . . ha, ha, clap!"

And somehow, they got the idea. I swear it worked, even if I looked like a demented ballet dancer whenever I was doing it.

The studio we were to use for recording the program was described to me as being "on the outskirts of Vilnius". It turned out to be not so much in Vilnius as "on the outskirts of another country" 130 km away. (No, I don't know why we had to go so far. Someone's cousin owned it probably).

The building used to be the regional headquarters of a soviet farmer's collective.

A driver in an ancient Mercedes picked me up from the hotel. The driver was also to be my bodyguard – you needed them in some parts of Eastern Europe. As in other countries, the only victims killed were those without kidnap and ransom insurance. Because, as one of the cheeky villains told the local paper when I was there, the kidnapping gangs were capitalists, not barbarians. Makes your heart glad to see them finally throw off the shackles of communism.

Because of the kidnap threat, the insurance company often insisted clients employ a local bodyguard. Anecdotally, most of them made a few dollars on the side tipping off the kidnappers about the best time and place to snatch you.

After collecting me from my hotel, the driver then picked up the TV station owner and the program producer from their respective offices and we headed off to apparently the only TV studio available in the entire country.

The driver, by the way, was a big burly guy who had an obvious bulge of a gun under his jacket. He drove like he'd get a ticket if he went slower than 160 kph. The roads were not great, even by Lithuanian standards. Being a nervous nelly, and getting ill from being thrown around the car so roughly, I made a comment out loud about how the driver must have been in training to become a Formula One driver. My new Lithuanian friends, who apparently wouldn't recognise sarcasm if it invaded their country with tanks and planes, laughed and translated the message to the driver, who took it as a compliment and an invitation to really test the old car out, while grinning madly.

Against all odds, we arrived safely at the studio. Back on solid ground, I asked my friends why we had been in such a hurry.

The producer shrugged, looked at me sadly and said "around here it's safer to go fast". Everyone in his group, he reported, had been robbed at one time or another and carjacking was so popular in Lithuania, they were thinking of applying to have it made an official Olympic event.

God, the places I get myself into.

Anyway, the rest of the day was a blur.

Judging by the size of it, the studio being used was normally where brooms were stored. I was told the technical staff earned less than $50 a week each, but considered themselves lucky to have a job, considering the bad economic environment. They were much more professional in their work than I would have been for $50, I can tell you.

The day was not all gloom. Turns out the Lithuanian television industry is full to overflowing with extraordinarily beautiful women – more than anywhere I'd ever seen anywhere.

I spent the day with my belly sucked in and my chin thrust forward in manly fashion, exhausting and ineffective as it turned out.

And no one can work in television in Lithuania, apparently, unless they have at least two mobile phones ringing continually. Why they don't take both sets of calls on one phone, I can't say. Probably the thing I'll remember longest about this visit, considering that I would probably need to go back to Lithuania soon to supervise more program recordings, was a question the producer put to me at the end of the long, long day.

We had just poured ourselves into the old Mercedes for the anus-puckering journey back to the city. No doubt we would also see our driver really make a good attempt to break his own personal best time for the distance.

The program we had made was called *Forgive Me*.

In the show, the presenter helped friends or family members who'd had a fight, to get back together again – by encouraging one of them to take the first step and say "I'm sorry". It was a very popular show in many places in Europe and generally dealt with family arguments, neighbourhood fights and such like.

I knew the producer had been mulling for some time on the question he wanted me to answer. Finally, he plucked up the courage and asked, "What do you do in the show if a guest wanted to say "I'm sorry" to more than just one other person?"

"You mean," I replied, "for example, if the coach of a basketball team wanted to say sorry to his team for not having coached them well enough to win the championship title? That would be a lovely item. Or a teacher wanted to apologise to her class for mistakenly teaching them the wrong subjects before their test? Another wonderful segment, full of emotion."

"In both cases," I advised, "it would be great to invite the coach, or the teacher, into the studio and then bring in the class or the team to surprise them so they could all hug each other as a big group. Great television. Very emotional."

The producer was quiet, nodding.

"What about if it was more people than that?"

"How many do you mean?" I asked.

"There's a former KGB agent who wants to say sorry to the people he sent to Siberia. He says there are about 200,000 of them." I still had my mouth open when I got to the airport.

"Lithuania, Oh Lithuania,
I love you, but you are insania."

21. The murder next door

L ook, I'd had a hard couple of days. I had been in Poland
  supervising a program and, like many programs in Poland
at that time, things hadn't gone to plan. It had taken me several
days to get things back on track, to the point that we finally managed to get a successful program in the bag. I'd had a
noisy dinner and a few hundred drinks in the hotel bar with
my Dutch colleagues. By the time I got to bed it wasn't so much
late in the night as it was very early in the morning. I was tired
and irritable.

I dragged my clothes off and turned the air conditioning
down to Arctic. For some reason I can never sleep in hotels
unless I have the temperature turned down to freezing level. I
also had this strange idea that a maid would find my body after
obeying the "Do Not Disturb" sign for several days. With the
temperature wound down to the minimum, at least my corpse
would still be in reasonable shape. Don't judge me.

But as I sank deeper into the pillow, a commotion started in
the corridor outside my room. And didn't stop. People shouted
and blundered along the corridor.

"For Pete's sake," I shouted out. "Shut up!"

But the banging and crashing continued.

I'm normally a patient sort of person and usually would have
allowed the drunks to make their way to their rooms without

complaining. But this night I was out of sorts.

I reached for the phone and dialled 9 for reception.

"This is Mr Bigg in room 131," I said. "There seems to be a drunken party going on in the corridor on this level. I wonder if you could send someone up to tell them to be quiet because some of us have had a long day today and face another one tomorrow. I need my sleep."

"Yes, of course, Mr Bigg!" said the man on the telephone, sounding hassled. "We will attend to that immediately."

But, of course he didn't. This was Poland. I lay in bed sighing dramatically. It didn't help. Luckily, after a while, the noise died down anyway, and I finally went off to sleep gratefully.

The next morning, bleary-eyed over breakfast, I noticed a lot more people than normal in the foyer of the hotel. But when you stay in as many hotels as I do, you learn to disregard what the rest of the world is doing and get on with your own business.

That was, until I got to work where the manager of our local office pointed out a story on the morning news.

"You've had an exciting night I see," he said.

"What do you mean?" I answered.

"Someone was killed in your hotel last night," he said.

"What?"

"A well-known Polish gangster was shot dead in your hotel.

Apparently, someone knocked and called out 'room service'. And he opened the door. He was shot three or four times. He hadn't even ordered any room service."

As if that was the worst part of the story. My God, I thought. That must have been what the commotion was about.

When I returned to the hotel that evening there were police in the corridor guarding the room just two up from mine.

I had been that close to a murder. And it must have happened just before I got to bed.

I may have even seen the killer downstairs on my way up. And there I had been – complaining about the noise.

What a dick!

No wonder the night receptionist sounded hassled.

For a time, after the Berlin wall came down, crime became an ever-present risk in Poland and, in fact, in all the former Soviet countries. Many of the men, terrifically trained by the Soviets to loot and kill, turned to crime to fund their purchases.

Early on there were many, many reports of young westerners being mugged for their sports shoes. Weapons were scarily available. When I made my first trip to Warsaw, I was told by a colleague I could get anything I wanted – "anything," he said with a knowing look, from the giant black market set up at the soccer stadium.

A Glock? How many?

They are cheaper in bulk.

Hand grenades? No problem.

An AK-47?

"Which sort? Russian or Czech?" I was asked.

Pirated software? Every single program written for every single computer in the world, including Sony's PlayStation, could be had for a US$1 each at the stadium.

The only problem was that with my gorgeous red hair and obviously western clothes, I wouldn't be welcome in the stadium because of the risk that I was a cop. And with everyone apparently armed, it was best not to be too visible.

One Saturday morning, I sat timidly in the car while a colleague went in to buy some things.

Hundreds of normal-looking Poles filed past me into the stadium. God knows what they were buying.

Home defence equipment, maybe?

At other times it was not funny. Going with a colleague to his mother's house for dinner one night, (yeah, I always live the high life as an international television producer, don't I?) we passed the burned-out wreckage of a suburban home. Apparently, a well-known bank robber had been holed up there hiding from the law. When the authorities discovered his whereabouts, they had surrounded the place.

As a SWAT team approached the front door, the criminal, a former high ranking Spetznaz (Soviet special forces) soldier, triggered the explosives he'd set up around the house and sent himself and half a dozen cops to the Polish version of heaven.

For a time, I had a bodyguard, of sorts.

Martin was my driver officially.

He was a small man who spoke almost no English. But he had a big pistol which he liked to store (if that's the correct word) on the floor behind his seat.

He drove like a maniac and, on the bumpy Warsaw roads, the gun would bounce around. I was always afraid it would go off accidentally and kill one of us (well, me to be honest).

As well, I lived in a house with both an interior and exterior alarm system. It was a bit of a joke for me, so I never activated them, thinking the locals were being a bit paranoid. That was, until the morning I got up and discovered footprints in the snow, all around the house.

Whoever it was, had tried to open the ground floor windows. Fortunately, I had locked them all securely. After that, not surprisingly, I set all the alarms.

It wasn't only in Poland that I brushed up against the new heavily armed capitalists. As I relate elsewhere, I had various dealings with them in Romania, Hungary and Lithuania.

There was a postscript to this story of the murder in the hotel room. Several weeks later, the newspapers reported an incident at another international hotel in the centre of Warsaw. Apparently, a Russian gangster took two prostitutes to his room late at night and, while engaged in nefarious acts, the ladies pulled out knives and tried to stab him. According to the newspaper, he managed to throw them off and shot them both dead before fleeing. The bullets in the dead prostitutes apparently matched the ones used to kill the man in my hotel. It seems someone was trying to get payback and the two woman failed.

By the way, I have never complained about noise in a hotel corridor again. Make as much noise as you like.

22. Learning a new language

I remember the moment I realised that living in a non-English speaking country could be difficult and that I should really attempt to learn the local language. At the time, I had lived in the Netherlands for only a few months. I was on a train and I thought my stop was coming up. I had carefully plotted the course before leaving home.

However, the sign on the station we approached was different to the one I was expecting. My stop, I thought, must be the next one. But when the sign at the next station appeared to be the same as the previous one, I dived for my travel dictionary. I discovered that what I had believed was the Dutch town of "Geldautomat" was, in fact, a sign advertising the device normally known in English as an automatic cash machine.

Damn.

One of the problems in learning Dutch, like with German, is the tendency of the fluent to just lump all their existing words together when they need a new word.

Take this example. When I went to the foreign police to have my residency permit renewed, the officer kindly pointed out that I had neglected to bring along a copy of my work contract.

Forgetting for a moment that, in any reasonable democracy, where I work and how much I earn, should be no business of the police, I pointed out to him that I had not been instructed to bring along such a document.

"Oh yes," he replied. "It says so clearly on the back of your existing permit card."

Sure enough, in plain letters on the back of the plastic card was the word 'tewerkstellingsvergunning'. Count them. There are 25 letters. How could I have missed it? Roughly translated it means 'to work position permit'. Of course. How silly of me.

And, just as English has stolen so many words from other languages, Dutch has also taken many words from English. It's hard to concentrate sometimes when listening someone speaking in rapid-fire Dutch.

You'll hear . . . "blah, blah, blah, blah, computer software, blah, blah, blah" or …"blah, blah, blah, so I told him, up yours! blah, blah." And my mind which has been trying to sample all the foreign sounds, clamps up at these familiar words.

It's the same for English words which have similar sounds in Dutch. The word for 'often' in Dutch is 'vark' (pronounced 'fark' – trying saying that out loud too often). It stops me every time. The word for 'more often' is 'varker' (pronounced farker) and the word for 'pig' is 'varken' (pronounced 'farken'). Not to put too fine a point on it, all these worlds sound to me like 'fuck, fucker and fucking.

If you get a couple of Dutch people talking about, for example 'how pigs are more often eaten', it sounds to my Australian ear like a group of Australian truck drivers discussing politics. "Fark this, farken that."

And a word of warning. Never tell a young Dutch lady she has nice visitors. The Dutch word for 'visitor' is 'bezoeker' (pronounced 'bahzooka'). The potential for miscommunication when the Australian and Dutch armies get together for anti-tank training is also alarming.

216

What all this led me to eventually, was a course at one of Europe's top language schools located in the south of Holland. They promise to take you in knowing nothing about a language and spit you out two weeks later speaking fluently.

I had only a week available this time, but was starting from a position of having lived in the country for a few months. I did my second week the following year and ended up quite fluent.

The language course was conducted in a former nunnery in a town called Vught (pronounced 'fooked' – which gives the people from the UK a real laugh). Students at Vught can learn English, Spanish, French and other European languages.

Every day started at 8:30 am with headphones and tapes. My first task was to listen and repeat the phrases recorded on the tape. From a booth nearby, I could hear a Dutch man learning English saying out loud; "I loaned him my tent for the third time last week."

Now there's a phrase he's going to use on his next trip to New York, I thought.

I concentrated on my sensible, useful Dutch phrases and said out loud, "als er een schaap over de dam is, volgen er meedere". Translated, this means "if one sheep goes over the dyke, the rest will surely follow". I noticed the Dutch guy smirking at me. What was his problem?

After the headphones, I had three lessons with private tutors. Lovely, patient women who were able to hear me murder and mutilate their language and pretend I was making progress. They weren't nuns, they were saints.

At lunch, I sat with six other students. The first day I thought, "Thank God, I can rest my brain and speak English for a while." But as I took my seat, the person on my right turned to the person on his right and said quietly in Dutch, "Thank God we can stop speaking English for a while." To my horror, the other five people at the table nodded their heads and began conversing quietly in Dutch. I'd picked the wrong table!

In the afternoon classes, it was more private lessons, more work on the headphones ("do you want my grandmother to bring her ice skates to the wedding reception?") and multiple-choice questions on the computer.

Dinner was conducted in Dutch again. Turns out the school does it deliberately, so you can practice your new language skills. I ate in sullen silence. Then there was a two-hour group discussion till 9 pm. The subject that night? "Why Dutch culture is different from the rest of the world." In my group of seven students there was an Italian, a German, a Frenchman, a Chinese, a Spaniard, a Canadian and an Aussie (me). All of us lived in the Netherlands and our group discussion quickly turned from "Why Dutch culture is different?" to "What pisses us off most about the Dutch culture?"

We went on for two hours without repeating ourselves. Everything from the expensive and awful food, to the way the bloody cinemas stopped every movie midway through so the audience could go out and smoke a cigarette. The teacher was somewhat taken aback but, as I told her on the way out, at least we did all our complaining in Dutch, so we were making progress . . . in a way.

By the time I staggered back to the hotel each night, my brain was bleeding. But I fell asleep feeling that at least I was learning. The next day though, I rose, switched on the radio (only Dutch language stations allowed) and discovered I had forgotten everything from the day before. I almost cried.

So, it was back into the tapes. ("Een ding is zeker. Een koe poept meer dan een apotheeker", which translated as "One thing is certain. A cow poos more than someone who works in a pharmacy." I couldn't wait to set my Dutch loose on an unsuspecting public.

And so it went – for seven days. We Dutch students bonded quickly after our bitch session the first night.

The Canadian lady and I took to sneaking out the back of the building at lunchtime while no one was watching so we could speak English to each other, both dreading what would happen if caught. After class we all hung around in what quickly became known as the Australian exercise gym in the hotel – the bar – drinking beer until closing time. And because we were all strangers, all of us were astronauts or millionaire financiers.

Not a car salesman, accountant or real estate agent among us. By the end, I felt as if I had really learned something. I was as fluent as I was going to get without more real-world practice. And it felt very relaxing being a student for a while. Just taking in information. Not needing to use it immediately. Eventually, though, it was time for home sweet home.

Back at work, the following Monday morning, my colleagues crowded round my desk.

"Wat heb je geleernd? – (What have you learned?)"

"Niets – (nothing)," I replied.

"Echt niets? – (Really? Nothing?)"

"Nay, ik heb niets geleernd – (No, I have learned nothing at all.)" What a waste of money, they muttered to each other and wandered off.

"Hey! I said all that in Dutch!" I yelled after them.

They didn't get the joke. Some Dutch people never do. It's another way their culture is different.

Next year I'm going to learn French. That should be fun.

23. Eating Out

I went to Lisbon to supervise the production of a Miss Beach Girl Quest program. The biggest Portuguese network, attractively called SIC, had staged mini quests along the coast during the summer and the 16 finalists were brought to Lisbon to feature in a big finale program.

Portuguese girls, as a purely subjective opinion, are not overly attractive when compared to other Europeans. Of course, there are some notable exceptions, but when God was handing out body parts, many Portuguese women skipped the line where She was handing out height and nice faces and, instead, got into the breast line twice. They went from there to the queue for the bottom counter, where they stayed and chatted for really far too long. And while waiting there, many of them accidentally leaned up against the facial hair counter.

But I have to admit, in a pathetic attempt to recover some credibility with you, among the finalists of this program were some stunningly beautiful women.

I went around during the rehearsals speaking loudly whenever one was in earshot.

"We judges have a hard time tonight! I wonder if my fellow judges are as open to bribery as I am?" But it didn't work.

As usual. I ended up working a long and hard day.

One problem when working in Portugal at that time was

that you rarely found crew members who were self-starters.

In most countries, television production staff know their next job depends on how well they do this one. So usually, staff take it upon themselves to get their own particular job done quickly, then help others with theirs. It helps a project get completed on time and efficiently.

In Portugal, historically the dictators punished self-starters. As a result there aren't many of them. This obviously changed as young people realised the old ways of doing things would not help them get ahead in the modern world. But there were still pockets of it.

As a really wide generalisation, a lot of the crews I worked with in Portugal appeared to prefer to take orders and not offer ideas of their own. It made television production very difficult in an industry which relied on people doing their bit, and a bit more, without being ordered to do so.

I found when someone in the crew didn't agree with the way I wanted something done, they nodded their heads and said "yes, no problem". Then they would go and do something that was almost, but not quite, what was required.

I had to constantly circle back and double check things to make sure I got exactly what was asked for. It was their way of disagreeing with me, without doing enough to get into trouble. It was also very time consuming and frustrating. And it wasn't just a problem in television.

To give you an idea. The night after the beach girl program recording, I wanted a quiet dinner and an early bedtime. I had a hankering for some Asian food. I know. In Lisbon, right? Spoiled rotten.

I asked someone in the office if they knew a good Japanese restaurant in the city and was given the name of a place I was assured was good. I wrote down the address. I always did that in Portugal after my first horror trip.

I hailed a taxi just on dark, as it began to rain, and handed the driver (a woman in her late 40s or early 50s) the piece of paper with the address I had written down.

"No problem," she said in Portuguese (at least that's what it sounded like) and off we went, deep into the bowels of old Lisbon where the poor people lived. After much twisting and turning through narrow streets clogged with traffic, she pulled over and hailed a man walking along the street.

"Do you know where Rua Des Trinos is?" she inquired in Portuguese. I'm assuming here.

"Yes," he replied, and pointed down the street, and waving his arms about like he was doing the Macarena.

"Great, thanks!" said the taxi driver, and off we went again.

Not more than 50 meters down the street, she stopped again and hailed another pedestrian.

"Do you know Rua Des Trinos?" she asked this man.

"Sure do," said the man who rabbited away in Portuguese, accompanied by much pointing and arm waving. It appeared to me he was pointing in a completely different direction to the first person the driver had asked. After minutes of this arm waving, the driver thanked him, and we charged off in the new direction.

You can guess what happened next.

Every 50 meters or so, she stopped and asked someone else. We were deep in the bowels of the poor section of the city by now. The streets were quite narrow and, despite the rain, there were a lot of people hanging around. I had my window up, my door locked and my hand on my wallet.

Eventually, I couldn't take it anymore and asked the driver

why she just didn't listen to the directions the people were giving her. In broken English she explained that most of them did not, in fact, know where Rua Des Trinos was.

What? Were they all merely pointing down the road and saying something like, "See that house down there? Well, around the corner from that house and four blocks up on the left, after the fruit stand, there's someone who may know where Rua Des Trinos is?"

Or maybe. "My brother lives two blocks up on the left, in the first house on the right after the place that was torn down in the late 1960s to make way for the new high school. He's lived here all his life and I'm sure knows where Rua Des Trinos is. Go ask him."

"Where the hell were they all pointing?" I politely inquired.

The driver conceded that people didn't like to admit they weren't able to answer her question. So they just made something up. She was hoping to run into someone who really did know where the street was.

"Stupid poor people," she remarked. I didn't remind her that when I first got into her taxi and showed her the address, she too had claimed to know the street I wanted.

We finally got to the restaurant, deep in the bowels of old Lisbon. But, as the taxi roared off into the rainy night, I noticed that the restaurant was closed. I mean permanently closed. And had been for some time by the look of it. (I suspect the person in the office knew it was no longer open but didn't want to admit to me he didn't know an alternative. "Poor stupid person," my taxi driver would have remarked.)

I tucked my head into my chest and bravely walked in the rain about 10 blocks back towards civilisation. Despite the downpour, the streets were filled with young Portuguese playing in the streets. They are wonderful people, except when they stare at you walking through their neighbourhoods. But I got out alive, thankfully, and managed to hail another taxi.

I asked to go back to my hotel. "Holiday Inn in Avenue Antonio," I told him.

"Okay," he replied. "No problem!" and drove off. Only to stop 200 meters down the road to hail a passer-by.

"Do you know the Holiday Inn in Avenue Antonio?"

I felt like crying.

I leaned over and asked him did he instead perhaps know of a Japanese restaurant? He got very excited.

"Sure do, good buddy," he said in Portuguese (or words to that effect) and we charged off in yet another new direction. Ten minutes later we arrived outside a grubby-looking Chinese restaurant. Chinese. Japanese. It was all the same to him apparently. Who cares? I thought, I'm hungry. It will have to do.

Amazingly, considering the evening I was having, the restaurant was open for business too. Inside I was shown to a table and discovered I was the only customer. Four Portuguese waiters stood staring at me (there were no Chinese waiters in sight, which was a worry).

Feeling decidedly cheeky now that I was out of the rain, out of the taxis and with a menu in my hand (albeit a Chinese, rather than a Japanese one) I asked the head waiter in a jaunty fashion, "What do you recommend?" I half expected him to say, "that you eat somewhere else, senor".

Instead he muttered "spring rolls".

Of course. Microwaved spring rolls. Sigh.

"How many do you want?" he asked, not even bothering to write my order on his notepad. Deep sigh.

It pretty much summed up how my evening had gone to

that point. As the waiter turned to take my order to the kitchen, another waiter emerged from the kitchen with my food. What?

How did that happen?

Of course it wasn't my order really.

I had ordered boiled rice and got fried rice; I ordered beef Sichuan and got beef in mushrooms. I came to suspect that, regardless of what I ordered, they were giving me the leftovers from the staff dinner. The only bright spot was they got my cold beer order correct. Did I complain? No, I didn't. By this time, Portugal had beaten me, so I acted like I was grateful to get it.

With the attention of the entire complement of waiters, and with no other diners in sight (everyone else in the city apparently knew better than to go there), they had me fed and packed out of the restaurant in under 20 minutes. Certainly, the fastest meal I'd ever eaten. As I left, I asked the head waiter if I had, in fact, broken the record for fastest customer they had ever fed. He looked at me with a blank stare.

Most surprisingly, considering the evening I was having, the taxi driver I hailed outside the restaurant actually knew my hotel. So I made it to my room and slept soundly despite the suspicious growling sounds all night from my stomach.

Next time, I will eat in the hotel.

24. And the winner is …

The call from Warsaw came through early in the day. It was a Thursday.

"Come quickly, Brian, our music show is a disaster. We are in deep trouble." I headed to the airport.

The new boss of our company in Poland had been given the job of producing the annual Polish music awards. He had taken what he believed was the safe option of hiring a Dutch director, but the local TV station had insisted on having its own line producer run the production. It was a recipe for disaster and anyone who had been in Poland for more than 10 minutes would have known it was never going to work.

As was often the case in those days, the local producer was someone's cousin rather than someone who could actually produce a television show. He turned up in a convertible sports car with his leather jacket draped elegantly across his shoulders and a plastic blonde in the passenger seat. It looked like he'd acquired all three only after getting the job.

He moved his brand-new Ray Ban sunglasses onto the top of his head (this was the middle of winter, mind you) and started issuing orders to a crew who didn't know who the hell he was. But the smart ones did know he was related to management (and therefore their jobs) so felt it wiser to follow his orders rather than those of the Dutch director. The Dutch director had flown in a week or two earlier.

Like most Dutch television people, he certainly knew how to make a good show, but didn't have a clue how to make a good show in Poland. It didn't work like in the rest of the world and certainly not like it worked in the Netherlands. The Poles, after years of living under a dictatorship of one sort or another, just did not like taking orders from foreigners.

It was an acquired art form to get them to do what you wanted, without them getting their backs up and refusing point blank to do what they were told. Like most people anywhere, they needed to be massaged and made to feel as if their contribution was important to the project. The worst thing you could do was waltz in and start waving your arms around like they were meant to jump to your whim. Quite understandably, the Dutch director had expected everything to run the same as it did in the Netherlands or Germany. He received a rude shock.

He immediately clashed with the producer because he could quickly see Mr Ray Bans didn't have a clue. So he tried to do both his job and the one he knew the producer wasn't doing correctly. But the clash trapped the crew between them. Not surprisingly, work on the production ground to a standstill.

Neither person was prepared to concede ground to the other. The director had Dutch arrogance and experience on his side. Mr Ray Bans had been appointed by the management of the television station and knew he couldn't be fired.

When I got there that afternoon, I found the producer, the director and two senior executives from the television station in a back room of the venue, standing nose to nose, poking each other in the chest and screaming at each other about where the fault lay. The four men turned to me as I walked in and started shouting at me all at once.

Talk about feeling wanted.

Outside, no one was working.

The crew had broken out their first beers. On a number of shows I did there, I was known as a dictator because I banned the crew from drinking beer until at least 9 o'clock in the morning. So harsh. But this time they were justified in opening a brew. Construction of the set had not been finished and rehearsals were a long way from getting started.

So, this was the situation with just over two days to go until we were expected to broadcast a three-hour live music awards program. It certainly was a disaster and they were definitely in deep trouble.

Part of the problem, surprisingly, turned out to be the venue. Warsaw's Sala Kongresowa (Congress Hall) is a beautiful building right in the heart of the city. It was a gift from Stalin to the lovely people of Warsaw in 1955. It was where the loyal Polish Communist Party held its annual conferences up until the time the Polish Communist Party wasn't loyal anymore.

During a break in our preparations, the caretaker of the building showed me underneath the main stage where a long, old fashioned conference table was set up, surrounded by a lot of old-fashioned chairs.

Apparently in the days of the loyal Polish Communist Party, the leaders would sit in the chairs and, at a signal, the entire stage would be lifted by some sort of hoist mechanism up into the main auditorium, where the loyal party members in the audience could applaud the sudden appearance of their leaders, as if by magic.

The caretaker also showed me the red phone, an old-fashioned dial-up handset, which apparently was the hotline to the Kremlin back in the day when Moscow told the local party leaders what to do and how to think.

I was entranced by the gorgeous old place. The problem for me was that because the Sala is a historic building it was not to be messed with, under any circumstances. A troop of old people, appointed as the building's guardians, wandered around where our crew was working, to make sure nobody touched anything.

Astonishingly, they told us we weren't even allowed to touch the seats or the carpet on the floor! That was going to make walking or sitting problematic for the audience of several hundred expected in the hall during the presentations.

Without consulting anyone, including the production manager who would have told him that we couldn't afford it, Mr Ray Bans had ordered a false floor be installed across the entire hall, on top of which new seats would be installed. As well as blow the budget to shreds, that decision had delayed the production by many days. They couldn't get enough carpenters to do the work. And the carpenters they could get – at great expense – had to work under the strict nit-picking supervision of the committee of old people.

Not surprisingly perhaps, in their efforts to get the work done quickly, the carpenters covered all the electrical outlets, and several doors, with wooden sheeting. That slowed the installation of the cameras and the other television equipment. No one had marked out the locations of the electrical outlets before the wooden sheeting was installed, so entire areas of sheeting had to be torn off so we could find where to plug stuff into. One of the camera operators illegally used an electrical saw to reopen a doorway to the men's toilet. I could understand his need.

Another problem was the teleprompter.

Television presenters like to make it look as if they have memorised all their words. In fact, the words which come out

229

of their mouths are usually written for them on a teleprompter screen, which normally sits in front of the closest camera. But the committee of old people insisted we couldn't put our cameras near the stage, so the closest camera to the presenter, where a prompter could be placed, was to be about 50 metres back.

The presenter would need binoculars to read the words. I ordered a large projector be set up at the back of the hall and we projected the words onto it in the largest font possible. Everyone in the audience could follow along as the words scrolled up.

During the broadcast, you could see the host squinting to read it. She didn't wear her reading glasses (obviously), and you could see much of the audience mouthing the words along with her. Hilarious to watch in any other circumstances.

Eventually, after two days of non-stop effort, hosing down problem after problem, solving personal disputes and production problems on average every 60 seconds, the broadcast slowly came into focus and it looked like we might pull it off after all.

A senior executive from the network took me aside several hours before the broadcast began and dropped to his knees in front of me.

"Tell me honestly," he pleaded, "is the show going to be ready?" I really had no idea, but I couldn't tell him that.

"Of course," I replied. "It's looks like it's going to be even better than we had planned."

"It has to be," he said. "The owner of the network told me he would be sitting in the presentation booth at the station tonight and if he saw any sign the broadcast was going off the rails, he planned to push a button, cut us off and swap the broadcast to an old movie. Then we will all be fired."

Crikey. I spent several valuable minutes assuring him that everything was on track. Then I went around all the associate producers to find out if, in fact, the show was really on track.

That's when I discovered the biggest problem of all.

It turned out to be a small, mousy, round-shouldered man with straggly hair in a cheap suit. He was the designated official from the music company which ran the contest each year to determine Poland's favourite songs.

In his shiny, expensive looking briefcase was the list of nominees for each category and, more importantly, the names of the winners. And he was angry.

In the hectic rush to get ready, apparently I hadn't paid him sufficient attention. He felt he had been ignored, and that had included his many, many great suggestions about how the show could be improved. He was obviously the most important person on the production – because of that list of winners in his impressive looking briefcase.

One of my associate producers drew me to one side and gave me the bad news. She told me that the music executive, let's call him Pavel, was refusing to hand over the list of winners to us ahead of time.

He would give us the nominees, she said, but under no circumstances would he let us know who the winners were beforehand. This was a potential disaster beyond all the others I had already faced.

When you produce an awards show, you prepare short video packages on all the nominees. When their names are announced, you run the short video package to remind the audience who the nominees are. You need a longer and more complicated video package on the nominee who wins. These packages take time to prepare and are quite important.

When the winner in each category is announced, the camera pointing at them captures the winner's moment of joy.

Then the winner has to make their way to the stage to re-ceive their prize. The pre-prepared video package covers the long and boring time it takes for them to rise from their seat, kiss all their friends and family and make their way to the stage. It's a journey which can take up to two minutes in some venues.

In awards shows where the television producer usually doesn't know the winners, the producer must prepare winning packages for all the nominees. The packages sit in the computer and, when the winner is announced, the director pushes the relevant button to trigger the appropriate package.

It's an expensive and time-consuming business when there are four or five nominees in every category. Mr Ray Bans had not prepared winners' packages for all the nominees. He'd ex-pected to be given the name of the winners in advance so he would only have to produce the one package in each category. But Pavel had dug his heels in.

I took Pavel to one side and quietly asked him what his problem was. I expected a small 'donation' would be requested, a normal tactic in Poland in those days. Surprisingly, though, Pavel made a valid point.

He explained that during the previous year's production of the show – not done by us, I should add – the producers had embarrassed him hugely. When the first nominee was an-nounced, there was one camera person standing near that nom-inee, pointing their camera at him or her. Same with the second nominee – only one camera in their face. But the third nominee had four cameras around them.

It wasn't hard for the audience to work out in advance who was about to win. Pavel had been criticised afterwards in the newspapers for it and he was determined not to get in trouble for the same thing this year.

We would have to prepare winners' packages on all the nominees, he explained, and we would have to wait, like the rest of the country, to find out who had won. I glanced at my associate producer, who was standing just behind Pavel, listening. She shook her head. We no longer had the time to do that. I asked Pavel to reconsider, but he stalked off in high dudgeon, having put me in my place.

I wracked my brain for a solution and came up with only one. I went and found two members of the production team who were sitting outside having a cigarette. They were two rather large Polish men. They were both great producers and the sweetest and gentlest of men. But because they were typical Polish men, they looked like gangsters.

Tall, heavily built and closely cropped hair – one of them even had a scar across his cheek that looked like a knife wound, but was really a scar from when he had fallen off a playground swing as a child. With their large builds, fierce countenances and dressed in their long heavy winter coats, they would have looked at home in a mob movie. Just what I needed.

I asked them to come with me to find mousy Pavel. I told them not to speak under any circumstances, but merely to look silent and menacing. With the two 'gangsters' stalking close behind us, I led Pavel by the elbow out to the car park behind the building, where it was dark and quiet, and explained to him the facts of life.

"I get judged on the quality of this production," I explained to him. "I cannot tell the owner of the network that the program looked poor because of something I failed to do properly. If the show looks bad, I get fired."

(I didn't, but he wasn't to know that).

I explained to Pavel, I was not prepared to get fired because of him. I would go to any lengths to ensure the show looked good. "Any lengths," I emphasised, nodding gravely and looking deeply into his eyes.

"Please consider changing your mind and giving us the winners' names in advance."

I turned to the two big producers, who had by now worked out what their role was to be, and told them to stick close to my friend Pavel – because I might need to "speak to him again" at the end of the show.

Pavel started sweating and clutched his briefcase to his chest. I promptly forgot all about him because I had a million other problems to solve. But a short time before the broadcast began, one of my two 'gangsters' called me to tell me the good news.

When they had crowded Pavel into the on-air broadcast vehicle where he was to sit during the show, the music executive had announced he had changed his mind about letting us know the winners in advance. He meekly handed over the list – fortunately just in time for us to prepare the video packages. Pavel had then announced to everyone he had decided not to wait around to watch the show go to air and had hurried away.

It was the news I'd been waiting for. A live television show is a lot like a duck on a lake. It is all elegant and calm on the surface, but underneath there's a lot of furious paddling. When the three-hour broadcast began, we were still writing scripts and preparing video packages to be used just an hour into it.

It was chaos, but organised chaos at least. And one and a half hours into the broadcast, we finally completed everything which had to be done.

The show then rolled towards its conclusion, just as if we'd spent weeks preparing it. It was a major success, a ratings winner and the station owner, back in the presentation suite at the network, got to save his old movie for another occasion.

The executive who had been on his knees, came up to me afterwards with a tear in his eye, shook my hand vigorously and paid me probably the nicest compliment anyone ever has.

"Working with you, Brian," he said, "is like taking a warm bath. You just feel so good afterwards."

After three days without sleep, I was exhausted. I headed back to the hotel and went to bed. The next day I returned to the Netherlands and thought no more about it.

Strangely enough, about six months later, I was in Warsaw again for another job. One morning, I entered my hotel on the way to my room to collect some papers. As I approached the bank of elevators, the nearest one opened and out stepped mousy Pavel.

When he saw me, he stopped cold in his tracks. His face went pale, his eyes went wide and before I could even say a friendly hello, he took off like a startled rabbit past me out the door of the hotel as fast as he could go.

What's got into him, I wondered? I never saw Pavel again and I'm told the following year someone else looked after the briefcase which contained the winners' names.

25. Delivering the good news

At one time we had a business venture in France, but my bosses never seemed to be comfortable with the deal. The French company was supposed to try and sell our formats to the French broadcasters.

But they hadn't sold any for ages and didn't appear, to us at least, to be trying too hard. It was almost as if they thought stupid studio game shows and cheap quiz programs were beneath their dignity. And they treated my bosses like French people treat everyone – with disdain.

As it happened, my bosses began making noises which, to me, made it seem they were thinking of getting out of the deal.

But care was obviously needed. It wouldn't be out of the question for the French company to launch legal action if they thought we were willfully breaking the agreement for no reason (bear in mind all this was way above my pay grade).

All I was told was that any programs of ours they were actively working on, if the venture was dissolved, they would get to keep. I should delay sending them more, I was told, until the future of the relationship was clarified.

Someone in our office must have said or done something to spook them soon afterwards, because after ignoring us for a long time, they suddenly got active with our shows. In the two weeks before I went there, I received calls from them almost daily, asking me to forward them tapes and details of different formats. I had to get creative with my reasons for why it was difficult to do so.

When I reported this upstairs, I was told to allay any French fears and assure them everything was fine. I was also instructed to go to Paris, ostensibly to supervise the recording of a landmark episode of a format of ours they had sold several years earlier. Over the years, I had spent a lot of time becoming best friends with the people in Paris. After all, that was my job in every country. And of everyone in my company, I think I had one of the better relationships with them.

So, I was given the job of flying to Paris, laughing at their jokes, make tut-tutting noises whenever the subject of the relationship between our companies came up, and generally reassure them.

As part of the task, my bosses thought it might be nice if I took them a gift. So, someone from the office went out and brought two big old fashioned 20-litre milk jugs (just like they use on dairy farms) and filled them to the brim with kilos of Dutch candy.

Putting aside for the moment, that the Dutch unquestionably have the worst sweets in Christendom, it apparently hadn't occurred to anyone that the gesture meant I was actually expected to board a plane to Paris carrying two bloody great big metal milk jugs! What? One under each arm?

To try and make it less embarrassing, I asked my assistant to find a big box to put them in. She chose a cardboard box which had previously held a Compaq computer. So, of course, as soon as I arrived in Paris, French customs thought they'd caught the mastermind behind an international computer smuggling ring and ordered me to open the box in the arrivals area.

They then upended the milk jugs and poured the thousands of candies out onto the counter to prove I wasn't smuggling contraband. It took me 20 minutes to load them all back in, watched all the while by the smug and smirking French customs bastards who refused to help.

The staff in Paris sent me a note later saying they appreciated the candy and that they'd eaten them all. Ha! I've eaten Dutch sweets – so I know they were just being polite.

The only highlight of the trip for me was that I met the niece of the producer of our program in Paris. I had been talking on the phone with the producer, a lovely and professional woman about my age. She mentioned her niece, named Anne, would probably be around the studio during the recording and might ask me some questions. Anne, she explained, was studying English in school.

She'd told Anne how she often practiced her English on me.

Would it be okay for Anne to practice her English on me?

No problem for me, I thought.

I speak English reasonably well.

As long as her niece didn't make a pest of herself.

At the studio, the producer and I were chatting when she looked over my shoulder and said, "Here's Anne. May I introduce you?" I turned around and all the air went out of my lungs. (Oh great, I hear you say – here we go again. This stupid man does nothing in his stupid stories but go on about beautiful women. In my defence I'm a lonely, sad man in an industry which puts me in the path of some of the most beautiful women in the world. Cut me some slack).

There, walking towards me in the middle of the room, was the second most beautiful woman I have ever seen, and I have worked all my life in an industry where beautiful women are a dime a dozen (See *The Most Handsome Man I know* for the most beautiful).

Anne was about 20 years old. A tall, willowy, blonde with classic French cheekbones and a body which would have had the Pope handing back his celibacy certificate, slicking his hair back, sticking out his chest and hooking his thumbs into his low-cut jeans.

Anne was talking, but I have no idea what she said. I pasted a lopsided grin on my face and what came out my mouth was not so much English as complete drivel.

Anne, no doubt used to this sort of reaction from men, quickly realised her English was better than mine. She also quickly got tired of standing there talking to a shambling, drooling wreck who was staring at her, grinning and not able to put two words in the right order. She excused herself politely and left.

During the recording, she volunteered to help the junior producers move the audience into their seats. But later, when it was discovered one of the models needed for the fashion parade segment had not turned up because of a car accident, Anne pitched in. I have to say she blew the professional models, each of them no slouches in the looks department, right off the stage. Sigh. Life continues to be cruel to me.

So cruel.

When the recording of the program ended and the audience had gone home, my French friends put on champagne to celebrate – both the milestone of the landmark episode we had just recorded and the obviously good relationship between our two companies. I was chatted to by everyone important, obviously deliberately. I reassured them all that our companies were cemented together in a bond not even death could break.

We raised our glasses several times to toast our Dutch-French friendship society.

During the drinks, one of my French friends asked me if I had ever seen the real Paris. I told him I had seen the Eiffel Tower and been to the Louvre, etc. That made them laugh.

No, I was told, I must see the real Paris, monsieur. So, after the post-recording drinks ended about midnight, a group of us drove to the city, into a rabbit warren of narrow, cobbled streets, to an old-fashioned looking, smoke-filled bar in what appeared to be the geographic centre of the red-light district.

It only lacked a sign warning me to hang on to my wallet.

Most of the ladies of the night lining the street outside were actually gentlemen, I was told. Apparently, you could tell the difference if you got up close, but I chose not to do that.

The bar we poured ourselves into was the size of the bathroom in my apartment and filled to the S-bend with what I was assured were real Parisians. Apparently, they were all training to be on the French Olympic Smoking Team, too. My clothes and hair stank the next morning.

Our group grabbed a big table near the back of the room under a small television set, which was deafening everyone with a soccer game, a game being ignored by everyone present.

A whiskey was thrust at me, and everyone looked at me as if to say, "Well? What do you think of the real Paris?"

As if I was going to suddenly don a beret and start belting out Charles Aznavour songs.

It was a tiny, smelly old bar like any other tiny, smelly old bar anywhere in the world. I've been in tinier and smellier bars, I can tell you. But, of course, I made all the right noises and the conversation continued loudly in the already loud room.

I ended up being stuck next to one of the junior staff members who, although he was working in television, assured me he was really a writer and penning the next mega-successful French movie. His appalling English and my appalling French couldn't disguise the fact he thought that Mr Important Australian man might have connections to get his script before some big, important movie people. I led him on quite wickedly, intimating that, of course, I could make him famous, but only passionate people wrote successful films. Was that him?

Of course, as you probably realise, it was the worst thing I could have told him. He sounded off passionately about his stupid film for about two hours, which eventually upset the heavily smoking French people at the next table.

They also hated me because they thought I was American. It was okay once I explained I was Australian.

"Ahh, kangaroos, Crocodile Dundee!" and we were friends again. I would really hate to be American and have to apologise for it wherever I went.

Very early in the morning I staggered out of the bar into a taxi, well soaked with whiskey. Despite the hour and my obviously non-attentive condition, the Senegalese taxi driver insisted on telling me how beautiful Senegal was for tourists at that time of year.

On arrival at my hotel, he quite kindly wrote out the name of his brother who lived in Dakar, the capital of Senegal and who was just about the best darn guide a tourist could ever hope to find there. I should be quite mad not to look him up whenever I was next on vacation in Dakar.

I still have the name and address of the guide if anyone is interested. I wonder if the taxi driver has ever generated any income for his brother. Senegal, is apparently quite nice during the winter when it's not so hot.

After only three hours of sleep, I was up and on the plane home, this time sans milk jugs. I felt liberated.

I believe my trip, just as my bosses ordered, successfully assured the French our two companies would have a long and happy future together.

I'm such a bastard.

26. Finnish sauna

I've worked in television for quite a few years and hosted and attended a lot of meetings. Most are in offices, and most are a waste of time. Thousands have been over lunch or dinner (and a few notable times over both). But until a particular two-day trip to Finland, I had never, ever, attended a business meeting stark naked.

Seriously.

You can't unsee that image in your mind, can you?

Because it's normally so cold in Finland, people don't like to move from building to building if they don't have to, so over time a system has built up where everything they might need during the course of the day is under one roof. They have combination conference centres/restaurants/saunas.

The Finns love their saunas.

It's estimated there are 2 million hot boxes servicing a population of just 5.3 million people. Most big companies and government institutions have their own. The president apparently has an official one, as does the Prime Minister. Saunas are to be found in most city apartments and country cottages.

I went to Helsinki for a meeting concerning one of our formats to be made there. The meeting was to be a full-day event, involving all the staff of the program and a couple of senior television station executives.

It also included the presenter and the director, along with most of the production and technical staff.

All the morning was spent in a stuffy meeting room before an electronic whiteboard. At lunchtime, we moved down one flight of stairs to the company restaurant for a big and tasty smorgasbord. Afterwards, we went back upstairs to continue the talking.

At 6 o'clock that evening, a staff member put her head around the corner of our meeting room and interrupted me mid-sentence to inform everyone that the sauna was now hot. Much to my surprise, smiles broke out around the room. We all stood up and trooped, as a group, downstairs to the changing rooms. There, even more to my surprise and growing concern, everyone stripped naked and went into the sauna.

I was very nervous.

I'd never been naked with such a large group of people before. Let's be honest, not even a small group of people. I was convinced more than one particular part of my body would embarrass me.

I thought I should try and hide in a corner, but no sooner were we all crammed into the small wooden room and starting to sweat, when the crusty old director of the program, turned his crusty old naked body and penis in my direction and said, "So Brian, you were explaining?"

And I was the centre of attention.

Forced to continue my discussion, only now I was naked (please no one look at my penis, please no one look at my penis, please no one look at my penis).

Everywhere I looked, there were naked people.

(Oh God, I shouldn't have looked there!

Oh God, I looked there again!)

The host of the program, a beautiful blond woman, had perched her naked self next to me and, during a break in my discussions, explained how, in a Finnish sauna, people took turns hitting each other with small clumps of tree branches. She explained how the exercise opened up the pores of the skin and made you healthier.

She offered to demonstrate, turned me gently around and started hitting my back and bottom with one of the branches.

Quite hard too.

Then turned me around again and started hitting my front.

I focused on the plight of the world's starving people, the vanishing rainforests and the cruelty of the live animal export trade throughout Asia.

On anything other than what was happening to me.

Then, when she mercifully stopped, she told me it was my turn to hit her.

Front and back.

Oh. My. God.

She was beautiful and I have to say it took all my power of concentration to remain aloof. I hit her gently all over. Front and back and she had her eyes closed with the pleasure of it.

Bosnian war victims, the cruelty of abattoirs, the best method of cleaning a clogged sewer system. I concentrated on these thoughts and sweated furiously. By the time the sauna was over, I was exhausted.

We all trooped outside, showered and dressed, and headed as a group to the restaurant again for dinner and to the bar upstairs for drinks, where we stayed until Midnight. All in all, a unique experience. Apparently, the Finns have a rule that there can be no dirty thoughts in the sauna. I broke that rule several times, but I didn't tell anyone. I sincerely hope it wasn't noticeable.

I'm told the normal thing to do in winter is to sit in the sauna for a while, then go outside, roll naked in the snow, then go back into the sauna and repeat that several times.

Very healthy apparently.

The presenter promised to take me to their sauna again in the winter. It's bad enough to sit in the gloomy darkness of a sauna, stark naked with a large of group of other stark-naked, people, many of whom are beautiful women.

Outside in the snow, quite a few parts of me would shrink with the embarrassment of it all. So I can't see myself doing that.

It makes me sweat thinking about it.

27. Lithuania all over again

So God, who obviously has a sense of humour, landed me for my sins back in Lithuania. And I had a day which seemed to last forever but was actually only 18-hours long.

Here's how it went.

The first few moments back in the former Soviet republic seemed to indicate my earlier impressions of Lithuania may have been a bit off the path.

Vilnius this time looked bustling and lovely.

The people were all smiling. My usual driver/bodyguard shook my hand like an old friend when he collected me from the airport. But of course, this being Lithuania, they were obviously waiting patiently for me to look away before springing the trap.

In non-existent English, the driver asked me where I wanted to go. It was noon and the four-hour flight via Denmark had meant I had been wrenched out of bed at 5:30 am in the Netherlands. My senses were not yet functioning properly.

"To the studio," I replied.

"Are you sure you wouldn't prefer to take your bag to the hotel, check in and relax for a while?" he asked.

Actually, he didn't ask that because his English was twice as bad as my Lithuanian. What actually transpired was this. He pointed to me.

"You." Then he mimed driving a car.

"Hotel?" Then he mimed putting his head in his arms and pretended to snore loudly. Then he looked at me hopefully.

I got the picture.

"Pray tell, my good man. What time do the proceedings officially begin in the studio?" I asked.

Nah. Actually, it went like . . .

"Me." I mimed an old fashion movie camera with the handle turning.

"Studio? Time?" and pointed to my watch.

"Ahh!" he replied and held up two fingers.

So, I asked him . . .

"Is okay, hotel?"

I mimed driving.

And "Studio" miming the movie camera,

"2 o'clock?"

"Yes, yes," he replied.

Okay then.

After checking into the hotel, I lay down. By now it was a 12:45 pm. I planned a short nap.

My phone rang. It was the local producer.

"Was I coming to the studio?"

"Yes," I replied.

"At 2 o'clock."

"Great, so you are already in the car?"

Uh-oh. "Why?" I inquired.

"It takes one and a half hours to get here," he replied.

I shot off the bed and rushed out.

God knows what the driver was thinking. I felt like going to where he was sitting in the car and miming a punch in his face. He would understand that all right. But he was armed, so

248

perhaps I should have mimed firing a shotgun at him.

Anyway, by breaking all current Lithuanian land speed re- (and my driver and I were already on the leaderboard for of those from previous trips) we arrived at the studio almost on time, the driver grinning broadly at me. I was sweating like a man who had narrowly escaped death, which I had several times. As with my last trip to Lithuania, we had travelled on the worst roads in Europe at 180 kph, because "it was safer".

The program being recorded was called *Forgive Me*, which you may remember from previous chapters. People come along to say sorry to each other and make friends again.

The studio is the size of a bread box and, from my first glance, it appeared they really had got value for money for the $35 they had spent on the construction of the set.

There were 50 people in the audience and the producer proudly told me that in the first two weeks of recording (this was the third), they'd had no audience at all. Word, he said, was obviously getting around that the show was popular. It must be hard to make a living in public relations in Lithuania. There weren't many cars parked around, so I wondered how the audience had made the long and dangerous journey from the city. They are a hardy folk.

The recording began on time and I started to forget about it being Lithuania. That was, until the producer received a telephone call midway through the recording.

It was his mother.

She was at home and had been watching a Russian news program. She was sure she had just seen the body of her husband (the producer's father) in a film clip about unsolved murders in Russia. Could the producer come home, please, so he could help her find out for sure? The producer told her he was busy recording the show and would be home later.

Seriously, that's what happened. In most countries you couldn't buy that sort of professionalism, could you?

Soon afterwards, the recording had to be stopped because of a police chase happening on the road outside. The chase ended directly outside the studio door, but the sirens continue to blare, until someone from the production was sent outside to tell them to turn the noise off.

They kindly did.

It turned out that the cops had been chasing a car thief. He had decided to surrender just outside the front door of the studio. Maybe he'd been the one to drive the audience there.

Back into the recording we went, until there was another stoppage. Some workmen at the back of the studio began drilling next to the air conditioning duct and the noise blared through to the studio floor.

The workmen were asked to stop.

And they kindly did.

But they stood in the same place, right at the entry to the air conditioning duct, and complained about it loudly. The noise of their complaining also came through and disrupted the recording. Someone else went out to tell them to shut up or move. Which they kindly did.

Within the show itself everything was going very well. Everyone was crying, which is what is supposed to happen. Even the audience was crying. At one point, a woman in the audience cried so loudly the recording was stopped so she could be taken outside to cry in private.

Which she was.

During the program, if the person who is asking for forgiveness (Person A) is forgiven by their friend (Person B), the friend (Person B) comes into the studio as a surprise for a tearful reunion with Person A. But, because the set was so small, the friends of Person A in the audience, could see Person B hiding behind the studio curtain.

They began to cry and call out to him.

Which not only disrupted the recording again but let Person A know what the surprise was going to be. The whole thing ended in a small riot which stopped the recording again.

Between recordings (there were to be two shows recorded during the afternoon), the producer asked me if I wanted something to eat.

"Will we be going out for dinner later?" I inquired, "because I won't want two big meals today."

"Probably not," he replied.

"I have to get home to my mother, what with my father's corpse appearing on the television and all."

Oh, right! Yes. Now I remember.

"In that case, I'll have something to eat now," I said.

There were 13 things on the menu in the studio canteen, all of them chicken or pork covered in something heavy and surrounded by potatoes (remember the national dish of Lithuania?). I chose the chicken and it wasn't bad.

Very filling.

Just as I swallowed the last mouthful, the producer came up to me, accompanied by one of the two presenters.

"Okay, so after we finish here, you and one of the presenters will go together to the restaurant and I'll meet you there if I can get away from my mother in time."

I had just eaten a meal heavy enough to make the legs of my canteen chair buckle.

Didn't we just moments ago agree …?

The second show recording went as planned, everyone crying and happy. It continuously amazed me to watch these three
people (the two presenters and the producer) make the whole
program themselves with no other production assistance. In the
Netherlands the same show needed a staff of 20.

In Germany they needed 25. And, although the technical
things like the set, the number of cameras and people in the
audience, were obviously much less than in the west, the Lithuanians actually made a program with as much feeling as in
many countries which had much bigger budgets.

The second program was in the bag by 8 pm. I'd been on
my feet for more than 14 hours by then, but still had a second
dinner of potatoes to look forward to.

My driver/bodyguard was long gone.

Kidnappers don't do shift work, apparently.

I got a ride back to the city with the two presenters in their
car. One was in the front seat with a mobile phone constantly
stuck to her ear. I thought she was merely being a busy socialite,
even though we were driving in a 10-year-old Datsun.

Then the other presenter explained that the show they had
recorded the previous week was just now being broadcast. Like
in every program which relies on getting contestants from the
general public, there was an announcement during the show
asking for people to call if they want to take part.

The telephone number given out during the show was the
presenter's own mobile phone number! She was actually speaking to potential contestants. And among the calls were those
from the usual crazy people who like to call television stations.

She was talking to those people, too.

Nowhere else in the world do presenters put their own mobile phone numbers on screen and say, "call me".

Nowhere.

It was a strange sight.

Two of Lithuania's most famous TV hosts driving along in a beat-up old Datsun with the interior light on so one of them could write down the names and numbers of people who wanted to be contestants on their show.

And it was raining and pitch dark outside.

The drive back to the city took a lot longer than my drive out to the studio but was a lot less stressful. I had a warm feeling.

At the restaurant, I couldn't face another chicken and potatoes, so I had half a bottle of white wine, which made me feel mellow. The hosts were great company too, but I was exhausted and wanted to go to bed.

At midnight, I asked to be driven to my hotel.

Just before I collapsed onto the bed, I had that same strange feeling as I had the first time I went to Lithuania. That someone was going to drill a small hole in the ceiling, lower down a wire and suck out my brains the minute I was asleep.

I got up and moved the bed.

Lithuania does that to you.

What an interesting country.

28. Doing backflips

People underestimate how athletic I have to be working as an international television producer. Of course, every time I try to argue this, people look at me as if to say, "Do you think I was abducted as a baby by flying monkeys?"

But it's true. No, not the flying monkeys bit. To do my job, you need to be very supple and lithe, words people don't normally associate with me. Devilishly handsome, yes, but not supple and lithe.

Take, for example, a visit I made to Turkey.

People say Istanbul was great in the Middle Ages. And you will meet people who say it still is. In fact, the serious young Turkish producer who collected me at the airport assured me Istanbul was the best city in the world. Further into the journey, though, he admitted he was originally from Macedonia and had not been to any other city than Istanbul. I had already guessed as much because Istanbul is dirty, crowded, noisy, and on occasion, dangerous.

On my first trip there a few years earlier, the Kurds had just issued a fatwa against westerners and killed a couple of British people to prove they were serious about it. The second time a few months later, a bomb killed 14 people in a marketplace in the same suburb as my hotel (although from the 15th floor of the hotel in the air-conditioned comfort of my executive suite in the Hilton, I wasn't struck by any shrapnel or body parts).

And on another trip, a big earthquake near the capital, Ankara, killed half a dozen people. I slept through the earthquake, as you already know from chapter 1 of this book.

So don't tell me Istanbul is exciting and vibrant. Those are just travel company weasel words to say it's not their fault if you die of something while searching for thrills in Turkey, like eating the food or crossing the road.

Istanbul traffic is appalling. The streets hadn't been repaired since the Italo – Turkish war of 1911, which we all remember that precursor conflict to World War 1.

(Seriously? You don't remember?).

Like everyone else, my driver created his own lane, rather than be restricted by the markings on the road. Instead of brakes, he merely used the horn. Like everyone else.

It's a form of primitive but effective communication.

"Toot. I'm turning right here."

"Toot, toot. I can see that and I'm making room for you, even though the light was red against you."

"Toot, toot. Was it really that red? From my perspective, it had more of an orange tinge."

"Toot, toot, toot. Well, never mind. See you at the mosque later tonight?"

"Toot. Yes, see you there."

Finding your way around Istanbul is a closely guarded secret known only to the 10 million locals. I could see no street signs and no numbers on any of the buildings. When I pointed this out to my driver and asked him how he found his way, he just shrugged and mumbled, "You just know". This was no comfort. There may have been tourists lost in the city.

And how the hell does the postal system work if there are no street names or numbers? If I want to send a letter to someone, do I address it to: "Ahmed Armedia, care of the big house with the nice windows, just up the road from the big yellow building in the suburb which has the great big warehouse near the sea?" Or what?

Do they perhaps every Monday call a meeting in a suburban square and ask each other, "Anyone know an Ahmed Armedia? I've got a letter here for him! Anyone know him?"

Or maybe they didn't have a postal system at all. Now I think of it, I'd never received a letter from anyone in Turkey. I guess my letters to colleagues over the years had been piling up in the warehouse near the sea, while embarrassed Turkish authorities tried to work out what to do with them. And here I was thinking they were just being rude.

The local authorities also obviously have a rule that traffic cops must pass a Saddam Hussein look-a-like competition before they are allowed into uniform. There are cops on every street corner and, after you've been driving for a long while (which is the only thing you can do in Istanbul traffic) you get to thinking, "Didn't I just see those same cops on the previous corner?"

They all look the same. Big fleshy faces with bushy moustaches and beer guts. It's going to be hell keeping these standards up when they finally grant women the right to join the force.

My first bit of real exercise during my visit happened about halfway to the hotel.

My serious young driver, having recently told me that Istanbul was heaven on earth, turned to me and asked, "What do you think of Istanbul?"

My first reaction is always to blurt out the truth.

Something like, "Are you kidding?"

But I never insult my hosts. I also prefer not to lie in these situations, because people can generally tell I'm lying by the stupid look on my face.

So, I have trained myself to perform a back somersault with a twist and come up with something that avoids the subject completely. Not a lie, but not the truth either. Something inane but adequate.

"It's certainly warmer than the Netherlands," I replied, and then followed up with "How could anyone not love Istanbul? The women here are the best looking in all of Europe."

I'd discovered this last statement, while strictly speaking a lie, worked very well in just about every country in Europe because it reaffirmed to the locals that not only their women, but their entire culture, was superior to all those around them. And it immediately diverted the (male) questioner's mind onto another subject … women.

It certainly worked in Istanbul and we finished the journey discussing what it was about Turkish women that, in the opinion of my driver, made them obviously the fairest in the world.

I don't know how he could tell. Most of the woman we saw on the street were covered head to toe in the proper Islamic fashion. Only parts of their faces were visible, so how could my driver even begin to tell they were good looking? He could be ogling his mother and never know it.

It was dark by the time we arrived at the hotel. Istanbul is a city full of mosques and at night, they are all illuminated outside. It's quite beautiful. I made a rather crass remark about how they were all lit up like Christmas trees, but my driver missed it, fortunately.

The hotel, not the same one I normally used, turned out to be an interesting choice. I was fortunate enough to get a room overlooking the Turkish National Car Horn Blowing Championships, which, I discovered began promptly at 6 am the next morning. I never found out who won, but I didn't get more than about four hours sleep, so I may have missed the item on the news.

I had been in Turkey to make a version of a program very popular all over Europe called *All You Need is Love*, which I've discussed elsewhere.

A quick reminder how it works. I like you, but I'm too afraid to ask you out. So, I go to the program. The host helps me create a message for you. In the message I ask you out on a date.

The host takes my message to you and, after you see the tape, you say "yes" or "no". If the answer is "yes", you and I have a joyful meeting in the studio. If the answer is "no", the audience gets to have a laugh while watching me squirm with embarrassment at the rejection. All light-hearted and very successful.

Particularly popular in Turkey. Since its launch six months earlier, it had been one of the country's most-watched programs.

As I explained in an earlier chapter, normally when I launch a program it stays the way I want it. But not always. It's an inexact science.

And somewhere in the time between my visits, this show had taken a strange turn.

When I had last seen it, the show was a fun and bouncy one-hour dating show, full of laughs and young attractive couples kissing and laughing.

The show I had been brought to see this time had the same name. But now it involved a succession of women, most covered head to foot, coming into the studio and telling the presenter and audience tearfully about a man they loved – and were often married to – who no longer wanted them.

Each guest begged the presenter to help them convince the

man to take them back. The program had become a non-fun and non-bouncy hour of sobbing, wailing and rending of tissues. And yet remarkably still hugely popular with the local audience. So, who was I to judge? What the hell do I know about television? Nothing apparently.

By the way, nine times out of 10 the man the woman was appealing to (fleshy-faced, bushy-moustached and beer-gutted) said no to the reunion and the bereft woman left the studio, to be replaced on the couch by another woman, dressed exactly the same, with exactly the same problem.

When one of the men surprised all of us by agreeing to take his sobbing woman back, he came into the studio and the couple hugged and kissed in the middle of the studio floor under the bright lights. All the while the studio band, featuring a man playing a South American pan flute, kept up a funeral dirge, which sounded like a blue whale dying.

The flute solo went on, long after common sense had strolled out the building and down the road. It was embarrassing to watch the happy couple finish greeting and hugging each other, then stand around wondering what to do, until the flute player eventually wandered to the end of his masterpiece.

In the control room the director had it all organised. She had been a production assistant when I had been there six months earlier, so had obviously done remarkably well in her career.

She had a directing technique I'd not seen before. Call a shot, light a cigarette, call another shot, chat to someone on her mobile phone, call a shot, sip on a Diet Coke and so on. The recording appeared to be getting in the way of her social life.

During the recording, a boss came into the control room and began overruling her decisions. Then the person whose job it was to push the button when the director called the shot, joined in, and started making his own choice of cameras. By halfway through the show, everyone in the control room except me was yelling. I had no idea what the problem was or who was putting the show together.

On the studio floor, the crying continued. Another woman had her plea turned down by her former boyfriend or husband. She was led tearfully from the set. The band tried to help by sending her off with a cheerful and jaunty polka.

"Good show, huh?" grinned the director at me.

I did a front somersault with a half pike.

"Very colourful," I grinned back at her.

From their discussion and arguments, it appeared I was missing something important about the recording of the show. I have not a single word of Turkish but maybe it was something in the language.

I concentrated more closely.

No good.

The director said something which sounded to me like "eating the kick-boxing item". Then the producer replied with something about "filming in a moustache" and then what sounded like "the sole bidder on the burgundy dip".

The director did not look convinced at that.

The producer turned to me.

"What do you think of our great show?" he beamed at me.

The locals often use me to prop up arguments they have with their staff. If Brian likes it, then it must be the correct way to do it. But I was all warmed up and athletic.

I did a forward double somersault with a double twist.

"The presenter is very sympathetic to the contestants," I offered.

"Yes, he is so warm, everyone loves him," said the producer.

"And the women!" I said.

"Are all women in Turkey so beautiful?" I never like letting a successful line go to waste.

The producer beamed. He knew I was telling it like it was.

Nobody in the control room seemed to have noticed the weirdest thing about the formerly happy, now gruesomely sad, show we were making. And of course, I wasn't brave enough to mention it.

Each of the very conservatively dressed, sobbing women was escorted in and out of the studio by a half-naked bombshell of a co-host. Her job was to beam her teeth and very obvious breasts at the audience, then glide out of the picture. Totally out of place.

In the dressing rooms later, I noticed she couldn't take her eyes off her own reflection in the mirror. Probably trying to re-assure herself that the face in the mirror was really hers. At the after-show drinks session, she draped herself over the presenter and giggled at his outrageously chauvinistic ways.

I was woken at 6 the next morning by the second round of competition in the Istanbul automobile car horn tests. They all passed. I'm never staying at that hotel again. I'm going back to the Hilton and the market bombs.

On my way back to the airport, the producer called me.

"Thanks for coming Brian. You were a great help."

I hadn't done much, but it was nice of him to say so.

"I was glad to have the chance to come." I told him.

"Istanbul is such an experience."

Front pike with a small twist.

"Brian, maybe you should come to Istanbul to work for me?"

Triple somersault.

"That wouldn't be work for me, my friend.

That would be more like a very long holiday," I laughed.

"I'd feel guilty taking your money."

We both laughed.

I wrenched my back with that last double back flip and pike.

When I got home, I had to lie down.

29. Bless you my son

My company had just bought a share in a production company in Rome. My task was to go there, find out which
of their formats we might be able to use elsewhere in Europe
and to let the Italians know about our formats that they could
try and sell locally.

I skillfully timed my arrival at the Leonardo da Vinci-Fiumi-
cino Airport in Rome moments after three packed jumbo jets
had landed. The queues in front of the customs barriers went
out the door and back towards the Netherlands. And forget
about your nice polite British queues. These international travellers (most of them returning Italians, it must be said) were as
unruly as a crowd of English football supporters.

We spent ages shuffling forward toward the customs barrier,
everyone moving at the same time, everyone elbowing to get a
millimeter advantage on the people either side of them.

There was no mercy shown.

Not even to the black-clad little old ladies among us.

These small gangsters were elbowing me just as roughly as
everyone else. Other old Italians cleverly slid around the outside
of the crowd. It was a vicious pit fight.

The customs officers acted as if every single one of the 1,000
people in front of them was a fanatical member of the Abu Nidal terror group and spent 10 minutes carefully questioning

each passenger before allowing them through.

It was going to take forever.

While waiting, I stood behind a small group of Italian men. As you know, I'm not one normally given to flights of fancy or to tagging people with cultural stereotypes (see the chapter on my visit to Romania as an example), but I'm sure these particular men were shifty. I mean, they exhibited all the signs of being members of the mafia.

There was a tall, gaunt, silver-haired gent with an expensive coat draped over his shoulders. The others in his group treated him with much respect. He put his hands on either side of their faces and kissed them 'Don Corleone'-style as a greeting.

One of the men standing next to him was dressed in a cheap suit. This undoubtedly 'made' guy was short, and completely round like a barrel, just like the mob enforcers I'd seen in the movies. Others in the group looked like goons as well. After an hour shuffling towards the customs barrier, I had convinced myself these men were mobsters.

But, you know what?

They were stuck in the hot, sweaty scrum with the rest of us. And the little old ladies elbowed past them just the same. Which made me feel warm and fuzzy.

After an hour had passed, the crowd began to grumble, but the lines showed no sign of moving. It was at this point that the wonderful Italian mentality came to our rescue.

A senior officer strolled up and took one look at the mass of irritated and complaining travellers.

He then moved to the customs barrier and yelled to the officials there to let us all through. Security was thrown out the window and the gates were opened.

Given our freedom, we all just charged on past the barrier

like a football crowd, including, I'm sure, several members of the Abu Nidal terror group.

The unseemly scramble through customs was led by the little old ladies. The mafia guys also jogged unceremoniously through the gate alongside me.

Out in the public arrivals area, I noticed the mafia guys were met by someone holding up a sign for people from Microsoft.

Sure. Sure. They didn't fool me. I knew it was a cover.

Welcome to Italy. Welcome to Rome in March.

Temperature a gorgeous 24°C (don't come in August, I was advised, when temperatures rose to 35°C and the pollution turned it into acid), beautiful blue sky and not too many tourists (again, as I was advised, don't come in August when most of the adult population of America drops by).

My driver from the airport was a suave and sophisticated-looking man who drove like he normally delivered kidneys to hospitals. He appeared well practised in navigating the unique Italian road system.

In Rome, the lines on the road to signify traffic lanes are merely meant as a rough guide to motorists and certainly not to be taken literally. Not at all. You can really fit four cars across a two-lane intersection if you know what you are doing. We did.

Traffic lights, too, have different shades of meaning in Rome than those used in other countries. At different intersections, apparently, you don't need to stop regardless of the traffic light colour at the time. We didn't.

'Stop' signs in Rome must originally have stated: 'Don't Stop'. Everyone still thinks of them like this even though the 'Don't' part has fallen off, or been eroded by the pollution.

Some intersections we blazed through at top speed were quite hair-raising.

Despite a number of exquisite moments of terror, Mr Suave delivered me to our office safely.

The company we had bought into in Rome was managed by Marco, one of nature's true gentlemen. A very nice, very smooth man from Milan, who became a friend.

His wife worked high up in the administration of the Vatican. Before this trip, I had no idea just how much power the Catholic Church had in this part of the world. Someone told me, quietly, that most television companies in Italy (broadcasters as well as independent producers) all had the church as a silent (or not-so-silent) partner.

Marco told me a story of once going to the office of a competitor and, while searching for a particular building, mistakenly opened the door of the wrong room and discovered eight red-clothed cardinals sitting around a table discussing TV business.

Marco had nice offices, about three metres from the television broadcaster, which was his biggest client. When I arrived, we had a quick get-to-know-you chat, then downed tools and headed off to a nearby restaurant for lunch.

They have their priorities right in Italy.

Spaghetti Roman-style, Marco explained.

Every district has its own distinctive spaghetti.

The Roman-style version tasted just like every other sort of spaghetti, I'd eaten, but I didn't mention that and made the right slurping noises.

Fish wrapped in spinach for the next course.

Delicious! But so much food. After lunch I felt like having a lie down. Or was that just in Spain you could do that? Instead, I spent the afternoon discussing business with Marco and one of his executive producers, Paolo, who spoke excellent English.

At the end of the day, Paolo asked if I had ever toured Rome.

No.

Would I like to eat something?

(Not really) Sure.

What do you, like to eat?

Sushi, I replied, cheekily.

No signore, not in Rome.

So as the beautiful day wound down, Paolo and I went out for a real Roman evening. He drove me to the centre of the city and parked in a convenient 'No Parking' zone.

On the way, we passed a small group of police, parked by the side of the road.

Paolo explained these were the 'bad' police. I asked him if they were criminals.

No, he replied, these were the police who gave you a ticket if you drove too fast or broke any of the road rules. Bad police, indeed. And there were so few of them in Rome that people knew who they were. After we parked illegally again, we strolled through the cobbled streets of the old city.

Past the grandeur of the French embassy, a 16th century palace. Past several famous landmarks, including the Piazza Navona and about a thousand fountains all with statues of galloping horses, naked maidens or boys pissing into the water.

The Romans love their fountains.

We ended up at what looked to be a normal suburban house, which had a black-clad, little old lady sweeping the yard outside. As we approached, she wished us "Buena sera" and ushered us inside where I discovered the house had been turned into a tiny four table restaurant.

This sort of establishment, Paolo told me, was called a Hosteria and it was a traditional way people in Italy supplemented their incomes.

It was like if you set up a restaurant in your own home, without letting your local health department know anything about it. You can see the potential for a lawsuit or two, can't you? But the Italians make it work somehow, probably because every woman in the country is a spectacularly good cook.

We were shown to a table and, instead of ordering from a menu, a little old man, probably the woman's husband, brought out a selection of small dishes.

If we ate what was on them, great.

If not, he just took them away and brought something else.

Sort of an Italian-style buffet.

Hilariously, at the end of one course, he picked up some bread from our table and wiped it through the spaghetti sauce remaining on my plate. He then handed it to me, saying that he wouldn't take the plate while there was still food on it.

Yes, mum!

You don't get that level of service at McDonalds, do you?

And he just took the cork out of an old bottle of white wine and brought it over to us. If we drank it, okay. If not ... well, we drank it, so I'm not sure what would have happened otherwise.

The whole meal came to about $30 for both of us and, when we left, it was like we were members of the family planning to migrate to America. We had our hands vigorously shaken and were wished well on our journey.

Then, full of food and wine, we strolled back to the car and went for a night drive around the city. Hopefully not to run across any of the 'bad' police while doing so.

First, we drove to the Tomb of the Unknown Soldier where Mussolini made all his big speeches. Then we walked past not one, but two colosseums, including the famous one that remains the largest amphitheatre in the world.

Quite awesome to think of the history in this place.

Then we went past the Lateran Palace, which was the home of the Popes for a thousand years before the Apostolic Palace, within what is now Vatican City, was built. The Lateran palace, which is really just a castle, has never been breached, even during World War 2.

Paolo told me there were rumours that tunnels under the castle led all over the city, including into the Vatican. Probably so the cardinals could sneak out for a beer, or go their meetings at the television production offices without anyone seeing them. And while on the subject of the church, it has to be said, you have never seen so many churches in one place in your life.

Talk about an oversupply of God.

Apparently, in the old days, the rich thought it rather too common to go to church with other people, so many insisted on having their own church and priest on their own property. And not just some little chapel either.

"We must have a bigger church than the Borghese's, dear."

Seriously, you could hop from church roof to church roof as you made your way across the city and never touch the ground. At the end of an evening's walking and driving, we ended up, as you do, full of wine outside the Vatican.

Thousands of statues and marble columns. The papal residence was right near the road, but no amount of yelling or throwing rocks at the windows by Paolo and me could get the Pope to tear himself away from the episode of *Italy's Next Top Model* he was no doubt watching.

Fortunately, the patrolling security guards were quite patient with us. They thought I was joking when I asked them to find out if the Pope wanted to come out incognito for a drink or see a show with us. I promised we'd have him home in time for Mass.

When it grew cold standing there gawking, we cruised back past the famous Roman ruin of the Temple of Diana to my hotel where we met up with a few other colleagues for a late drink.

I commented on the poor state of the roads we had driven over in the city. Paolo told me the Roman city council had big problems whenever it needed road work or building renovations.

Every time council workers dug down more than a metre or two, they discovered ruins of some kind and the work had to stop for weeks or months until the archaeologists cleared the area of relics.

Until the early 1990s, apparently, the builders were unaware of the value of relics or so blasé about what they were doing, that when they found any historical artefacts, they just tossed them aside and kept on building.

The government was trying to save recovered relics, but builders still trashed relics or sold on the black market, anything they found remotely valuable. But it all meant that road works were a slow and expensive business. I flew back to the Netherlands the next day.

Marco, by the way, offered me a job in Rome, which was really nice of him.

I replied in real Roman style:

"Bless you, my son."

I'm going to need to borrow a red Cardinal's cape.

30. Forgetting

It wasn't a sign of encroaching old age. It was just that I was really, really late for my flight.

Things had gone wrong from the first thing that morning. I slept through my alarm and, by the time the usual traffic snarl heading into Amsterdam had freed my car, allowing me to drive onto the highway to Schiphol Airport, I had only moments left before the plane's scheduled departure time.

Normally, making a flight is not such a big problem. My job involved hundreds of flights each year. At one stage while supervising *Who wants to be a Millionaire?* I was visiting up to three countries a week. In one noteworthy year, I actually took the company record from my travel-weary boss with an arse-flattening 112 return flights. That was 224 flights in 365 days. Nearly killed me.

So, I was well experienced in getting to flights in all sorts of cities, the great ones and the shitholes. Each city had its own procedure and timing. I had the art of getting from my home or hotel to my seat on the plane, mastered to fine precision. I rarely spent more than a few minutes sitting in the terminal with other commuter drones and sweaty tourists.

I prided myself on having missed only one flight in all that time, and that wasn't even my fault. That failure was down to a bone-headed but polite Parisian taxi driver and a stubborn mule of an Air France employee. Just to delay my current departure momentarily, this is what happened the day I missed that one and only flight.

I had run from our office in Paris into the street, hailed a taxi and flopped into the back seat.

"Airport Charles de Gaulle, s'il vous plait," I told the elderly driver in my masterful French.

"Certainly sir," he replied in perfect English (I wasn't fooling anyone). "What time is your flight?"

"Six o'clock," I told him.

"No problem then sir," he answered. "We have plenty of time."

Satisfied with the answer, I buried my head in the notes of the meeting I had just left, marking what follow-up I would need to do in the days ahead.

At some point I looked up and noticed we were on the free-way to the airport and, in due course, we arrived there,

"Here you are, sir. Well in time. It's 10 minutes to six."

What the hell? In my wrapped-up world, it never occurred to me that a taxi driver wouldn't know you had to be at the airport at least a half an hour, and usually up to an hour, before a flight was due to leave. It took half an hour for the stewards to get the passengers into their seats, and their stupidly large number of bulky carry-on bags in the overhead lockers. Every moron knew that – except my friendly taxi driver, apparently. And, of course, I hadn't told him of that fact. I did now.

"Sorry sir," he said, appearing to look apologetic.

"I didn't know that. I've never been in an aeroplane. But that's good information for the future in case I do get to go for a holiday somewhere."

Can Parisian taxi drivers do passive aggressiveness or sarcasm? It certainly seemed like it, but he was so polite and so apologetic I didn't have the heart to call him names. I just grabbed my bag and ran.

I still had a chance. Evening flights in the busy UK/Netherlands/France corridor were often late. As I approached the check-in area, I could see passengers milling around the departure gate I knew was used for flights to the Netherlands. The flight hadn't left. There was still a chance. I trotted over to the check-in desk and had to wait, hopping from foot to foot, while a French family of four discussed their entire fucking life story with the only staff member manning a computer in the long row of 12 check-in computers. French working hours clash horribly with modern life.

Eventually I got to the front of the line only to be told by the snooty woman, in a snooty tone, that my flight had indeed closed.

"But the people there, see those people? They are on the same flight and they haven't boarded yet. I have no check-in luggage. I can still easily make it."

"I'm sorry sir, but the flight is closed for check in. I will book you on the next flight in two hours."

And that's what she did. Fuming, I strode up to the departure gate of my original flight and approached the staff member behind the desk there. I wanted to make one more attempt.

"I was originally booked on this flight. Can I get back on it?"

"Sir, you are booked on the next flight."

"Yes, I know, but can I get back on this one instead please?"

"Sorry sir, this flight is closed."

So, I flopped down in one of the hard, concrete blocks Airport Charles de Gaulle calls a chair and watched angrily as my original flight took forever to board including, no doubt, some smug bastard who had my seat. I could have made it easily.

My arse was cold and numb by the time I got home that night. And that, of the many hundreds of flights I've taken, has been the only one I ever missed. (And I only had to wait two hours, at no further expense, for the next one.)

Of course, I've had a few near misses over the years.

My nearly unblemished record was almost broken once for a flight booked from Heathrow in London to Australia.

An autumn leaf had apparently fallen onto the track somewhere along London's Piccadilly Line, which, of course, meant the entire train system had to be shut down. That delayed my train from the city by an hour. By the time I got to the check-in desk, the flight was closed and, to all intents and purposes, gone.

I was shattered.

I had no accommodation any more in London and almost no money left. I was saved by the man whose job it was to transport handicapped people through the airport in the little car with the orange flashing light.

He'd been parked near the check-in desk as I somehow convinced the nice English woman behind the desk (unlike the stubborn French check-in person) that I could indeed make it to the plane, despite the fact it was leaving in two minutes from gate Z435 which looked to be about 4 km away.

The man waved me aboard his little car and we barrelled down the departure halls of one of the worlds biggest airports at well over the little car's safety speed. Narrowly avoiding killing strolling passengers, he successfully got me to the gate where we found, surprisingly, the aircraft was still there.

You know you're late when you see the head steward standing with the half-closed aircraft door propped open, looking angrily at his watch. Someone must have called ahead to tell him we were on our way. No packet of peanuts or cool pre-take-off orange juice for me. I got a stern look and a pointed glance as I shuffled guiltily past him.

This was followed by a plane load of angry business class looks as I made my way down the aisle.

The steward must have announced they were all waiting for one really late dickhead.

But I made it.

On another occasion, I was so late getting onto a small commuter plane from the Australian snowfields, I was forced to run across the tarmac in full ski gear, including hat, gloves, ski goggles and ski boots (not an easy task I can tell you), as the stairs were pushed back in place and plane door reopened just for me.

An hour or so later, still kitted out for a blizzard, I was standing in line for a taxi at Sydney Airport in 30°C heat, attracting no end of puzzled looks. Some of those in the taxi line with me took careful looks at the sky, no doubt worried they had missed something important in the weather forecast that morning.

But back to Holland.

On this morning, despite being really late, I was determined not to miss my flight. I ran through the departure area to the travel desk used by my company. They knew me by sight. I was a regular. As I approached the desk at speed, the woman behind the counter held out my tickets and I snatched them, barely slowing my pace.

"Thank you," I called over my shoulder.

My trips were booked several days, and sometimes even several weeks, in advance by my office, based on my schedule. Just another journey in a long line of journeys. As I jogged, I noted my flight number and could see on the departure board the gate I needed to aim for.

When I got to the customs line, it was joyously free of tourists and other assorted morons who make business travel such a pleasure. I rushed towards the border guard and held out my ticket and passport.

"And where are you going today, sir?" he asked politely as he reached for his stamp. I stared at him. I had no idea.

The tickets had been booked days ago.

I had the flight number and departure time in my diary.

But where was I going?

"Um …"

"Your destination, sir?" his eyebrows started to climb.

I was a blank canvas. I tried a shit-eating grin and got a fierce stare in return.

"You must know where you are going this morning, sir?" he tried again.

"Of course, er …"

Maybe he thought I was one of those people who liked to come to the airport and jog up and down the corridors to get some exercise.

They have those sorts of people, don't they?

For the life of me I couldn't remember where I was going.

I really couldn't.

"Um, isn't it written on there?" I asked, gesturing to my ticket which he held.

I remained polite.

The last thing I needed was to be called a loony and be dragged off to some office somewhere for questioning. I'd miss my flight for sure.

"Yes, it is sir. It's written very clearly on the ticket," he said.

"Then help me out, mate by giving me a hint.

I'm running really late."

The use of "mate" was my way of starting the first steps towards playing the stupid Aussie in the hope he might put me down as a fool of a tourist, or some such.

"You must know where your flight is going, sir. Somewhere in Scandinavia, perhaps?"

Light bulb.

"Sweden, I'm going to Sweden," I declared proudly, like a toddler who has wiped his own bottom for the first time.

"Yes, you are, sir. And you'd better hurry. The flight is about to leave."

You have to hand it to the Dutch border police. They are remarkably civil, considering the number of idiots they are forced to deal with in the course of a normal day.

I'd love to say that not knowing where I was going that time was a one-off event, but it wasn't. It was depressingly common in my line of work.

I got a good start on my Alzheimer's disease diagnosis in those days. It was because of the sheer amount of travel I did.

I spent a lot of time on planes and sleeping in hotels.

One after the other, after the other. Unless something happened to break the monotony, they became an endless blur, barely noticed as I went about doing the things I did during the in-between-travel times.

I remember once walking down the departure lane at Aéroport Nice Côte d'Azur in the south of France and suddenly realising I didn't know where I was.

Simple, I thought.

I would look for clues in the signs around the arrivals area.

Nope. All bloody airports these days are designed to be easy for people of all cultures and languages to navigate and therefore tend to be all cut from similar blocks.

It wasn't until I went outside and had to negotiate with yet another bone-headed but polite French taxi driver that I realised my location at the blue coast airport at Nice.

Many is the time I woke up in my hotel bed and my first thought was "Where the hell am I?" Because the 'looks all the same' problem is much worse in hotels than it is at airports.

At one point I became convinced that the more aircraft I travelled on, the more likely it would be that I would be on one that would crash. My reasoning went that if I bought enough tickets in a lottery, one day I might just win it.

The thought terrified me for months and I only overcame it by concentrating during take-off on counting the seconds it took from brake release to when the front wheel left the ground.

It was always 38 seconds for a Boeing 737.

The counting calmed me. As did my eventual realisation that I couldn't do anything about a plane crash anyway. It was all in the laps of the various gods.

In the same school of nervous nelly-ness (which is a word, isn't it?), I became convinced that because I stayed in so many hotels, I would one day die in one of their anonymous rooms. I dreaded the sight which would confront the Filipina maid who would let herself in, having first knocked, called out "House-keeping!" and received no answer.

Because they often do that, I've actually come out of the shower naked to find them in my room. It's not as attractive a scene as the movies might have you imagine.

There's no "Oh my, sir. I'm so sorry. But perhaps I can stay a little while and wash your back."

Far from it.

It's usually a hand flying to the face and a startled "Jesus, Mary and Joseph!" (in Tagalog – the Filipinas are good Catholics) before they flee, the wheels of the toiletries cart jamming in the door in their haste to get away.

It must happen to them a lot.

It can't be just a naked me. Can it?

So, I always slept with something on. That was a given.

I had to think about the maid's feelings. And, as I told you earlier, I kept the air conditioner on chilly. That was to prevent my body from decomposing too rapidly.

You can laugh, but mine will be the best-preserved corpse ever carried out of that hotel.

It's not just flights and anonymous rooms which I forget.

One time I left the Netherlands at 7 am, arrived in Lisbon, Portugal, before lunch and took a taxi directly from the airport to the studio, which was a damned long way out of town. Then we had a long, long day recording several shows.

At 2 am, I fell back into a different taxi and gave him the address of the hotel where I usually stayed. When we arrived there, I wearily trudged towards the elevator, past the night clerk, who looked up startled as I pushed the elevator button.

But which floor was I on? I couldn't remember. Which room for that matter? Couldn't remember that either. I fished around my pockets and bag but could find no room key.

I was really tired. So, back out of the elevator I trudged and approached the night clerk.

"I'm sorry. I can't remember which room I'm in and seem to have misplaced my room key. The name is Bigg."

After a long time clacking at his keyboard, the clerk looked at me and said, "You aren't registered at this hotel, sir."

"But I always stay here."

"You aren't on the register, sir, and we are full tonight."

"Then which hotel am I registered in?"

He gave me that look. You know the one.

"How would I know that, sir?"

Can Portuguese night clerks do passive aggressiveness and sarcasm? I think so but he was very polite.

Luckily for me there was not much for night clerks to do at 2 am. When it dawned on him that I wasn't going to leave, he rang other hotels in Lisbon and soon found I was booked into one further up the same road.

My office had discovered this hotel was full and had re-booked me. But they had not told me of the change. More likely, they had told me of the change and I hadn't listened.

Outside, I climbed back into the same taxi which had dropped me there moments before. The driver looked at me strangely (oh, I always visit international hotels in the middle of the night just to check on them, you know). Then I got to the other hotel, checked in successfully and was asleep before my head hit the pillow.

That was after first making sure I was wearing clean underwear and the air conditioning was turned right down.

Can't forget that.

31. An old saying

In case you think the stories I've been telling you are made up or merely designed to make me look like the best television producer there ever was, I should tell you about something that happened to me which could change your mind.

It's a story which proved the old saying: "A quick trip to the toilet can cost you a pile."

Actually, that saying is not so old.

Is it even a saying? Well, it is now.

The boss of a company I'd dealt with a few times, let's call him Bob, called to invite me for lunch.

It was a bit of an unusual request, because we had never done that much business together, but Bob knew about me from the work I'd been doing around Europe. His invitation smacked of a prelude to a job offer. I thought, "What the hell. It's a free lunch." I accepted the invitation.

On the appointed day, we turned up to the nominated restaurant in the middle of a particular city which shall remain nameless. It was an expensive eatery. The steaks cost the equivalent of a child's semester school fees. Bob's company obviously had money to burn, I thought.

This was looking up.

The lunch confirmed it.

Out came the $100 bottles of wine, one after the other.

Bob brought along several of his senior executives and, by the way they laughed at my jokes and agreed with my every stupid opinion, once again I was the most devilishly handsome and smartest man in the room. Of course, it was a job offer.

Bob wanted me to take over a particular branch of his company which dealt with creativity and format creation, two things I had proven to be good at over the years.

Creating and protecting intellectual property remains one of the most important functions of a successful production company. And Bob was prepared to offer me a great deal of money to do it for him.

But I was reluctant.

The company I worked for, Endemol, was blessed with two absolute geniuses for owners. John and Joop were not only brilliant businessman, but they were also black-belt creative masters in their own right.

I could walk into John's office with an idea for a new show. Before I was even finished explaining it to him, John would have understood the concept and mentally improved it in 100 ways. While I sat there, he would reach for the phone, call up a television station in another country and sell 13 episodes of his great new show on the spot. The program would be in pre-production before I got back to my desk. You have to see him in action to believe it. We are not worthy.

Joop was more of a people person. He made you feel like it was a total privilege to work 16 hours a day for him. If you did he rewarded you generously and you did it happily because he always noticed you. I loved him like a father. As I said, they were geniuses and working for them was a delight.

Under these two men, Endemol went from being a relatively small Dutch outfit to the fastest growing television production company in the world in the 1990s.

We kept turning out the most number and the biggest television formats the world had ever seen. Big Brother anyone? John and Joop fostered and promoted creativity and allowed me the freedom to operate how I thought best. I travelled the world creating new formats, supervising or producing huge television shows and having a real impact on the industry. Why would I want to give that up?

The other issue was that Bob had a reputation as a 'hands on' boss. He paid his staff very well, but I'd heard that no one else in the company was allowed to make decisions. He was also well known for yelling at his staff in public, even his senior people. No one likes that. Even for a big salary. His company had a big staff turnover.

It so happened that, at the time, I'd been reading a book about the evolution of companies. Most businesses start out as Level 1 companies. The owner and their family or friends in a garage or small office, trying their best. If the idea is good enough and the owners work hard enough for long enough, the company grows to profitability. Eventually it grows to the point it becomes a real thing, with a reputation in whatever industry its been trying to break into.

The future of the company hinges on that point, when it turns from being Level 1 to Level 2. When owners, and family and friends, must let go of the reins. They must hire professional people, then step back and let those people do the things they used to do themselves. When it reaches Level 2, the company must expand or go bust. There is no point at which things can just stay the same.

Endemol International had reached that second stage just before I joined it. John and Joop had stepped back and let the people they hired, such as me, take things forward while they retained the all-important overview and future vision.

John later told me he hated the moment when he realised he no longer knew the names of all his employees, but it had become necessary as Endemol grew and grew.

He and Joop accepted that they needed their staff to make important decisions, accepted they needed to trust their people to take their company forward. As I said, they were geniuses.

Bob's company too, was just reaching the same stage of development. It had grown just enough to be on the verge of Level 2. But it seemed Bob was scared to let go of the reins. From his behaviour, it appeared he didn't trust anyone.

The book told me that when a Level 2 company had an owner who wouldn't let go, the company would keep growing for a while before collapsing in on itself.

The owner would inevitably become too stretched to keep track of all the decisions that needed to be made.

So, despite the generous money on offer, I made my mind up to say 'no' to his overture. But I thought I'd wait until the end of the lunch, so as not to spoil the convivial atmosphere.

The wine kept flowing and the lunch heaved on into the afternoon. The midday crowd had long since disappeared and the restaurant staff started setting up tables for the dinner session.

The restaurant owner wasn't stupid.

He made no attempt to kick out the group at table 1, who had spent $1,000 on food and was busy chalking up another $1,000 on wine. The staff could whinge about their overdue rostered break all they liked, but the noisy group at table 1 was going to put his kids through college if they stayed a little longer.

By mid-afternoon I was plastered.

We all were.

And having put away my body weight in steak and wine, it was time to finally get rid of some of it.

I staggered to my feet and, with the help of a lot of arm waving and finger-pointing by the manager, I found the way to the toilet.

In my condition, I had some trouble working out if I was to use the stalls marked with a seagull or those marked with a crab.

Why didn't they just use "men" and "women"?

The delay nearly caused me an injury.

Inside the stall, I felt it would be safer for all concerned if I sat down to do my business. I did and promptly passed out. What seemed like moments later, I came to. I finished the proceedings and returned to the restaurant.

It was empty.

The place was empty, other than a very surprised looking restaurant manager. The group I was with just moments ago was nowhere to be seen and, when I went outside, the car they had arrived in was also gone.

"The bastards," I thought. "They waited until I went to the toilet and then took off without me. How mean."

I was angry. I hailed a taxi and went back to my hotel where the unfortunate guests in rooms near me got to enjoy my well-earned 10-hour noisy slumber. The next day Bob called me. He was also angry.

"If you didn't want to work for me, you only had to say so. You did not need treat me so rudely," he said. "It was unprofessional to just walk out without saying goodbye."

I had no idea what he was talking about. I hadn't done that. I had just gone to the toilet.

"We waited for a long time, thinking that you might've been having trouble in the toilet.

We were worried you might have had an accident or something. We even got the owner to go in and check, but he said you weren't in there, so we left."

"Thanks for nothing. My offer is rescinded."

He hung up.

I never heard from him again.

He later sold his company to a multi-national and retired from the business, much to the delight of his staff.

Turns out I was asleep on the toilet for three hours.

It was a new record for me.

And do you know what?

I realised it was probably time for me to consider giving up my glamorous but hectic life as an international television producer for a simpler life. Before it killed me.

And soon afterwards I did that. I was forced to. The universe took care of the decision for me. But that's probably a story for another day.

32. The trouble with being a 'yes' person

One of the common themes in this book is how often I get into trouble saying "yes" to things.

I don't know when it started – me automatically saying "yes" to every half-arsed idea that came before me. Perhaps when I was a teenager. Teenagers do stupid things, don't they? But now it is so built into me, I couldn't consider living my life any other way. My girlfriend knows the way to get me to go somewhere is to tell me I have never been there before. That works for everything except shopping for new clothes.

When I go on holidays, for example, I often don't book accommodation in advance, because I like the uncertainty, adventure and risk in having to find somewhere odd, or out of the way, when I get there.

Sometimes, the place I find is a shithole. One night in Germany many years ago, my then wife and I accidentally ended up booking a room in a brothel. The owner looked open-mouthed at me when I asked if the room rate included breakfast.

He had to fumble around in his paperwork to remind himself what the price would be for guests who wanted to stay for more than an hour.

The next morning, we came downstairs after a terrifying and sleepless night of screams, fights and ugly sex noises from the rooms around us, to discover the owner had asked his elderly mother to come in specially to cook us a big German breakfast. She was lovely. The breakfast was terrific. The experience was priceless and much funnier in hindsight.

More often than not, the place I stumble across is somewhere I would never in a million years have chosen, but which turned out to be the perfect place I couldn't have found any other way.

And the people I meet there invariably turn out to be amazingly interesting, funny, scary or entertaining. I got such adventures, as those you read about here, by choosing to go places most people never consider.

Or places slightly off the beaten track.

Once, travelling in southern Europe, I didn't book a bus ticket in advance and, of course, the last bus of the day to the next town was full. I was bemoaning my stupidity as I walked through the countryside, with the prospect of a long, hot and tiring hike.

Late in the afternoon, I walked past a stereotypical Swiss-style alpine house and noticed an old man sitting in a chair in the shade, at the side of the house. He was whittling wood. He said a friendly hello to me. I said an equally friendly hello back to him and, on the spur of the moment, I wandered in and sat down next to him.

It turned out he was an expert wood crafter who, for more years than I had been alive, had made parts for those irritating cuckoo clocks the Swiss sell to stupid tourists.

He offered me a drink of water, which I accepted. I sat with him most of the afternoon, learning about how stupid Swiss wooden cuckoo clocks were made, which I can tell you all about if you have a couple of hours to spare. No, I thought not.

It was an experience which has remained strongly in my mind. And one I would never have had, if I was the sort of sensible person who booked his ticket in time to catch the last stupid bus.

But being a "yes" person is, honestly, much harder work than the alternative.

Most people prefer to say "no". Life is very comfortable for "no" people. Every day is pretty much the same. Every routine enjoyed by its repetition.

People who prefer to say "no" often go to the same place for vacation every year (pitching their tent or parking their caravan next to the same people they did last year – shoot me in the head). Tuesday is always bowling night, the parents come over for dinner every Thursday and the car gets washed every Sunday morning, regardless of the weather.

Life is safe, the world ordered and, as a result, life seldom deals them nasty surprises.

"No" people are a perfect television audience. They are there, every week, in front of the set to watch the shows I make.

They are usually fans of the aspirational reality shows, such as the garden or house makeover programs. They will never actually do any of the extravagant makeovers they see on the programs, but they enjoy watching others doing it. They love to watch travel shows, knowing they will probably never visit any of the exotic destinations. ("We always go to the coast at Christmas, don't you know")

They watch the quiz programs, answering all the questions out loud, knowing they would never go on the program themselves as a contestant. That would mean overcoming their natural conservative nature. They worry what their friends and neighbours would say if they got on the show and made a fool of themselves. It's easier to say "no".

I'm not claiming that saying "no" is a bad thing.

Who would you rather have as the captain of your next flight? A "no" pilot who was sensible and went to bed early, because they were to be the captain of a jumbo jet the next day?

Or a "yes" pilot who stayed a little too long at the bed-and-breakfast hotel bar the night before?

Once or twice a year, you read about "yes" pilots who fail an alcohol or drug test on the way to the cockpit. You can also watch Denzel Washington in that movie. I want a "no" pilot in charge of my flight, thank you very much.

So, I'm not saying a "yes" person is better. The two personality traits merely sit at opposite ends of life's seesaw.

But "yes" people are the ones who call you at 2 am from a remote hut on the top of a mountain in Africa, to tell you about the great sunrise they have just seen. They are the ones who, at a moments' notice, will load three friends into their car and set off across the country to visit every town starting with "A", just because no one has ever done that, and it seemed a sensational idea over a few glasses of wine.

A "yes" person will quit their job and sell their house in the city, to fund a bed-and-breakfast in the hills above India. And who, when the business goes broke, as it always was going to, will admit they "just wanted to see how things would turn out".

Life for a "yes" person is enough to give a "no" person a case of hives.

A "yes" person never goes to the same place twice for holidays. You can forget regular Thursday night dinner with the parents. Mum and dad will go six months before they hear from you (which is also when mum and dad learn that their "yes" child is living in Thailand with a French scuba diving instructor and has a whole new sleeve of tattoos).

"Yes" people have a sometimes misplaced confidence in their

own abilities and an optimism that everything will turn out all right in the end. Because, of course, it's impossible to live out on the edge without occasionally stepping over it.

"Yes" people will tell you about the amazing adventures they had in a country you've never heard of, but then admit they got a nasty foot fungus which laid them low for three months. If they live long enough, they will, of course, be the ones who gain the most life experience.

I feel the pressure of my personality type each time I accept a new job.

When I go into the new office for the first time, I rarely feel like it's an exciting opportunity. Instead, I feel as if I have just closed myself off to other opportunities which would have come past me, had I not accepted the job. But I always reconcile it by understanding that, because I said "yes", the job will lead me down a new path anyway.

And the next opportunity might well be the one which changes my life again. If you read my book *"Walking the Camino: My Way"* (and you should, by golly) you will see that it sometimes does.

Because, ultimately, life is all about conquering fear. Which is hard for most people, including me.

Saying "no" is easier, but doesn't lead anywhere, except to the couch, getting fat and old. Saying "yes" means I have to push myself a little harder, get up earlier, be a little busier, with both big and little things in life.

Here is a list of some of the things I've set out to do in recent years. As well as walking the 850 km of the Camino Frances (because it sounded like a lark), I've taken intensive German language lessons danke schön' with the umlaut (German girlfriend insists); applied for jobs in the Netherlands and Switzerland because I wanted to work for an international charity in some god-forsaken hell hole (I didn't get the jobs which was probably for the best); I've lost 10 kgs by changing what I eat and the times of day I eat it; I taught myself the ukulele (God help the neighbours); I'm up to 50 sit-ups a day; I have made several attempts to brew Viking mead, which my daughters thought would be cool (it tastes like old bath water but at 2 am will keep a party going strong); and I am planning one day to start a beehive and raise chickens, all of which are stupid and which make it look like I'm just getting older. And yes, that's true too.

But I also continue to say "yes" to a lot of less age-related, things. I sold my beautiful little aeroplane, which I built in a backyard garage a few years ago and which I used to fly all over Australia (I have my eye on a new one). I've fallen in love again (which I swore I'd never do. It is truly a terrifying experience). Against all sensible advice, I headed off to live in Europe again, just as the worst pandemic in 100 years went viral across the continent, and not in a good way.

I'm two thirds of the way through writing three books, which is something I've had on my list to do since I was a boy (you are reading one of them). I'm planning to write three rom-com movie scripts, just to see if I can sell them (I just love rom-coms). Oh, and I want to produce another feature film, which won't make any money, like the first one didn't. This one will be about two snakes who fall in love – which sounds like a big Disney hit, doesn't it?

I am a terrible example to my children, I think. For obvious reasons, none of them have had the "You must get a real job" speech other fathers give their children.

In my defence, I always make friends easily, in a wide variety of cities and countries, and those friends generally stay with me for life. People, like me, who are not afraid of change, and always look at the positive side of life, are usually fun to be around. People prefer optimists and, from everything I've read, scientists say optimists are more successful and happier than pessimists.

Life is, of course, made up of both sorts, and the world would be a completely stupid place if we were all the same. The trick is knowing which one you are and making sure you compensate.

It's not just me with this opinion.

Google's Executive Chairman, Eric Schmidt, once famously advised a group of graduating students to, "Find a way to say 'yes' to things."

"Say yes to invitations to a new country, say yes to meet new friends, say yes to learning a new language, picking up a new sport. Yes, is how you get your first job, and your next job. Yes, is how you find your spouse, and even your kids. "Even if is a bit edgy, a bit out of your comfort zone, saying yes means that you will do something new, meet someone new, and make a difference in your life, and likely in others' lives as well. Yes, lets you stand out in a crowd, to be the optimist, to stay positive, to be the one everyone comes to for help, for advice, or just for fun. Yes, is what keeps us all young. Yes, is a tiny word that can do big things. Say it often."

I've been trying to live that philosophy for most of my life.

Being a "yes" person is difficult.

But I wouldn't want to be any other way.

33. And finally

Those, then, are some of my stories.

You will have to wait until another time to hear about other adventures I packed into some hectic years criss-crossing the world making television.

Remind me next time to tell you about when I met Jean-Claude van Damme in Sofia, the capital city of Bulgaria. I had gone there to advise a television production company about a game show invented by me and a couple of others. Watching the former big Hollywood star interact with members of his own film crew at the end-of-filming party (which I snuck into uninvited to get a free drink), was educational.

Sad but educational.

Also remind me to tell you about how I ended up in a farmhouse in Lapland one winter weekend, watching the wedding ceremony of a man who was the spitting image of Vladimir Lenin. I'd met the groom in a Helsinki pub the night before. Sigh.

Or the time in Moscow, when I stupidly ignored warnings about the brutally toxic polluted summer air outside and nearly died, before managing to stumble into an Orthodox convent and playing the stupid dying tourist to avoid being arrested.

And I guess I should also tell you of the time I was looking for a couple of new staff members in a particular large Eastern European country.

I was advised by the owner of a small television station in a small city that within his ranks, I would find some likely prospects. Curious, I went there and discovered the owner wanted me to hire his entire staff, more than 50 people.

Otherwise, he told me, he would have to fire them in the next few weeks. He had sold the broadcasting license and hadn't told his people yet that they were to be out of work.

I could also tell you about how I learned to ignore the tourist brochure which advises tourists to stay at a particular hotel near the cathedral in Mainz in Germany. The rotten bells go all night.

And, the other time . . . well it's getting late, so I'll stop.

As you will have realised by now, just like in real life, I'm not often the hero in my own stories.

But all these things happened to me in one way or another, just as I've related them here.

Thanks for reading.

Acknowledgements

Most of these stories were written down because Harry Basham, the father of my ex-wife, had some terrible luck towards the end of his life. He was a school headmaster, who lived a sober and responsible life. He saved much of his salary towards his eventual retirement.

His plan was to finish work at the allotted time, then withdraw from the bank all the money he'd saved so he and his wife, Madge, could travel the world until one of them went face first into their bacon and eggs.

A great plan and one which many people have. Harry had travel books scattered all over their living room as the two of them planned all the places they would go and the things they would see. However, a few months before the big retirement day, Harry had a heart attack.

It wasn't fatal, fortunately, but it laid him low. And what was worse, the doctors told him his weak heart meant a long aeroplane flight wouldn't be good for him.

Okay, no problem, Harry and Madge thought, their plans were easily changed. They would take a long boat ride to Europe instead. They had enough money to do it and a long cruise would be just as much an adventure.

Then, two other things happened in quick succession, which kicked Harry in the testicles.

The Australian government ruled that retiring people could no longer withdraw all their savings in one lump sum and just spend it how they liked.

The government was sick of retirees spending all their money (like Harry and Madge were planning to do), then coming back to the government asking for a public pension for the rest of their lives. From now on, the government ruled, retirement money could only be taken out in small regular amounts.

If that wasn't bad enough, soon afterwards, the financial institution where Harry and Madge had invested all their savings went bankrupt because of a huge fraud. The couple was left almost penniless.

Harry was heartbroken. Instead of cruising the wonders of the world, he and his wife were now sentenced to spend the rest of their lives in their small suburban house going nowhere, eking out their existence with a small public pension from the government. He struggled to make sense of his life. It was a tragic story which always brought me to tears when I recalled it.

About the same time as Harry and Madge's lives were unravelling, I was about to drag my own family from the comfort of our lives in Sydney to the Netherlands, where I had just accepted a job as an International Supervising Producer with a small Dutch television production company called Endemol. My ex-wife suspected it might have been a company making pornos. Fortunately it wasn't.

When in Europe I began visiting weird and wonderful places and started experiencing strange things, I thought it might be nice to write them down and tell Harry about them. Every adventure I had, I wrote a glowing report and sent it to him, hopefully so he could vicariously enjoy Europe with me. After a few months however, Madge told me to stop.

Every letter from me, she said, was a dagger into Harry's heart, a regular reminder that he was sitting at home, slowly and pointlessly dying, while I was out there living his adventure.

So I stopped sending them to him. But I kept writing them, because by now I had a growing group of friends and family who seemed to enjoy the stories. This way I eventually recorded the details I needed for this book.

By the way, Harry and Madge, by living frugally for a while, were eventually able to save enough money to go on a bus holiday to Australia's Northern Territory. It's a very long and tiring journey by bus from New South Wales, where they lived.

Midway through the holiday, outside the city of Katherine, in the middle of Australia, Harry had another heart attack, this one fatal.

He was buried there, where he fell.

He would have liked that.

I'm glad he managed to get that last adventure.

Madge went home and died there a short while later. So I must say thank you to Harry and Madge for the inspiration.

Thanks also go to my regular editor, Jennifer Cooke, who saves me from making too big an idiot of myself in words, even if she can't stop me being one in life.

She takes valuable time from her own busy life to ensure my words tell the story I want them to and point out where I might have insulted all and sundry. Those are the bits that have already gone.

Thanks also to my muse, Stephanie, the surgeon from Stuttgart, who has the uncanny ability to notice mistakes which have sailed past eight sets of eyes before hers. She also encourages me to keep going when the burden seems too much.

Thanks also to my regular designer, Karin Middleton, whose creativity and talent makes me look better than I really am.

Making a Millionaire: My Way

*Want to learn how to make a million dollars the hard way?
Here is a sneak preview of Brian's next book "Making a Millionaire: My Way". It's all about his adventures making television's most
successful program "Who Wants to Be a Millionaire?" in more than
20 countries. It's full of tips on what makes that great show work
and how you might improve your chances to win it.*

Physical triggers: The Contestant Farm

So a contestant, let's call her Carol, makes it to the chair in the centre of the studio and is about to play for $1 million.

Her face is going to be the only thing on the screen for the next 15 minutes, so how does the producer improve the chances he or she will get good, gripping drama from Carol in exchange for the show's money?

Let's be clear about something up front. The producer is happy for Carol to win a lot of cash – really, truly they are – but only if the show gets an appropriate amount of excitement and entertainment in return.

If Carol is boring, it won't matter how intelligent or clever she is. She won't get much airtime, so logically, not much prize money either. It's probably not polite to say it aloud, but to get the level of drama the program requires (and, of course, help Carol win some money) the producer and presenter need to get tough with her. They need to break down her self-confidence, quickly and completely, then hope and pray Carol is brave enough to fight back. If she is, she can win the million and the show will get a ratings hit. If not, she will never win enough to buy the private jet.

So how does the producer break down Carol's self-confidence? By getting into her head and body and physically putting her personality under extreme duress.

Obviously, the arena itself is designed to look like the Colosseum. All the lights, sounds and audience attention are focused on that one chair. Sitting there as the centre of attention, even the most confident person can expect to feel nervous.

But the producer doesn't leave things to chance. A great deal of thought has gone into the show's environment.

You will have seen on the show that the centre of the Millionaire set consists of two chairs and an electronic console where the questions and answers appear. You may not have noticed that it is all constructed on top of a translucent glass floor, under which is filled with bright, swirling, rapidly moving lights. Most people get nervous walking above a glass floor. The swirling lights make the feeling of vertigo worse. Everyone, even the show's staff, get a palpable sense of uncertainty walking across the floor when the lights are twirling.

The contestant's chair is a high and narrow barstool. It's deliberately designed to be just a touch higher and narrower than is comfortable for most people, especially when you consider it is sitting on top of a translucent and vertigo-inducing glass floor. The barstool's seat also has an uneven base, which allows it to wobble slightly when the contestant is sitting in it. The goal is to make the contestant unconsciously unsteady and nervous.

They are sitting too high, on an unstable base, above an unstable floor. Brrr.

Sometimes, the arms of the barstool are removed to make the contestant's perch even more precarious.

Nothing to hang onto.

In some countries, in the lower back of the chair, a bass

speaker quietly pumps out a deep heartbeat sound. It's not sub-liminal exactly, but it's not far off. The beat goes directly into the contestant's spine.

In one unnamed country, on the centre console, just underneath the screen where the questions and answers appear, a small heater is installed on the contestant's side, to pump heat at their legs. The heat adds to the increasing level of stress they are beginning to experience.

By the way, on the presenter's side, there's a small fan or air-conditioner, which allows the presenter to look cool and calm throughout the process. The contestant becomes aware they are getting hot and bothered, but they can see the presenter is seemingly unaffected. The contestant worries it's their nerves, which makes them more nervous.

You've heard the heartbeat which the show plays during the question-and-answer session. What you might not realise is that the computer, which triggers each of the questions for the contestant, also triggers the heartbeat sound.

The beat is fed into the speakers in the studio (and sometimes into the back of the contestant's chair). This heartbeat continues as long as the contestant takes to lock in an answer to the question.

The heartbeat starts slowly for Question 1, at a level slightly above a normal person's resting heart rate. But the beat gets faster as the questions progress. By Question 15, the rapid, panicky heartbeat sound booms out across the audience and into the head and spine of the contestant. It creates an amazing amount to stress for them.

And it appears the contestant's own heartbeat increases to match the sound she is hearing. But that's not the end of the pressure applied by the physical environment.

The studio lights join in to ratchet up the tension even further, as if it needed it.

You've seen the lights dim when it's time for each new question to be asked. But what you might not have noticed is that the spotlights, which are focussed only on the contestant, also pulse at the rate a normal person breathes.

For Question 1, the lights pulse quite slowly, at a resting breathing rate. But with each question they speed up until, by the end, they are pulsing much faster. The contestant's body matches the pulse and, by the end, is breathing like they have run a race. Inhale, exhale. Pulse, pulse. Faster and faster. Our minds associate faster breathing with stress which triggers a fight-or-flight response.

The end result of all these (I call them physical triggers) is that the contestant becomes strongly physically and mentally affected by the studio environment. As the show goes on, her body reacts more and more to the stimuli, her heartbeat increasing and her breathing becoming more and more rapid and ragged. These factors add to the growing sense of panic in her.

And all this before a question is asked or an answer demanded.

Increasingly panicked and nervous, she looks to the friendly presenter for support, but this is the moment which has been primed for the presenter to move in, like a shark, and rip away her increasingly fragile self-confidence.

Oh, and a couple of final things about the physical triggers.

The noises and lights also affect the audience in the studio and the viewers at home. I've seen many studio audiences completely hypnotised by the throb of the heartbeat noise and the gentle inhaling and exhaling of the lights.

On-screen, the camera stays on close-ups of the contestant and the presenter (no wide shots at all).

The combination of the lights and heartbeats with the close-up shots, creates a tangible sense of claustrophobia for viewers at home.

It's the same technique movie directors use in horror films to build tension.

In the studio, the audience reacts to the triggers by sitting forward in their seats and breathing more shallowly and quickly. At home, I've seen viewers unconsciously sit forward in their lounge chairs and grip the arms of their seats, just as if they, too, were watching a horror film.

It's fun to watch everyone when a commercial break begins. The sounds and lights go bright and loud. The shot moves away from the close ups to a wide overhead view showing most of the set. Everybody, contestant, presenter, studio audience and home viewers, all take a big breath and sit back in their chairs, as if they've all been asleep.

The physical triggers are powerful cues and responsible for much of the success of *Who Wants To Be a Millionaire?* But not all. For that, you need to consider the questions the contestants get asked.

Walking the Camino: My Way

Here is a sneak peek at Brian's book "Walking the Camino: My Way" detailing his epic and hilarious month-long pilgrimage along the Camino Frances in Spain.

Sneak peek: Walking the Camino: My Way

If you gave me the choice right now between repeating the walk I did today or getting kicked in the nuts by the entire Real Madrid soccer team (excluding their interchange players), I would have to consider long and hard before I could give you an answer. Real Madrid has a lot of strong kickers.

I have done long walks before, including quite a few with a full pack. But the first day of the Camino Frances nearly did me in.

The first 16 km to St-Jean-Pied-de-Port was a doddle. A beautiful stroll through a beautiful valley – chatting with fellow walkers with a hale fellow attitude. The light rain was not off-putting, all part of the experience, we all chortled.

But at the 16 km mark, the trail left the valley and began to climb the hill towards where we knew the village of Roncesvalles, our first night's stopover, would be.

The track became steeper and steeper with each passing kilometre. The nice paved road became a chewed up, muddy, sloppy, goat track.

The happy talking soon dried up. I started puffing. For a while I followed a Scottish doctor called James. We'd had a great chat down lower. Not anymore. I stopped breathing through my nose, as per my fitness-obsessed son's instructions, and started using both nose and mouth to suck in air.

Eventually, I was forced to suck in air through every orifice, just to get enough oxygen into my system. As I climbed, the air got thinner and thinner. The older and less committed of us fell behind. I was put out by an 80-year-old Korean man, who fair belted past me like I was standing still. I didn't even have enough energy to throw something at him. And, to be fair, I was actually standing still.

The track went up and up and up.

It also got colder and colder.

About the 22 km mark, I entered the snow zone and the temperature plummeted to well below zero. It was no real problem for me, because I was blowing steam from every opening, enough to power every home in the valley.

Eventually, me and a bloke called Brian Black from Canada were down to clawing our way 50 metres higher, then standing for a minute to drag in more air before staggering another 50 metres, then stopping to repeat the process. I thought I would die for sure. It would have been a relief.

The climb seemed to go on forever. Around every corner, the muddy, wet track kept going up. I kept gulping mouthfuls from my water bottle.

The other problem was my pack. Someone had, without me noticing, slipped a 2019 VW Golf into my rucksack, including the optional seat covers. The 7 kilograms I had blithely hoisted onto my back this morning somehow doubled in weight the higher I went, then doubled again.

It was incredibly painful and made breathing even more difficult. I was nearly done in by the time we Sandakan death march survivors finally reached the top, where we were blessedly greeted by a howling, freezing gale and snow storm.

Who the f@+* cared about that?!!

I had reached the top. I stood happily in the storm, sucking in the freezing air like it was honey. I had only a lazy 1.5 km downhill to go, to get to my bed for the night.

I was so chuffed about not having to go uphill any more, I actually skipped for joy a couple of times. Until I lost my balance on my bone-weary legs and nearly toppled into a creek.

The accommodation is amazing, staffed by wonderful Dutch volunteers who seem to understand and sympathise with us about the brutal journey we have just completed.

I have been able to practice my appalling Dutch with them. I am warm, I have had a lovely shower, I have on clean clothes, I'm just about to hobble out to find food and my legs and arms hate me. It's all downhill for the next week or so. They say this first day is the worst day of the entire journey. They'd better be right, otherwise I'm calling Zinedine Zidane (the Real Madrid coach) and opting for the much less-stressful nut kicking.